SPECIAL P

D0000197

"Anne McTiernan has written a gripping, deeply personal memoir that often reads like some of the best dramatic fiction out there. *Starved* is both a search for understanding the complications of family and a parallel exploration of our relationship with food, as either nurturer or torturer. Anne's history as a young girl growing up in 1950s Boston and her drive to both heal herself and break free from a toxic relationship is framed through both the eye of the clinical researcher and the heart of great author in this fantastically well-written memoir bursting with intelligence and hope. An absolute achievement."

—DOMINGO MARTINEZ
New York Times best-selling author of *The Boy Kings of Texas* and 2012 National Book Award in Nonfiction Finalist

"As a leading obesity researcher, Anne McTiernan has conducted some of the most groundbreaking studies on nutrition, exercise, and health. But in this book, she provides extraordinary insight into her own personal struggles with food. It's an emotional and riveting life story, and one that anyone who has ever had a strained relationship with food—which is most of us—can find solace in."

—ANAHAD O'CONNOR
Bestselling author and health writer for the *New York Times*

"*Starved* is an absorbing, and sometimes shattering, primer on abuse and resilience. Anne McTiernan mines her past to bring up the

CALGARY PUBLIC LIBRARY

NOV 2016

painful, real details that make this memoir sing—even as it breaks our hearts."

—CLAIRE DEDERER
New York Times best-selling author of
Poser: My Life in Twenty-Three Yoga Poses

"A heartbreaking and inspiring story of a young girl who faces neglect and punishment by her family and church but survives through sheer will and goodness—and intelligence."

—MIRIAM E. NELSON, PhD
Professor and author of the international
best seller *Strong Women Stay Young*

"McTiernan's absorbing memoir details her early abandonment and troubled relationship with family and food, and readers will cheer as she completes her difficult journey to self-acceptance."

—STEPHANIE CLIFFORD
New York Times best-selling author of *Everybody Rise*

"Dr. McTiernan's remarkable life story is a testament to the power of human resilience and the determination to do good. Instead of spending her life seeking vengeance for the abuse and hardship she endured as a child, this inspirational physician has dedicated her adult life to helping people and improving their lives. I am in greater awe than ever over her enormous accomplishments."

—JOANN E. MANSON, MD, DrPH
Professor of Medicine, Harvard Medical School

"Anne McTiernan is a master storyteller who writes with great wit and insight. If you grew up without the support you needed to survive and yet somehow still thrived, you will likely see yourself in her story. But no matter how you grew up, you will find yourself rooting for her."

—THEO PAULINE NESTOR
Author of *Writing Is My Drink*

Starved

Starved

A Nutrition Doctor's Journey from Empty to Full

Anne McTiernan

CENTRAL RECOVERY PRESS
Las Vegas

Central Recovery Press (CRP) is committed to publishing exceptional materials addressing addiction treatment, recovery, and behavioral healthcare topics.

For more information, visit www.centralrecoverypress.com.

© 2016 by Anne McTiernan
All rights reserved. Published 2016. Printed in the United States of America.

No part of this publication may be reproduced, stored in a retrieval system, or transmitted in any form or by any means, electronic, mechanical, photocopying, recording, or otherwise, without the written permission of the publisher.

Publisher: Central Recovery Press
3321 N. Buffalo Drive
Las Vegas, NV 89129

21 20 19 18 17 16 1 2 3 4 5

Library of Congress Cataloging-in-Publication Data

Names: McTiernan, Anne, author.
Title: Starved : a nutrition doctor's journey from empty to full / Anne McTiernan.
Description: Las Vegas : Central Recovery Press, 2016.
Identifiers: LCCN 2016025978 (print) | LCCN 2016028636 (ebook) | ISBN 9781942094289 (paperback) | ISBN 9781942094296
Subjects: LCSH: McTiernan, Anne,--Health. | Eating disorders--Patients--United States--Biography. | Abused children--United States--Biography. | Mothers and daughters--United States--Biography. |
BISAC: BIOGRAPHY & AUTOBIOGRAPHY / Personal Memoirs. | PSYCHOLOGY / Psychopathology / Eating Disorders. | SELF-HELP / Personal Growth / Self-Esteem. | BODY, MIND & SPIRIT / Inspiration & Personal Growth.
Classification: LCC RC552.E18 M423 2016 (print) | LCC RC552.E18 (ebook) | DDC 362.19685/260092 [B] --dc23
LC record available at https://lccn.loc.gov/2016025978

Photo of Anne McTiernan by Susie Fitzhugh. Used with permission.

Every attempt has been made to contact copyright holders. If copyright holders have not been properly acknowledged please contact us. Central Recovery Press will be happy to rectify the omission in future printings of this book.

Publisher's Note: This book contains general information about eating disorders, family trauma, and related matters. The information is not medical advice. This book is not an alternative to medical advice from your doctor or other professional healthcare provider.

This is a memoir—a work based on fact recorded to the best of the author's memory. Our books represent the experiences and opinions of their authors only. Every effort has been made to ensure that events, institutions, and statistics presented in our books as facts are accurate and up-to-date. To protect their privacy, the names of some of the people, places, and institutions in this book may have been changed.

Cover design and interior design and layout by Marisa Jackson.

To my husband and our daughters

Table of Contents

Acknowledgments

In training to be a doctor, you learn that without the wisdom, teaching, and support of others, you will fail, and your patients will suffer. This book exists thanks to so many people who have taught and helped me over the years.

First, I thank my husband Martin, who encouraged me throughout the development of this book, edited several versions, and said "it's great" every time. He has guided me on a route through life with meaningful destinations, exhilarating vistas, exciting side trips, and safe landings. I thank also our two beautiful daughters, Rachel and Cassandra, and their wonderful families for tolerating my life-baring narrative. They keep me grounded in the present when I stray into agonizing about the past or worrying about the future.

I am so grateful to my wise agent, Anne Devlin, for her encouragement and support. I give special thanks to Janet Ottenweller at Central Recovery Press for shaping and improving the book. Thanks also to Eliza Tutellier, Nancy Schenck, Valerie Killeen, and Patrick Hughes for believing in the book and including me in the Central Recovery Press family. And thanks to Marisa Jackson for the beautiful and meaningful cover and interior designs.

"See one, do one, teach one" is a half serious pun on learning to perform medical procedures. In contrast, writing creative nonfiction takes years of education and practice. This book would not have been possible without the outstanding teaching of Theo Nestor, from whom I learned the art and science of memoir. As she helped me with overall book design, Claire Dederer taught me to think first about the reader, which is eerily similar to another medical education truism, "the patient comes first." Jennifer D. Munro taught me how to see the patterns and content of a manuscript. She saw what I was saying before I realized it and used brilliant surgical technique as she performed her editing operation. Jennifer Worick and Kerry Colburn taught me critical nuts and bolts of the writing business.

The women in my writing group—Rosemary Gregory, Margot Page, Joyce Tomlinson—are all expert writers who generously shared their knowledge and experience with me. They honored me by accepting me into their group; I was the straggler to their strides.

I thank the many family members, friends, and colleagues who have asked at some regularity about the progress of this memoir and were mollified with my meager responses. Finally, I am grateful to Deborah, Frank, Jack, and Marcia for restoring my sanity of sorts, without which I could not have written about my difficult beginnings.

Author's Note

Four and a half decades have passed since I left home. I married early and well, and my husband and I have two daughters and several grandchildren. Along the way, I collected several academic degrees—too many probably—which led me to my career as a medical doctor and researcher. Throughout my career, my personal experiences have shaped my passion for research.

This book is a memoir, and as such, reflects my recollection of events during my life. I reconstructed conversations from my memory, which may differ from other people's memories. In some cases, especially when recounting scenes from my early childhood, I created dialogue to support the narrative. The names and characteristics of my immediate family are real, but I changed the names and physical characteristics of many other people in the book to preserve their privacy.

The Obesity Society, whose mission is to advance the science-based understanding of the causes, consequences, prevention, and treatment of obesity, recommends that physicians and researchers use "people first" language. That is, they recommend that we refer to "persons with obesity" rather than "obese persons." This helps create positive, productive discussions about weight and health, reduces chance of bias against persons with obesity, and underscores the medical community's classification of obesity as a disease rather than as a failing.

As a child and early teenager, I was labeled as "fat" and other derogatory terms. I thought of myself as a fat kid, and that made me inherently ugly, undesirable, and a failure. In this memoir, I have chosen to use those terms to show my own experience with weight bias. However, I fully support the Obesity Society's position on working to reduce the use of pejorative words to describe individuals with weight issues or obesity.

Prologue

I answered the phone, expecting the usual telemarketing call telling me not to hang up. Instead, a woman's voice asked if I was Dr. Anne McTiernan. Most people calling my home don't know I'm a doctor, unless they are friends or relatives.

"Yes," I said, looking out at Lake Washington's steel gray water under an equally drab sky, a typical Northwest November sunset. Any minute now, I'd hear my husband open the garage door to bring in his bike after pedaling home from teaching his last university class of the day.

"Hi, Doctor, my name is Joan McGinn. I'm the social worker at your mom's nursing home in Plymouth."

"Hello," I said. I didn't want to deal with this tonight. I had returned late the previous night from giving a talk on obesity, exercise, and breast cancer at an American Association for Cancer Research conference in Washington, DC. Today, I'd risen as usual at 5:00 A.M. for my morning workout followed by a full day of meetings.

"Your mother asked me to call you."

My stomach twisted into an imitation of sausage links. This was not the first person to phone me on my mother's behalf. Over the years I'd been called by neighbors, doctors, nurses, and lawyers. I took a cleansing breath, trying to decide how much to tell this stranger about my relationship with my eighty-seven-year-old mother, how I had discontinued my visits with her ten years before and had stopped taking her calls five years ago. And I did that because every contact with my mother brought up painful memories I was unable to handle. Before I said anything, the social worker continued.

"You mom has decided to go off dialysis," she said.

The sausage links burst. I knew what this meant. My mother had end-stage kidney disease. Without dialysis, she'd be dead within days.

"Oh, God," I said.

"Your mom told me she's suffered enough. She is ready to let go."

I stayed quiet, thinking then not thinking.

"Would you like to speak with your mom? I know the two of you have been estranged."

"No," I said quietly. I didn't want the last words I heard from her to be the usual accusation that I was a horrible daughter. "But please tell her that we talked," I added.

"Okay, I'll do that. The nurses will make sure your mom is comfortable."

"Thanks."

"Do you want me to let you know how she's doing?" she asked.

"Yes, please, that would be nice."

"Okay, I'll be in touch."

"Tell her I'm thinking of her."

"I will."

And indeed, I was thinking of her. I thought of her most days.

The social worker called as promised, two days later. "I'm sorry to tell you that your mom just died," she said.

I decided to go to her funeral. I wanted to see for myself. I needed to make sure she was dead.

CHAPTER 1

Starving

"You need to look pretty today," Margie said with pursed lips. "It's a very special day."

I sat on the edge of my bed in the room I shared with my aunt Margie (pronounced with a hard "g"). I liked the crinkling sound my shiny blue dress made as I swung my feet back and forth. With each swing forward, I could see the tip of my black patent leather Mary Jane shoes. Still, I listened carefully to my aunt's words. The catch in her voice told me the special day, a sunny September afternoon in 1957, might not be a fun day.

Margie brushed my hair so hard I would have cried if I wasn't already used to it—every morning she pulled my hair into a perfect, tight ponytail with an ink-stained rubber band she'd saved from the rolled-up *Boston Globe*. This day, she added my straw hat with the strap that dug into my chin if I opened my mouth. Then she gave me my white cardigan sweater to hold in case it got chilly. I felt hot with my stiff blue dress and shoes and didn't want to put on the sweater anytime soon, but Margie always knew what I might need in case of an emergency.

Margie led me to the living room sofa in our third-floor walk-up apartment on Boston's Commonwealth Avenue. I lived with my mother and Margie, her sister, when I wasn't staying at one of the boarding homes my mother sent me to from the time I was three months of age. Very few mothers worked in 1953, and daycare was scarce. The few women who did work usually had a relative or babysitter take care of their children in the home, but it was rare for a mother to send her child to a boarding home.

"Sit quietly now, Anne. Don't mess up your dress, or the sisters will think you're naughty," Margie said.

I didn't know what sisters she meant and I didn't understand why they'd think I was naughty if my dress got a little wrinkled. But my mother was home, so I knew that I had better sit still. While I waited, I held my doll—I named her Ruthie—close to my side with her legs sticking straight out just like mine.

The yellow taxi pulled up to a four-story, light brick building in Watertown, just west of Boston. We climbed out of the cab and stood on the sidewalk while the driver went around to the back and struggled to pull a long box out of the trunk. My mother opened her black purse, counted some money carefully into the driver's hand, and asked him to carry the box up to the building.

"That wasn't part of the deal, lady," he said, "and if you're not going to give me a tip, why should I do you a favor?"

My mother's face contorted into the look she got right before she slapped my face, so I hid behind Margie's skirt and held Ruthie's hand tight.

As the taxi pulled away, my mother said, "Well, we'll just have to carry the damn thing."

She and Margie each grabbed a handle on the box and lugged it across the sidewalk to the building's entrance, their faces scrunched with the effort. They wore almost-identical black skirts and white blouses with pearl costume necklaces and earrings. The seams of their nylon stockings rose perfectly straight up the backs of their calves. Crimson lipstick provided their only spots of color. Both women had dark brown hair and deep brown eyes—the latter rare among the Irish. "Black Irish," they might have been called, although they considered their pale, freckling skin proof of their Celtic roots. My blonde hair and blue eyes contrasted sharply with their coloring. Years later, my mother would tell me this came from my bastard of a father, making me regret my palette.

My mother pushed a button next to the front entrance. After a few minutes, a woman opened the tall, wooden door. She wore a long black dress that covered her feet and a funny black cloth wrapped around her head so it looked like she didn't have any hair. I'd never seen anyone in such strange clothes.

"Hello," said the lady, "I'm Sister Mary Joseph. Welcome to Rosary Academy. You must be delivering one of our new boarders."

"Yes," said my mother. "I'm Mrs. Mary McTiernan, and this is my sister Miss Margaret Smith." She emphasized the "Mrs." and the "Miss."

"And who is this?" Sister Mary Joseph asked as she looked down at me, smiling.

"This is Anne Marie McTiernan," my mother said.

"How old are you, Anne Marie?" the nun asked.

I looked down at my shoes.

"Anne, tell Sister Mary Joseph how old you are." My mother pinched my shoulder.

I held up four fingers. It bothered me that I didn't know how to show with my fingers that I was four and a half.

"Four years old? That will make you our youngest boarder."

"Make sure you don't spoil her," my mother said.

"Hmm," the nun said. "Well, then, you'd better follow me."

Sister Mary Joseph led us down a dark hallway. My Mary Janes tapped the tiled floor. We climbed up four flights of wide staircases; my mother and aunt stopping at each step to lift the box between them. The smell of Lysol permeated the cold air. I shivered.

"This is the dormitory," said Sister Mary Joseph. "We have only girls boarding at Rosary."

We entered a long room. Thirty identical beds, covered with white chenille bedspreads, lined the room. Whitewashed walls contrasted sharply with the black linoleum floor and dark wood wainscoting. The room was silent. Sister Mary Joseph led us over to the first bed on the left. My mother pointed to a sign I couldn't read taped to its foot.

"This is your new bed, Anne Marie," she said. "This is where you'll be sleeping from now on."

I looked up at my mother and asked, "Where will you and Margie sleep?"

All three grown-ups laughed.

"Margie and I will sleep at home," my mother said.

Panic shook me. I was being sent away again. For the past year, I'd lived in the apartment with my mother and aunt. Margie's lingerie sales salary was so low that it was cheaper for her to work evenings and Saturdays, and take care of me on weekdays, than for my mother to pay for me to live at a boarding home. I loved being with Margie every day. She and I slept in the same room—so I wouldn't disturb my mother's sleep—and I knew that she'd comfort me if I called out for her at night. Now I felt sick to my stomach.

A brand-new doll sat on the pillow. It had perfectly curled brown hair, brown eyes, and a stiff pink dress. I hated it immediately. I hated the lady with the weird black clothes. I didn't want to stay in this place. I wanted to go home with Margie to my own bed. I wanted to hear Margie breathing if I woke up scared in the middle of the night.

My mother opened the long box and showed me the contents. All my clothes and shoes were folded and stacked neatly, along with pink towels, white sheets, and a green blanket. My mother and aunt made the bed.

"There, honey," my mother said, "now it's all ready for you." Then she put my clothes into the two drawers of a small metal cabinet that stood by the head of the bed.

"All your things are in here," she added. "Your pajamas and underwear are in the top drawer, and your dresses and sweaters are in the bottom drawer. Your toothbrush, toothpaste, and hairbrush are here on the top of your cabinet. I'll leave your jacket in the trunk." She closed the lid of the trunk and slid it under the bed.

"My tummy hurts," I said.

"You'll be fine," my mother snapped.

I looked at Margie. Her eyes were wet, so she looked around the room and at the nun, not at me.

"Has Anne had her dinner today?" Sister Mary Joseph asked.

"Yes, I cooked a big Sunday dinner. She ate a nice meal."

"Good, then we'll just give her some sandwiches in the dorm later. The cafeteria won't be open until tomorrow."

I wondered what a cafeteria was.

Sister Mary Joseph brought us back down the stairs to another, smaller, room. It had books, several tables and chairs that looked about my size, and bright-colored things like blocks, pegs, and crayons. On the other side of the room, a door and two windows looked out on a playground.

A different lady, dressed exactly like Sister Mary Joseph, greeted us. Her black shoes with black laces peeked out from under her dress. This new lady smiled and talked with my mother and aunt, but I wasn't listening. Instead, I looked around at the things in the room, wondering what they all were. There were no other people around, just the four of us. The room echoed a little as the three women talked.

After a while, my mother announced, "It's time for us to go, Anne Marie. Be a good girl now."

"No, don't leave me," I cried.

"We'll be back real soon, Anna Banana," said Margie. "On Friday. I love you."

I cried while my mother and Margie walked out the door then watched as they walked through the playground. Margie turned around and waved. My mother didn't turn back. I thought I'd never see them again.

"There now, Anne Marie, it will be okay," reassured the nun as she picked me up. "No need to cry. You'll have fun here at Rosary. Tomorrow you'll start school and meet the other children who will be here for you to play with."

I should have been used to institutional life by that time. Throw my things into a duffle bag on Sunday afternoons and say, "C'mon, Ma and Margie, gotta get to Rosary on time." But, being four years old, I wasn't quite up to being a trooper about this leaving home stuff. I'd certainly had a lot of practice at it in my short life, though.

My mother later told me that I began my semi-incarceration at three months of age. I lived at the first group home Sunday afternoon through Thursday night and at my mother and aunt's apartment for the rest of the week. The facility's owner devised shortcuts to handle the dozen or so babies in her charge. Toddlers and older babies sat on potty chairs while they ate—to accomplish two functions at one time. Diapers were changed once a day. Babies were fed in their cribs with bottles propped on their chests. Crying babies were left alone.

By the time I was eight months old, I had a diaper rash severe enough for Margie to bring me to the family doctor despite the five-dollar charge—about a quarter of my mother's weekly salary. Later in medical school, I shuddered when I saw pictures of bacterial skin infections that developed in severe diaper rashes, as I remembered Margie describing the raw, red area stretching from my upper legs to my waist, covering front, back, and sides. It would have been swollen and oozing a yellow liquid with areas of bleeding and peeling skin. After the doctor examined me, he told my mother to take me out of that home.

Years later, when my mother told me her side of this story, she talked about the difficulty of finding childcare in a time and place where women were expected to stay home with their babies. "That doctor made my life hell," she said.

Now as a doctor myself, I can see the influence this man had on me. Some people become physicians to follow a family tradition or because they aspire to wealth and status. A few enter the medical profession in gratitude for excellent treatment through an injury or illness. I chose medicine in part because I wanted to save people—similar to how my childhood doctor rescued me from neglect. My research extends this desire to the general public; if I can discover whether diet changes, weight loss, or exercise reduces risk for cancer or other illness, then hopefully some people will be saved from suffering.

Within a month, my mother sent me to a home for physically and mentally handicapped children near Boston. Teresa Burns took care of babies and children with diverse conditions, such as polio, rheumatic heart disease, water on the brain, cerebral palsy, brain injury, and Down syndrome. In the 1950s, many of these children had life expectancies of only months or years. Their parents could not, or would not, care for them.

I'm not sure how I managed to get admitted to her facility. Maybe our doctor pulled some strings, saying I needed special treatment for the skin infection from my diaper rash. I certainly fit the criteria of having parents who did not want to take care of me. Full of love and warmth, Teresa was as wide as she was tall, her body as soft as a feather pillow. To this day I love the comfort of being hugged by a chubby woman. This helps as an obesity physician and researcher, as I've never thought of obese patients as ugly, but rather as people with a health condition. I stayed with Teresa until I was three years old. For the following year, Margie babysat me on weekdays while my mother worked. The comfort and joy I experienced with Margie during this period made the move to Rosary Academy even more wrenching.

Rosary was my third institutional home. It was as if I was a repeat offender. Go to an institution, do your time, get a short reprieve at home, commit a crime against your mother, face more time. My mother would often slap my face when I cried, or was sick, or wet the bed, or if she didn't like the way I looked at her. I tried to be a good girl so she wouldn't hit me or send me away, but it was difficult to know exactly what I was supposed to do to make her happy.

Many of my memories of Rosary are hazy with its Gothic-like settings of dark hallways, classrooms, dormitory bedrooms, and bathrooms. Other memories are crystal clear like it's happening to me right now in such bright light that I can see details without my bifocals.

The Rosary boarders slept in one large dormitory room. The beds were arranged by age with the youngest girl's (mine) closest to the bathroom and the oldest girl's on the other side of the room. The room's windows were close to the ceiling. No one could see in or out.

That first night, I lay awake, unable to sleep. I clutched Ruthie tight against my chest and curled myself into a ball while the hated new doll sat on the cabinet by my bed. I wore my favorite pajamas, pink with little dark pink roses on the yoke's ruffle. My head lay on my bunny pillow toy, the one with the big floppy ears and a pink pocket in the back.

Margie had shown me how to put my pajamas into the pocket in the morning so they'd stay neat during the day. Although my sleeping things were with me, I didn't have Margie and I didn't have my own bed. I wanted to be at home so Margie could read me a Peter Rabbit story, rub my back, tuck me in, and give me a Kleenex to put under my pillow.

As I lay in bed, listening to the sounds of the other girls sleeping, I couldn't understand why my mother and aunt didn't want me to stay at home with them. I decided that I needed to try harder to be a good girl so that my mother would love me, then all three of us could live together.

At some point during the night, I fell asleep because I woke to the sound of ringing. Through a brain fog, I saw Sister Mary Joseph, moving a small bell up and down as she walked between the rows of beds.

"Time to get up, Anne Marie," she said over my head.

I sat up, confused. Girls were going in and out of the bathroom, toothbrushes in hand. Others were slowly dressing by their beds, their backs to the room. All wore identical cotton undershirts, underpants, and full slips; those further dressed had donned blue uniforms.

"You'll want to visit the bathroom first," Sister Mary Joseph explained.

I inched out of bed and stood up. Sister Mary Joseph took my hand and walked me over to the bathroom. The other girls giggled but stood aside as she led me into the long room with its row of six sinks opposite a row of toilet stalls. She told me to go into a stall and shut the door behind me. I could see her feet under the door, waiting. When I emerged, she led me to a sink and showed me how to mix hot and cold water in the sink so I wouldn't burn myself. There were no bathtubs here; the bathing room was down the hall. Back at my bed, she told me to find some clothes in my cabinet, get changed, and fold and store my pajamas. While I was doing this, she told one of the older girls to make my bed. Sulking, the girl did as told. I noticed she didn't make it smooth and neat the way Margie always did, but I didn't complain.

"Hurry, Anne Marie," Sister Mary Joseph said. "You have to get to the cafeteria in five minutes."

I couldn't imagine eating anything now. My stomach felt like a big fist was squeezing it shut—no food could get through that stricture. But I sped up my actions because I wanted the sister to like me. The buttons on the back of my dress gaped open—my arms were too short to reach them. I didn't yet know how to tie my shoes, so I left the shoelaces loose. My hair remained tangled on one side of my head.

"Jane, take Anne Marie down to the cafeteria," Sister Mary Joseph said. Another older girl walked over to my bed. She said nothing as she escorted me down the long, dark staircase. As we descended to the bottom floor, sounds of girls' chatter swelled and acrid smells of overcooked oatmeal and powdered eggs grew stronger. I stopped.

"Please," I whispered, "don't make me go down there."

"Come on," urged the girl. "Sister told me I have to bring you downstairs. I'll get in trouble if I don't do it."

"I feel sick," I moaned.

She dragged me down the stairs even as I begged her to let me go back up. Once at my assigned seat at the little girls' table, I couldn't eat. I could barely look at the neon yellow scrambled eggs or the congealed brown oatmeal the girl put on a tray for me.

"You'd better eat or Sister will paddle you," she said.

With this threat, I lost what control I had over my stomach and spit up bile onto my lap. An old nun appeared quickly, gave me wet dishrags to clean myself, then told me to go back upstairs. Feeling very ashamed, I climbed the stairs. Sister Mary Joseph took one look at me, told me to get changed, and then brought me down to my new classroom. She barely spoke to me. I thought she must be mad at me and hoped she wouldn't hit me.

This reaction to food at Rosary repeated itself daily, and I threw up most mornings, sometimes before breakfast, sometimes afterward. I would proudly inform Sister Mary Joseph on the rare mornings that I didn't get sick.

I recognized the kindergarten room where my mother and Margie had left me the day before and I looked around, hoping to see them. Before I could register my disappointment, a lady in a blue dress walked over to me.

"You must be Anne Marie," she said. "I'm Mrs. O'Doyle. I'll be your teacher." She smiled as she looked at me. With her brown hair pulled up into a bun on top of her head, she looked like the picture of Cinderella from the book Margie read to me, all dressed up for the ball.

"Come meet the other children," she said.

She took me by the hand and led me over to a table where three other girls sat. Each chair had a piece of paper with letters written on it.

"That's your name, Anne Marie," she said. "This will be your seat. And these girls are Nancy, Diane, and Maria."

The morning went quickly. We colored, listened to the teacher's songs, colored again, played at recess on the concrete playground, and heard a story. At 11:30 A.M., the teacher told us to clean our places and get our lunchboxes. Then she gave everyone a little carton of milk with a straw. I still didn't feel hungry, but I wished I had a lunch and lunchbox like the other girls at my table. Seeing that I had no food, the teacher told me I'd eat in the cafeteria. I wanted to heave the milk I'd just drunk.

Soon, several ladies arrived. As each walked in the door, a child would get up and run over to her. Usually the lady would bend down and either give the child a hug or pick her up. A couple of ladies had big bellies, so they just reached down to rub their child's hair. I watched as each mother-child pair walked out the door. I stayed, wondering when my mother or Margie would arrive—but they never came.

"Oh, Anne Marie," said the teacher. "One of the older boarder girls will come by soon to get you for lunch."

"But I want my mommy or Margie to come get me."

The teacher squatted down until her face was in front of mine. "I know, dear. But you'll soon have lots of friends among the boarders. And today you'll have a nice lunch waiting for you in the cafeteria."

Finally an older girl arrived at the door.

"I'm supposed to bring her to the cafeteria," she said, pointing to me.

"You're fifteen minutes late. Next time you need to get here on time."

After we were out of the teacher's sight, the big girl pinched my arm.

"Ow," I cried.

"That's so you don't tell on me," said the girl. "Or next time I'll pinch you harder."

I arrived at the cafeteria in tears.

"What's wrong with her?" asked the nun who monitored the lunchroom.

The girl shrugged.

I wasn't averse to all food at Rosary. I coveted the cream cheese and jelly sandwiches that another kindergartner, Marie, brought each day. Her mom cut off the bread crusts for her, which made the sandwiches even more enticing. One day Marie gave me a quarter of her sandwich—she must have noticed my hunger. The taste was even better than I had imagined. The next weekend, I asked my mother to make me a sandwich like Marie's.

"Cream cheese is Jew food. We don't eat cream cheese."

I didn't know what Jew food was. She made me cottage cheese and jelly sandwiches instead, and she didn't cut off the crusts. The bread was soggy, and little curds fell out the back of the sandwich when I took a bite.

My morning sickness at Rosary wasn't an early case of bulimia—my fingers were too short to reach the back of my throat. No, this was real, honest-to-goodness heaving my guts out, like I was trying to exorcise something evil inside myself, something that made my mother banish me. I don't recall lunches or dinners at Rosary, but I must have eaten very little. Over the next several months I steadily lost weight and soon looked like a skeletal version of myself. I was starving to death.

I learned in medical school that pediatricians refer to this experience as "failure to thrive." With just basic needs met—food, shelter, and loving caretaking—most kids will eat, grow, gain weight, and develop cognitive and emotional skills. Failure to thrive occurs when something goes very wrong, and it can be deadly: children raised in orphanages with minimal human touch have an increased risk of dying. The nomenclature is unfortunate, implying culpability on the child's part. More appropriate would be to label the adult with "failure to parent" or "failure to care."

The nuns must have been concerned about my not eating and weight loss because they began to give me a sandwich each afternoon in the dormitory when the older girls were still in class. Sister Mary Joseph cut it into quarters just the way I liked it. Sometimes it would be spread with molasses, which made me gag, but other times it would be filled with peanut butter and honey, which I liked. None of the other girls were given food in the dormitory. I knew they would have been jealous.

The kindergarten class was half-day. As the only boarder in that class, I was on my own in the afternoons. One winter day, I ventured on to the playground. I shivered in my coat and wool hat, as I sat on a wooden merry-go-round and idly pushed myself around with one foot. An image of a man scurrying away sticks in my mind. He wore a brown overcoat, a thick scarf, and a brown fedora pulled low on his head. Later, I'd tell my mother a boy put a stick into my bottom and it hurt to go to the bathroom. I wonder what really happened to me that day. Was the stick just a stick, or was it something else? Was the boy just a boy, or was it an older male? Whatever did or did not happen that day, it's clear that I was vulnerable. No one was watching out for me.

Frequently, I wandered the hallways at Rosary, not sure what to do with myself, feeling lost. The nuns did have me take a nap in the afternoon, so someone must have tracked me down occasionally.

Sister Mary Joseph supervised the dormitory. At night she wore a white muslin gown with matching robe and cap. As with her daytime costume, a string of beads hung from a black rope around her waist. She told me these were rosary beads. I thought maybe they were named after the school and wondered if they hurt her legs when she slept on them.

The dormitory followed a bedtime ritual. The girls went in small groups to brush their teeth. Sister Mary Joseph stood outside the open bathroom door to make sure they were making progress, while also keeping an eye on the rest of the room. After all the girls finished in the bathroom, Sister Mary Joseph told us to kneel by our beds with our hands folded, our heads down, and our eyes closed.

"Hail Mary, full of grace, the Lord is with thee. Blessed art though amongst women . . . " After Sister Mary Joseph finished the Hail Mary prayer, she would be quiet for a few seconds, and then say, "Dear Lord, thank you for our blessings today. Please help us to be good and holy girls. Amen."

"Amen," the girls said in unison. I wasn't sure what "amen" meant, but I said it too.

"Girls," she said, "remember that nighttime is for sleeping. All lights need to be off now. If you have to go to the bathroom, be quiet and don't turn on your light. The nightlights will be on, and you'll be able to see your way. Be quick and then go right back to bed. No stopping to see your friends. If any of you need me in an emergency, you know where my room is, right at the end of the dormitory."

It felt comforting to hear her say these things, but she didn't come over to each girl's bed to tuck us in. I didn't dare get up because Sister Mary Joseph had said that we were supposed to stay in our beds unless it was an emergency. Some nights the bigger girls would sneak into the bathroom after Sister Mary Joseph's room went dark. I'd hear them whisper and giggle. One night, through the open bathroom door, I could see them eating toothpaste. Sister Mary Joseph suddenly appeared.

"What are you girls doing up?" she asked. "You know you should be asleep."

"We were hungry," said the six-year-old whose bed stood next to mine.

"Come along now," said the nun. "Breakfast will come soon enough. You need to make sure you eat all your dinner so you won't be hungry at bedtime."

I could understand why they were hungry. I'd barely tasted any of the congealed food the kitchen workers glopped onto the boarders' trays. But even if the meals had been as good as at home, I wouldn't have wanted them. My throat clamped up at the thought of eating there.

I lay awake most nights at Rosary. The nightlights around the room caused dark shapes and shadows to appear on the walls. I tried closing my eyes, but the darkness under my eyelids frightened me even more than the shadows. I could hear various noises: a bed's springs squeaked as a girl tossed around in her sleep, an arm hit the wall, a doll's head thudded on the floor, a girl called out "Mama." In the months I spent there, my only deep sleeps were on the weekends at home.

On particularly bad nights, when I'd cry from terror, Sister Mary Joseph would take me to her room and let me sleep in her bed. She wasn't Margie, but it was so comforting to have her nearby that I'd drop off to sleep as soon as my head hit the pillow. I doubt if Mother Superior would have approved. Maybe Sister Mary Joseph came from a large family, or maybe she'd learned over the years how challenging boarding school was for the little girls.

Looking back from the perspective of a mother and grandmother, I am grateful that Sister Mary Joseph cared for me on difficult nights. While I found it comforting, it could be a dangerous situation for a vulnerable child at a boarding school. If my mother knew about my sleeping in the nun's bed, it didn't seem to concern her.

In my thirties, on night call during medical training, I'd again sleep in strange institutional beds. It might be a cot in a dingy, dirty room with peeling paint; a bunk bed in a dorm; or even an empty intensive care unit bed. The difference was that I chose to undergo the rigorous training and was free to leave. I couldn't leave Rosary—I was a prisoner.

One afternoon an eighth grade girl came over to my bed as I woke from my nap. She had short, curly, dark-blond hair and thick pink-rimmed glasses. Her royal blue school uniform blouse fit tightly around her arms. The top of my head reached to her waist.

"Come with me," she said. "I'm supposed to give you a bath."

She led me down the hall by the hand.

This bathroom looked as large as a ballroom. Like the dorm, the walls were white with dark wood wainscoting. Several overhead lights hung down with bare bulbs sticking out of silver cone fixtures. The black and white square floor tiles were several times larger than my feet. Little light got in through the narrow windows. A large, institutional bathtub sat in the middle of the room. A bar of Ivory soap lay in a silver tray near the water taps.

The girl turned on the water tap and helped me undress. She showed me where to hang my clothes on some hooks. She walked over to a metal cabinet and took out a white towel, which she placed on the floor near the tub. She turned off the water. Steam rose from the high surface of the water like the wisps of smoke from my mother's and aunt's cigarettes. I hugged my arms around my chest to warm myself in the cold air.

"Get in the tub," the girl said.

I felt the water with my hand, the way Margie taught me to do at home.

"It's too hot," I said.

She swished her hand through the water.

"It's fine," she said. "Sister said to give you your bath or neither of us will get any supper." Her voice was louder now. I thought she must be angry.

I couldn't move, stiff like one of my dolls. I didn't want to get into that hot water because I knew it would hurt me, but I was also afraid of this girl. On the other hand, the threat of missing supper didn't bother me at all.

"It will burn me," I cried.

Suddenly the girl picked me up and put me into the bathtub feet-first. I screamed from the pain of the scalding water, but she held me down. Her fingers dug into my arms as she struggled to push me farther into the burning water. I screamed, "Please, please, please let me out."

The bathroom door crashed open. Sister Mary Joseph ran in, yelled at the girl to get away from me, and picked me up out of the water. She gently wrapped me in a stiff towel. She inspected my bright red legs, which stung the way my face did after my mother's slap.

Still carrying me, Sister Mary Joseph rooted around in the metal cabinet draws and took out a big jar of Vaseline. She sat down on the floor, held me in her lap, and gently spread the Vaseline on my legs. I didn't complain that it hurt every time she touched my skin because it felt so good to lean against her and have her take care of me. I almost felt safe.

If my mother noticed burn scars the next time I was home, it didn't bother her enough to take me out of Rosary. It's unlikely that Sister Mary Joseph reported the incident—the Catholic Church keeps such things secret. After this, though, only the nuns gave me my baths.

Medical school would help me realize how much I'd suffered as a child. I'd learn in a pediatrics lecture how to recognize the signs and symptoms of child abuse. I listened in a frozen state, remembering my own abuse at the hands of people who were supposed to take care of me.

I'd learn in microbiology about a condition called *scalded skin syndrome*, in which an infection with certain strains of *Staphylococcus* bacteria causes skin to blister and peel off, as if boiling water had been poured onto it. Until they heal, patients are vulnerable to dehydration and infection with other bacteria. After my scalding at Rosary, I felt exposed, as if my protective coating had been peeled away. Until I could escape that school, I was vulnerable to attack.

At Rosary, there were safe times of day and there were dangerous times. I felt safe with my kindergarten teacher and the other students in my class. Sister Mary Joseph wasn't the cuddly type, but she had a kind voice and smiled frequently. But when I wasn't around these people, I tensed with fear for stretches of minutes or hours.

One day I was walking down the hall from my classroom toward the girls' bathroom. Two bigger girls approached from the other direction. I looked at the floor, hoping they wouldn't notice me. Suddenly I was looking at two big pairs of black and white saddle shoes. I moved to the left to get around them, but they blocked my way.

"This is the little brat who told on me to Sister Mary Joseph," said one of the girls.

I looked up and recognized the girl who had given me the scalding bath. Her face squished into a sneer. She pushed my chest with her fist.

"Know what happens to tattletales?" she asked.

I shook my head. She pushed me again.

"They get hurt, that's what," she said.

Finally they left me. Afraid to be alone in the girls' bathroom, I ran back to the kindergarten room. The teacher asked me what was wrong. I stood there holding my legs together tightly, afraid I'd wet my pants. The teacher must have realized something was wrong because she called over to another classroom for a teacher to watch the kindergartners while she brought me to the lavatory. After this, the teacher took all the children to the bathroom at one time.

On Friday mornings, Sister Mary Joseph would tell me to come up to the dormitory after school to pack for the weekend at home. I would be so excited during the school day that I couldn't concentrate. The nuns often found me wandering the halls outside of the kindergarten classroom as if I were trying to go home early.

Several of the girls didn't leave on weekends. Some of them lived too far away for their parents to make two trips each week. Some, my mother told me later, were so wild that they had been sent to Rosary because their parents couldn't handle them. I felt sorry for these girls but thought they must be really bad if their parents wouldn't let them come home at all. They had a haunted look on Friday afternoons as we lucky ones packed up our weekend suitcases and laundry bags.

Not much happened at home on the weekends, but I loved being there all the same. After enrolling me in Rosary, my mother and aunt moved to the first-floor apartment of a brick duplex in Watertown. My mother and Margie worked, so weekends were for housecleaning. I loved helping with the cleaning because I got to follow Margie around.

On Sundays we went to 8:00 A.M. Mass. Afterward, my mother made Sunday dinner, which we ate around two o'clock. Then it would be time to get ready to go back to Rosary. As soon as my mother put my suitcase on my bed, I'd feel sick to my stomach. She called it "butterflies in my tummy," but it didn't feel like butterflies to me. It felt like I was going to throw up all the Sunday dinner I'd just eaten.

One weekend late in December, my mother didn't tell me it was time to go back to Rosary. She didn't bring me back on Monday, nor on Tuesday. I knew that Christmas was coming soon because Margie had put up our few decorations—antique ornaments she hung on a tree and an old crèche. Three personalized Christmas stockings my mother had knitted lay across the cherry veneer coffee table because we had no fireplace. Tuesday night Margie told me that Santa would bring me presents that night.

"What do you want for Christmas, Anne?" she asked.

"To stay here forever with you and Mommy," I replied.

Margie bit her lip but said nothing. I don't remember what presents I received but I loved being at home with Margie, who took the week off as vacation time. After a breakfast of French toast, we'd walk to the local park. Margie loved the seesaw and swings as much as I did. After a couple hours of play, we'd drag ourselves home for a grilled cheese sandwich and a bowl of Campbell's tomato soup. Then I'd cuddle next to Margie on the couch while she read me a story. She'd tuck me in my bed for a nap and give me a little back rub to help me relax.

My mother was home during part of the Christmas break. I loved seeing her too, although I could never figure out why she got so mad at me. I wanted her to love me so she wouldn't send me away again, but I couldn't figure out how to make her love me. Too soon it was Sunday afternoon again. When my mother said it was time to get ready, I burst into tears.

"I don't want to go back to Rosary!" I cried.

"You have to go. I don't have a choice," said my mother, firmly. She stood tall, hands on hips.

"But why can't I just stay here?"

"Don't be difficult, Anne. You have to go back to school. I can't stay home with you. I have to work."

"Margie could stay home with me."

"Margie doesn't want to stay with you. She's not your mother. Now, go to your room and open up your suitcase so we can pack it."

"Please don't make me go." I couldn't stop the tears from welling up in my eyes and pouring down my cheeks.

"Oh for Christ's sake, Anne, if you don't stop this bawling I'll really give you something to cry about."

My mother didn't wait long; before I could catch my breath, she swatted me across my face. Then she did it again and again until I stopped crying. I went to my room, opened my suitcase, and threw up into it. My mother rushed in, and after she saw what I'd just done, slapped me even harder. That made me sick again, but I still had to return to Rosary.

My mother and Margie never visited me at Rosary, even though they lived within a couple of miles of the school. Sister Mary Joseph helped me compose a weekly letter to my mother. I told her what I wanted to say, and she printed it on a piece of paper. Then, I copied it over carefully onto another piece of paper. She put it in an envelope, let me lick the envelope and stamp, and mailed it for me. I don't remember receiving any letters from either my mother or aunt, but on Valentine's Day my mother did send me a card printed on a puzzle. Sister Mary Joseph read the message: "To my daughter, please be my Valentine. Love, Mom." I loved pulling the puzzle apart and putting it together, over and over again. I had the message memorized and pretended to read it every time I assembled the puzzle. It was as if I was trying to piece together my fractured family, attempting to make sense of my life.

One afternoon in May of 1958, I woke up on a couch in Mother Superior's office. The sun streamed in the windows and hurt my eyes. My head throbbed the way your hand hurts after being caught in a drawer. I desperately wanted to sleep, but a nun shook me each time I nodded off. I wished she would just leave me alone. To my surprise, my mother's voice appeared at the edge of my consciousness. *Maybe I'm dreaming*, I thought. One of my knee socks was bunched around my ankle. I wanted to pull it up but didn't dare move.

"She's hurt her head, Doctor," I heard my mother say. She must have been using Mother Superior's phone. "The nuns couldn't wake her up for an hour."

There was a pause, then she added, "I don't know why they didn't call you sooner. They called me first to come over. I had to wait for a taxi to pick me up at work."

Then there was another pause until she said, "Okay, I'll bring her right in."

Slowly, my memory cleared like a cloud-filled sky making a slit for the sun to push through. I'd climbed the ladder to the top of Rosary's playground slide. I'd sat down at the top of the slide and carefully arranged my wool skirt under my legs. I gave myself a gentle nudge down. The third grade girl behind me, impatient at my cautiousness, bore down on me without waiting. She body-slammed me a third of the way down the slide, sending me over the side, headfirst onto the concrete. No nuns patrolled the playground—perhaps they were at afternoon prayers. The next thing I knew I was flat on my back on Mother Superior's couch with two nuns looking down at me as if I were a science lab specimen.

A yellow taxi took us to our doctor's office in Brookline. The doctor asked me all sorts of silly-sounding questions: What is your name? Where are we? Who is this lady here (pointing to my mother)? How old are you?

I must have gotten the answers right because he smiled and patted my head. Then he examined me. My head still hurt, and I wanted to curl up and sleep. But I felt less groggy than I had in the Mother Superior's office.

"How long has she been at Rosary?" he asked my mother.

"Since September," she said.

"I saw her last August, when she was four." He looked at his notes. "She weighed forty-five pounds then. Today she's only thirty-five. What the hell have you been doing to her for nine months?"

"Nothing, doctor. She says she feels sick a lot."

"Didn't you notice that she's lost weight? She looks like a goddamn concentration camp survivor."

"It's not my fault. I can't help it if she doesn't eat at Rosary."

The doctor looked at her over his glasses.

"Is she at Rosary on the weekends?"

"No, we take her home on the weekends."

"Does she eat at home then?"

"Yes, she seems to enjoy eating. Except on Sundays, when we have to get her ready to go back to Rosary. She'll often throw up her Sunday dinner."

"Jesus Christ, I've never seen such neglect. You need to take her out of Rosary immediately."

"But what am I going to do? I can't take care of her. I have to work."

"I don't know what you're going to do. But, if you send her back to Rosary, I'll have no choice but to call social services. I've a good mind to do that anyway. They could take her away from you, and you could get arrested for child neglect."

My mother was sobbing now, but she agreed to follow the doctor's instructions and took me out of the school. I never returned to Rosary. The doctor insisted on seeing me each week. Sometimes my mother or Margie brought me to his office, and sometimes he made a home visit. He always weighed me and asked what I was eating. He asked who was taking care of me and seemed satisfied when my mother told him about the various ladies who watched me during the day. After about a month, he started to smile when he read the numbers on the scale.

I could have died that year at Rosary, yet I had no medical problems to account for my nausea, vomiting, reduced eating, and subsequent weight loss. I was just sad. So I wasted away. In my medical school psychiatry class, I'd learn that loss of appetite and weight loss can be signs of severe depression. My sadness at Rosary was starving me.

Years later, my mother told me that her decision to send me to Rosary was financially driven. It was less expensive to board me there than to send me to a day school and pay for after-school care. It seems that in those days the Catholic Church, with money to spare, had special interest in holding children captive round-the-clock. The Church subsidized the indoctrination of its children. And for my mother it was a welcome relief not to have to deal with me on weeknights.

Soon after I left Rosary to live in the Watertown flat with my mother and aunt, I found myself standing alone outside our front stoop, face-to-face with three brilliant red tulips. I was struck at being able to see such beauty so close. Usually, I had to crane my head up to see something pretty, such as gilded statues at Church or a lady's necklace. The sun beamed down and warmed me while it released a faint fragrance of spring from the tulips. It felt good to be home.

Chapter 2

Fattening Up

I stood next to my mother in front of a large, dark-red brick building. It was July, 1958. We had just moved from Watertown to a flat in Brighton, a working-class section on the western edge of Boston. I was so happy to be living with my mother and Margie again that I didn't much mind the move to a new apartment. As long as I could be with them, I'd live in a shack. When I was home, it was always my mother, Margie, and me. Margie held a variety of amorphous roles in the family. She was a second mother to me, the one I ran to for banishing the pain of cuts and scrapes. She sometimes acted like a daughter to my mother and a sister to me. Then, when she was angry with either my mother or me, she'd pull back and act like we were roommates.

I now shared a room with my mother. Sometimes she made me lie next to her in her bed for a morning snuggle. I hated being that close, hated the vinegary smell of her before she washed and applied perfume. I didn't dare complain about this new arrangement for fear that my mother would get mad and send me away again. At least Margie still gave me big hugs at night and rubbed my back to help me get to sleep.

Some of my dresses that used to hang loose were snug around the waist, now that I'd had five months of my mother's cooking and Margie's goodies to fatten me up. My shape was getting closer to its genetic roots—my mother was always overweight. She'd bemoan her girth frequently. "You just have big bones, Mary," Margie would say.

"Where are we?" I asked my mother as we gazed up at the brick facade.

"That's your new school, God willing."

I shivered in spite of the heat. School meant being sent away and sleeping in a strange room with children I didn't know. It meant I would hardly see my mother and Margie.

"I feel sick," I said.

We had walked the mile to the school, keeping to the shady sides of the streets. On our block, we passed two- and three-family houses that housed typical, large Irish Catholic families, each with a father, a mother, and half-dozen kids. We avoided the Projects, a public housing development filled with the larger Irish families, often with twelve or thirteen kids. Many would be "Irish twins," born ten months apart. We walked along a street of single-family houses that my mother said were where the well-to-do lived, the middle-class couples who might have only two to four children. These were a mixture of Catholic and non-Catholic, Irish and non-Irish families. The fathers were professionals—doctors, lawyers, accountants—but not making quite enough to live in the wealthy suburbs to the west of Brighton.

My mother dressed nicely today, like she did for work, even though it was a Saturday. She wore a yellow shirt dress that reached just below her knees. A thin belt matched her white patent leather pumps. Pearl clip earrings, a single-strand pearl costume necklace, and white cotton gloves completed her outfit. Her short dark hair rose straight back from her forehead, and pancake makeup reached perfectly to her hairline. She made her thin lips visible with a careful application of red lipstick, and her eyeglasses with turned up corners matched her hair color exactly.

My blue and green plaid taffeta dress crinkled as I moved. I carried a miniature version of my mother's purse, which housed my white cotton gloves. A tight ponytail and plastic headband controlled my blond hair. I felt very proud to be all dressed up and walking with my mother.

If I'd known how to read, I'd have seen "St. Columbkille School" engraved in large letters over the rounded stone alcove. My mother hesitated, took a deep breath, and opened the dark wooden door. Inside, cool stale air and red linoleum-covered staircases greeted us. I stopped, unable to move. The dimly lit stairs and strong Lysol scent reminded me of Rosary Academy and caused a wave of nausea.

"Come on, Anne Marie," my mother said. "We'll be late."

I climbed the steps slowly, my feet like blocks of wood. My mother grabbed my arm, her fingers pressing in deep. We stopped at a door to our left. My mother opened her purse and pulled out a piece of paper on which I recognized her sloped handwriting in blue ink.

"I think this is it," she said.

She pulled off her gloves and knocked on the door once, softly. There was no response. She knocked again, louder this time. After a minute, the door opened. A lady appeared, dressed in a black gown like the Rosary nuns. A stiff white material framed her face and reached upward like a small pastry box, topped with a long black veil. Her black eyebrows stretched out in front like cat whiskers. I wondered if this nun would give me baths and put me to bed at night.

"May I help you, dearie?" the lady asked.

"I'm Mrs. McTiernan. I'm here to see Mother Superior about my daughter."

"Oh, yes, dear, I'll tell Mother Superior. You can have a seat right there."

We sat side by side on a wooden bench, each with our hands in our laps holding onto our purses, me with my legs swinging, my mother with her legs crossed at the ankles. My mother looked straight ahead, her face expressionless.

"Stop moving around, Anne," my mother said. "You're rocking the bench."

Sitting as still as I could, I decided to count the tiles of linoleum around us. I had reached thirty-two when the door opened. The nun said Mother Superior could see us now. She led us into an inner office with narrow windows covered with dark green shades that didn't keep out the hot sun. Another nun sat reading papers on her desk. Suddenly she looked up, as if surprised to find someone else in her room.

"This is Mrs. McTiernan, Sister," said the older nun. "And this is Anne."

"Hello," said Mother Superior. "Have a seat." She motioned to two wooden chairs in front of her desk. My mother sat in one. I shimmied myself up into the other. My mother held her purse so tight the pink went out of her fingers.

"Well," said the nun, "I understand that you'd like Anne to attend Saint Columbkille's in the fall."

"Yes, I . . ."

"You know she's younger than our first graders usually are," Mother Superior interrupted. "From your application I see that she's only five years old."

"Yes, Sister," my mother said. "But I have no other choice than to send her to school. Her father and I are separated, so I have to work. And I can't afford a babysitter."

"What made you choose St. Columbkille?"

"Anne's father went to school here."

My ears perked up. My mother rarely mentioned my father; she only told me that he had gone away. I couldn't understand why she wanted to send me to his old school. I wondered if this lady had been my father's teacher.

"And did you attend parochial school?"

"No, Sister. My family lived out in the country, in the town of Kingston, near Plymouth. The only schools were public. But I went to Sunday school."

Mother Superior pressed her hands together like the statue of the Blessed Mary that sat on my mother's bureau. The nun looked at me for what felt like a long time. I jumped when she addressed me. "Anne, what did you learn in kindergarten?"

I felt like crawling under the chair. I looked at my mother. She was sitting at the edge of her seat, leaning forward.

"She knows her ABCs," my mother said.

"Can you say your ABCs for me, Anne?" asked the nun.

I didn't respond.

"Answer her, Anne Marie," my mother said. "Sister asked you a question."

"ABCDEFGHIJKLMNOPQRSTUVWXYZ," I said quietly without pausing.

"Very good, Anne," the nun said. Then turning to my mother she asked, "Is she a good girl?"

I held my breath as I waited to hear what my mother would say. At home, she often told me I was a bad girl.

"Yes," said my mother. "Anne is a very good girl."

I smiled when I heard this, even though I knew it was a lie.

"Well," said the nun, "you know that we have to charge you tuition and fees. For one child that will come to a total of thirty dollars a year. Can you pay that?"

"Yes," said my mother. "I'll manage."

"Is her father involved in her care?" Mother Superior asked.

"No. I'm on my own."

"Does Anne have any sisters or brothers?"

"No, she's an only child."

"So it's just the two of you living together?"

"My sister lives with us. She's never been married."

"Do you both go to Church and keep up with the sacraments?"

"Yes," my mother said. "We go to confession every Saturday and Mass every Sunday, and we take communion every week."

"There are no male friends visiting you or your sister?"

"Oh Lord, no," said my mother. "That's out of the question for either of us."

"Good," said the nun. It sounded like she was calling my mother and aunt good girls. "You'll need to send a lunch with her every day."

"You don't serve the children lunch?" my mother asked.

"Most of the children go home for lunch. Those who live too far away stay for lunch. So Anne won't be alone. But we can't send her home to an empty house for lunch."

"No, of course not. I just thought maybe you had a cafeteria."

"We closed our cafeteria several years ago. We found that the families couldn't afford to pay for prepared lunches and preferred to have their children come home in the middle of the day."

I didn't want to be different from the other kids who got to go home in the middle of the day, but I was very happy to hear that I wouldn't have to eat food made at the school.

"Who will take care of Anne after school?" Mother Superior asked.

"Our landlady, Mrs. John Reilly, has agreed to watch her. She's home with her seven children."

"Ah, yes, the Reillys are blessed with a large family. I see that you live on Turner Street. That's quite far from school. Will you walk her to school in the morning?"

"She'll walk to school and home with the Reilly girls."

That seemed to satisfy Mother Superior, who nodded slowly while looking at me. She stood up.

"Well, we're happy to welcome another child of Christ to our family. We'll send a letter before school starts letting you know who her teacher will be, her classroom number, and the times and days of classes and holy days. We'll also send information on where you can purchase Anne's school uniform."

I didn't like the idea of a uniform. The uniforms worn by the older girls at Rosary had made it difficult to tell them apart. I wondered why I couldn't wear my own dresses like I did at Rosary.

"Thank you for allowing Anne to come to St. Columbkille. She'll be a very good student for you, Sister." My mother stood up.

"Do you have any questions for me, Anne?" asked Sister.

"Where will I sleep?" I asked.

The nun laughed. "In your bed at home of course, dear. What a funny question."

Margie walked me to my first day at St. Columbkille. She had pulled my hair into a ponytail so tight that I had trouble closing my eyes. My classroom, one of three for first grade, had fifty-three children. A single nun taught us; there were no assistant teachers or interns or parent volunteers. I listened carefully to everything the sister said, afraid I'd get sent away or slapped if I was not a good girl. The nun rewarded me with gold stars on my papers and all As on my report cards. These were something tangible, something I could show my mother, so she might like me a little more or hate me a little less. The nun assigned me to work with the children who were lagging, so at age five, I became an unpaid assistant teacher. I couldn't understand why the teacher chose me to help others—I felt insecure and lost, not capable at all. All my life I'd experience what psychologists call *imposter syndrome*. Even when I'd succeed at a difficult endeavor, such as finishing medical school, I'd feel as if I didn't deserve the rewards of my hard work.

Living at home, my weight quickly rebounded and shot up. I went from resembling a concentration camp survivor to a chubby kid. A condition called the *refeeding syndrome* is caused by rapidly replacing nutrients in someone who has been starved. The person can develop severe electrolyte abnormalities if fed too much, too soon, and the risk of serious complications, including death, is high.

I don't know if I starved enough at Rosary to have had this level of risk. Studies of people exposed to starvation as children show an excess of fat accumulation in the period of refeeding and catch-up growth. Looking back, I can see that this is what I experienced. Finally living in a more stable environment, food represented comfort rather than terror, and I was able to eat. My body, still in a state of metabolism caused by the Rosary starvation, was too efficient at using calories. So my body ballooned up, and I became a fat girl.

The Reilly family had so many kids that to an outsider I blended in—just one more Irish face—although I felt more like a stray kitten nursed by a mother dog along with her litter. Mrs. Reilly's care pretty much amounted to a benevolent smile whenever I ran through her flat on the heels of her kids. But she never hit or scolded me. One of her daughters was in first grade with me, and her closest sister was a year older. The girls looked similar enough to be twins—both with pale skin, freckles, and mousy brown hair cut short. My mother said Mrs. Reilly cut her kids' hair around a bowl, as if this was shameful. I pictured her seven kids lined up with cereal bowls on their heads waiting for their trim. I thought they looked cute and wished Mrs. Reilly would cut my hair, too.

The Reilly girls taught me how to eat peanut butter out of the jar with a spoon and how to make mud pies in the backyard. Sometimes we played Red Rover or Cowboys and Indians with their brothers. We rode all over the neighborhood on our roller skates tightened to the bottom of our sneakers with special keys, skinning our knees when cracked sidewalks tripped us. I always went to Margie with my banged-up knees—she knew just what to do and say to make the hurt go away faster.

My mother arranged one of her week's vacations to coincide with my Easter break. This didn't mean that I saw much of her. There were no family-goes-to-amusement park types of vacations for working-class Boston Irish. Rather, we roamed with the neighborhood kids all day until our stomachs growled for supper. One evening, after climbing the stairs to our flat, I found the door ajar. This was odd, but being six years old by then, I didn't worry about it. I just shoved it open.

"Ma!" I called. "I'm hungry."

The flat was silent. I walked through each room, calling for my mother. I couldn't find her. I didn't think to see if her things were gone. I knew that she'd had enough of me and decided to leave. *I must have been a bad girl*, I thought. I wished I knew what I'd done wrong so I could make sure never to do it again. I wished I knew where my mother was so I could tell her I was sorry and loved her and would never be bad again.

When Margie arrived home an hour later, she found me standing in the living room, crying.

"What's the matter, Anna Banana?" she asked.

"My mommy's gone," I said.

"What do you mean *gone*?"

"She's gone. She wasn't here when I came home from playing with the girls."

"Oh dear God, I hope nothing's happened to her. Let's go ask Mrs. Reilly if she's seen her."

We walked downstairs and knocked on the Reilly's door. Mr. Reilly answered. His face held a scowl and a two-day stubble.

"Hi, Mr. Reilly. Have you or Mrs. Reilly seen my sister Mary? She wasn't home when Anne came in, and she didn't leave a note."

"She's gone off to the hospital with my wife and daughter. The stupid kid got her fingertip sliced off on her bicycle. So now I'm taking care of all these brats on my own." Behind him we could see a blur of kids shoving each other in the kitchen.

"Stop that now or I'll give it to you," he shouted. He closed the door in our faces.

"That rude, ignorant man," Margie muttered as we climbed back upstairs.

My mother finally came home after Margie fed me hot dogs and beans and got me ready for bed. I heard them arguing.

"Where in hell have you been?" Margie asked.

"Little Mary Reilly cut her finger badly," my mother said. "Mrs. Reilly took her in a taxi to the hospital. I went along with her. I had to help."

"Well, you left Anne here without anyone to watch her," Margie said. "I found her sobbing in the living room."

"I had no choice. Mrs. Reilly needed my help."

"You couldn't even tell Anne where you were going? You couldn't even take time to leave me a note? What was I supposed to do? For all I knew, you were lying in a gutter somewhere."

"Oh for Christ's sake, Margaret, I was just trying to do the right thing and help that little girl. Nothing bad happened to Anne. And you were coming home soon."

"What if I'd been delayed? Who would have given Anne her supper? Who would have gotten her ready for bed?"

"Jesus, Margaret, I knew Anne would be fine on her own for a while."

"She's only six years old! She's a little girl."

"You just want to baby her. It's about time she did more around the house for me."

"I'd like to see how you could manage without me. I've a good mind to get my own apartment."

"Oh, stop being such a martyr, Margaret."

There was silence after this. I heard plates rattling in the kitchen, presumably my mother making herself supper. Now I had two things to worry about. Earlier, I worried that my mother had left me because of something I'd done. Now I was petrified that Margie might move out. I didn't know what I'd do without Margie. Who would kiss my skinned knees? Who would play Go Fish with me? And who would rub my back at night and tuck me in so that I could sleep?

I crept out of my bed to the bathroom and saw my mother from the side of my eye as I passed. Margie's door was closed, but light leaked from underneath. Back in bed, reassured that they were both home, I slept.

April arrived with cool mornings and warm afternoons. I let myself into the apartment after school using the key I kept on a ring with a picture of Saint Anthony. The saint was supposed to guard against losing things. I threw down my book bag, hung up my winter coat, and grabbed the sweater I'd just pushed out of the way to make room for the coat. I didn't stop to change out of my school uniform—I had very few clothes anyway, so I couldn't see the point.

Outside the back door, I fastened the roller skates onto my shoes, giving the key an extra twist so they wouldn't fall off. I quickly caught up with the Reilly girls and off we went. After two hours of strenuous play, we skated into our backyard in response to Mrs. Reilly's call. We trooped into the kitchen, where a half-dozen kids were trying to grab early tastes of dinner. Mrs. Reilly, baby on one hip and toddler pulling her nylons down her calf, was swatting the bigger kids away from her stove with a big wooden spoon. At 5:15 P.M. sharp, my mother walked in. My mother smiled and thanked Mrs. Reilly for once again watching me.

I followed my mother up the stairs to our flat. I was tired and hungry, glad to be home. My mother was quiet. We walked into the apartment.

"Shut the door," my mother said.

After releasing the knob, I turned, ready to head for the bathroom. The blow to the side of my head stunned me. I couldn't figure out what was going on. My mother held her big black leather purse in both her hands. Then she hit me again with the purse, this time striking my face. I didn't dare react. I knew by now that whatever she was doing would only escalate if I cried or tried to protect myself.

"You little shit," she finally said. I remained silent, afraid to ask why she was angry.

"How dare you wear your good white sweater outside to play? You'll get it filthy, you'll ruin it, and how am I supposed to replace it? Do you think I'm made of money?"

"Sorry. I didn't think."

"Of course you didn't think. You never think. You certainly never think about me, working so hard with no thanks coming from you."

I stood there, head down, in part to hide the flowing tears, in part to avoid her eyes. If I looked at her, she might start up again. Now I can see that my reaction was real animal behavior, victim pacifying the aggressor. If a menacing dog threatens you, stand still and avoid looking it in the eye because it reads movement as aggression. My stand-still-head-down stance was to avoid the wild dog's bite.

I didn't understand the level of her anger. I didn't see why wearing a sweater outside to play bought me a beating. There was no dirt on the sweater. But I was only six years old and didn't discriminate well among clean, smudged, and filthy. So maybe she saw something I didn't.

As an adult, I rarely wear white. I tell people it's because I dribble tea or coffee on most things I own, and light colors won't forgive my sloppiness. Or I say that my skin is too pale—I'd look like a monochrome painting. But in reality I avoid wearing it because it reminds me of getting bashed in the head with a heavy black purse. This became a problem for me in medical school. While most of the students were excited to don their white jackets that marked them as doctors-in-training, I was ambivalent and wore it only when required. The saving grace was that it was okay to get it dirty.

My mother disappeared that summer for two weeks. At first, I didn't know where she was and thought I must have made her really mad to leave for good. Mrs. Reilly took care of me during the day and in the evening when Margie said she had to go to the hospital. I didn't know what a hospital was.

"Your mother had an operation," she explained.

"What's an operation?"

She paused. "It's when some doctors open you up to fix things inside you."

"What did the doctors fix?"

"They took out one of her kidneys."

"What's a kidney?"

"It's what helps you go pee-pee."

"Why did they take it out?"

"It was sick."

I wondered how the doctor opened my mother up. Was it like unbuttoning a jacket? And would she still be able to pee? Did something I do cause her to have this problem?

Mrs. Reilly took me with her kids to St. Elizabeth's Hospital one night after dinner. However, children were not allowed in the hospital. While she went inside, I caught fireflies on the hospital's grassy tiers with her kids, which diminished some of my disappointment at not being able to see my mother.

When my mother finally came home, Margie and Mrs. Reilly helped her up the stairs to our apartment. My mother sat in the pink Queen Anne chair, frowned, and closed her eyes.

"Anne, you'll need to be quiet so your mother can rest," Margie said.

My mother looked very weak sitting there, but I wasn't sure whether she could still hit me in her condition. Just to be sure, I resolved to do whatever Margie told me so I could stay out of trouble.

"Okay," I whispered. I really wanted to know what the doctors had seen when they opened my mother up but didn't dare ask. I don't think this was an early sign of interest in human physiology. Rather, it was as if I wondered what my mother was made of, what was her essence. And would she be less angry with me after having this sick kidney removed? I hoped she would get better soon.

My mother groaned. "Oh, Dear God, I'm in pain."

"What can I do for you, Mary?" Margie asked. "The doctors said you were weak but you'll get stronger every day."

"They were just saying that. I don't know how much longer I'll be on God's green earth. I'll be dead soon, I'm sure."

This shook me. If my mother died, what would happen to me? My mother told me that Margie wouldn't stay home to take care of me. Would I have to go back to Rosary? I started to cry. My mother turned her eyes to me without moving her head.

"For Christ's sake get her out of here, Margaret. I need my rest."

"C'mon, Anne," Margie said. "Help me make your mother some tea."

She hustled me off to the kitchen, where she gave me milk and Toll House cookies while she made tea for my mother and herself. Tea was prescribed whenever someone was sick in our house. The Irish imbue tea with almost mystical powers of rejuvenation, and Irish-Americans continued the tradition. My mother and aunt drank it strong and black, unless they needed a special treat, in which case they'd add a dollop of milk. They preferred the modern teabag over tea leaves, happy to adopt time-saving methods.

My mother stayed out of work for almost a month. She lay on the couch most of the time in her nightgown and bathrobe. When Margie was at work, it was my job to get things for my mother—her cigarettes, the lunch Margie left in the refrigerator for her, the newspaper. I even learned to make her tea. I had to stand on a chair to reach the stove. My hand would shake from the weight of the kettle after I'd filled it, and it would shake even more as I poured the boiling water into the teacup. The steam would burn my arm as it traveled up from the kettle spout. My mother wanted the teacup nice and full, so I'd have to walk very slowly to avoid spilling. A few drops would usually fall, but they hit the top of my Keds, so they didn't sting for very long.

I prayed for my mother. I prayed that she'd get well soon. I prayed that she wouldn't die. And I prayed that she'd see how helpful I was and let me keep living with her and Margie.

I'd later learn that my mother suffered from recurrent kidney stones and infections. At the time, there were few treatment options, and her case was compounded by poverty and lack of access to specialists. After her surgery, her kidney specialist instructed her to limit intake of calcium to prevent formation of new stones. Every time we had ice cream, she'd say, "I'm not supposed to have this. It could kill me." It kind of spoiled the pleasure of my hot fudge sundae.

Later that summer, my mother had returned to work but was so weak that Margie had to do all the cooking, cleaning, and shopping. But on one particularly hot day, Margie, home on vacation, said she and I should go to Revere Beach. She packed us a lunch of bologna sandwiches, potato chips, and a thermos of cold orangeade. We stood in the back hallway, packed beach bags leaning against our legs. Margie stretched out her right hand, key poised a hair's breadth in front of the lock.

"Did I turn off the stove?" she asked.

I didn't say anything. I knew she wasn't asking me. A kid would never know the answer to such an important question, even a mature six-year-old like me.

"I have to go back in and check."

Her mouth was set as tight as it could be given her lower teeth overlapping her top teeth. She looked at me. The iris, normally brown, was practically all black, which meant she was having one of her "nervous" feelings. She opened the kitchen door and walked over to the stove. I trailed behind her. The big black line on each of the burner and oven dials pointed straight up in the off position. One by one, Margie grasped each dial and made the motion of turning it to the right. She repeated this two more times.

"I'd better make sure the front door is locked," she said.

I waited in the kitchen while she went to check the door we used only on the rare occasion of the doorbell ringing. I heard the lock slide back and forth three times. It was always three times. Margie returned to the kitchen. Beads of sweat sat on her forehead. She blew air up from her mouth.

"Anne, are the lights all out?" she asked.

"I think so," I answered.

"I'd better check."

We passed through each room of the apartment: the living room with its dark green brocade-covered couch and little black-and-white television on the rolling metal stand; the dining room dressed with my mother's cherry table, chairs, and hutch; the room my mother and I shared with our twin beds pushed too close together for my liking; Margie's bedroom with its mahogany bureaus and double bed. Margie pushed each light switch down, as if to make it more off than it already was. She checked every unlit lamp. She pressed the dials on unmoving window fans to their off positions. She performed all these checks three times. We returned to the back door. Margie paused. "I forgot to check the window locks."

I tried to keep my face placid. I was sweating but I knew that if I complained about how long this was taking, Margie would start her routine all over again. This time I waited by the door. Hopefully she'd remember to check the faucets on this turn around the apartment. Her routine never wavered: stove, front door, lights, window locks, faucets, back door. In the summer, she added the fans.

Margie appeared again. She opened the door and started to go out.

"Wait," I said, "I have to go pee-pee."

"Well, hurry up, then," she said.

Finally, we were outside. As we walked, I scanned both sides of the street to see if any of the kids from school were around. I hated meeting my classmates, afraid they would laugh at me or point out my fatness. But I also felt proud to be walking with my aunt. I wanted the world to see that an adult loved me enough to spend time with me.

We didn't meet anyone on our journey. We had left the house at nine o'clock, after the morning commuter rush, so we had seats next to each other all the way to the beach. I loved sitting close to Margie. Neither the streetcar nor the subway train were air conditioned, so my fat little body must have made Margie even hotter, but she didn't seem to mind and even let me put my hand in hers. I couldn't kiss her in public though—she said it wasn't right.

At the beach, Margie spread out our old navy wool picnic blanket and put something heavy on each corner so it wouldn't fly away. We stripped to our bathing suits, and I ran toward the water.

"Anne," Margie called after me, "don't go in over your knees."

"Okay," I yelled back. I didn't understand this rule. At the YMCA summer camp I'd attended for two weeks, I was the best swimmer of the Minnows. My fat body floated very well in water, which made swimming easier for me than for most of the skinny kids.

But I knew better than to argue with Margie. The water petrified her, along with heights, open-slatted stairs, bridges, cars, planes, thunderstorms, fires, horses, speaking to strangers, and electricity. My mother's fears were more about health—every symptom, ache, or pain portended immediate death. My own fears were a mixture of theirs and some of my own:

being sent away, my mother, speaking to strangers, speaking in public, other kids, boys, men, being sick, spiders, and bees.

My later decision to become a doctor might have derived from an innate desire to heal my mother in order to heal myself. I felt so powerless as a child, so dependent on my mother's moods. If she was angry, I flinched. If she was sick, I fretted. If she was frustrated, I tried to do better. In my immature mind, I connected these together. She was sick, therefore, angry, therefore, frustrated with me. I wanted the power to cure her illness, calm her anger, and heal her frustration. A healthy mother would allow me to be a healthy child.

Margie sat on the blanket, smoking her Chesterfield cigarettes and reading a paperback novel. She looked up and smiled every time I called her to watch me. I emerged only for lunch and to build sand castles with the pink pail and shovel we had brought with us. Later in the afternoon, we strolled along the boardwalk, chocolate ice cream cones in hand. After five minutes I was covered with sticky brown residue. Margie wiped what she could with the single-ply napkin the clerk had wrapped around the cone.

"You'll have to go back in the water to wash off," she said. I didn't complain at this. Too soon, Margie called to me that it was five o'clock and time to go home.

"Please, can we stay a little longer?" I pleaded.

"I need to make dinner for your mother. We don't want to keep her waiting." She had that nervous look again, so I didn't protest.

On the ride home, I leaned against Margie and enjoyed every minute of it. She made me feel safe and protected on our outings. With her, I could be a little girl.

Chapter 3

Crumbs

Screams woke me one October evening in 1959. I lay there listening, my thoughts as thick as vanilla pudding, not knowing where the screams were coming from. If I'd still been at Rosary, my first guess would have been the seven-year-old girl whose night terrors we mostly learned to sleep through. But I had been living with my mother and aunt for the past year and a half. I realized the screams came from outside my bedroom. Looking over at the other twin bed, I saw that my mother's form was missing. I sat up in bed and listened while I decided what to do. Suddenly my mother's voice loudly declared that she'd go get Mr. Reilly. Her footsteps passed my door, down the hall that led to the rickety back porch and stairs to the landlord's first-floor flat. I cracked the bedroom door open to hear better. My mother didn't have to knock very hard or long; Mr. Reilly was a fireman and could wake easily even when medicated by a six-pack of Schlitz.

I stepped into the hall. Light streamed out of the bathroom. I crept toward the light and found Margie bent over next to the toilet, her hand pressed down on the plush toilet cover that almost matched the sky blue bathroom rug.

"What's the matter?" I asked.

"There's a rat in the toilet. I almost sat on it."

Margie had the wide-eyed look on her face I'd only seen during thunderstorms, when she'd unplug the phone and all the electric appliances and make me sit still, away from windows and doors. I didn't understand why she'd fear a small animal. I'd never seen a rat up close, but if it fit into our toilet, how big could it be? I bent over to peer in the crack between the lid and the toilet bowl. Was that a whisker sticking out? I moved closer, hand stretched out to open the lid.

"No!" Margie's voice felt like a blow. "Don't open that, Anne. It could bite you."

Just as I started to understand the seriousness of the situation, my mother arrived with the scowling Mr. Reilly. Margie pulled the belt of her thick pink chenille bathrobe tighter. Identical pink rollers poked out all over the two women's heads.

"I don't see why you had to wake me up for this," Mr. Reilly growled.

"Oh for God's sake, John," said my mother. "We need the rat out now, so we can use the toilet. Plus what if it got loose in the apartment and attacked Anne?"

Now I was getting scared and I shivered in the cool night air. Two people had said I was in imminent danger from this thing. In my mind's eye the rat grew bigger by the second. I pictured him curled into a tight ball in order to fit in the bowl, ready to spring out when the lid was raised. He'd spray everyone with toilet water as he aimed his teeth at my neck.

I never did get to see that rat. My mother scooted me back to our bedroom after taking me downstairs to use the Reillys' bathroom. My mother seemed very happy to leave the rat caretaking to the landlord and Margie.

The next morning, as I searched for words in my Alpha-Bits cereal, my mother and Margie talked about the previous night.

"I didn't want to lift the toilet seat this morning. Are you sure Mr. Reilly really took care of the thing?" my mother asked.

I found a word short enough to fit onto my spoon—*rat*.

"Yes, it was horrible. And he had the nerve to complain that we couldn't do it ourselves. He said he had to be the man for his own family and now for ours, too."

"Jesus, we don't ask a lot of him. We pay him good money for the rent. It doesn't seem unreasonable to ask him to take care of rats and a few little repairs."

They were silent for a minute. Then my mother said, "I wish to God I had a decent man to take care of me."

"All men are scum," Margie replied. "Most of them are lazy, good-for-nothing drunks."

"Well, our father and Anne's father were that way, so you're right about some of them. But there are decent men out there."

"Humph," Margie said.

The landlord was no stranger to our flat. My mother and aunt had found doors and bureau drawers left open and said it had to be Mr. Reilly because he and his wife were the only people besides them who had a key. They knew that sweet Mrs. Reilly would never do that, and besides she was too busy with her seven kids. They didn't know why Mr. Reilly snuck in—they never left money lying around and didn't have liquor or valuable jewelry. Then one night after collecting me from Mrs. Reilly, my mother found our front door ajar. A week had passed since the rat visitation.

"That's strange," she said. "Anne, you didn't leave it open when you went out to play today, did you?"

I shook my head seriously because I knew from the sound of my mother's voice that this was a serious situation. My mother's hand trembled as she pushed the door open. She told me to stay in the front hall while she walked around the apartment.

"Well, nothing seems to be missing," she said.

When Margie arrived home thirty minutes later, my mother told her what she had found.

"Do you think it was Mr. Reilly again?" Margie asked.

"I'm going to go talk to him. He has no right to come in here."

She pounded down the stairs. After five minutes we heard her raised voice, then Mr. Reilly's voice, but we couldn't make out the words. My mother soon stomped back upstairs.

"You won't believe what he told me," my mother said. "He said he let himself in to make sure we weren't having any men in."

"What?"

"That's right. He said that no woman would be able to live without a man, so we must be trying to sneak men in. He said he didn't want his kids to see any sinful goings-on up here." My mother's voice broke as she continued. "He said Anne was a bastard, and he didn't want his pure little girls associating with her."

My head spun at this. I couldn't imagine not being able to play with the Reilly girls.

"What's a bastard?" I asked. They ignored me. Or maybe they didn't hear my small voice.

"Jesus," Margie said. "That's crazy. Was he drunk?"

"I think so. I could smell booze on his breath."

Suddenly they noticed me listening. My mother began making dinner. Margie set the table and put in a load of laundry. I hung around the kitchen, waiting to hear what else they would say about the Reillys, but I was to be disappointed with their silence.

At 7:30 P.M., my mother sent me to bed with the usual stern instructions to go to sleep. As soon as I closed the bedroom door, I pressed my ear to the cool wood. I heard things like "sneaking up here," "maybe he was looking for food," and "filthy." I couldn't tell if they were talking about the rat or about Mr. Reilly.

The following Saturday afternoon the mail slot in the front door clanged. Margie went downstairs to collect the mail. She returned, leafed through several items, and handed most of them to my mother.

"Bills," she said.

"What's this one?" my mother asked.

They peered at the front of the envelope. Frowning, my mother sat down on the living room couch and ripped open the envelope. She read the letter inside and, to my great shock, started to cry. She handed the letter to Margie, who read it and also began to weep.

I sat on the couch close beside my mother.

"What's wrong?" I could feel my lips quiver. I'd never seen either of them cry.

"The landlord is kicking us out," my mother said. "We have to be out in two weeks. Jesus, how in hell will we find a new place right before Thanksgiving?"

"But where will we go?" I felt panicked that I'd have to leave home. I'd finally been allowed to live with my mother and Margie. At the same time it surprised me to see my mother and aunt so distraught. If being evicted upset them so much, I wondered why they'd sent me away so often.

"Don't worry, Anne," Margie said. "We'll find a place to live."

I hoped there would be room for me.

Our new apartment was the bottom flat of a converted farmhouse. The landlords, an elderly couple, lived upstairs with one of their adult sons. Mr. and Mrs. Johnson weren't as fun as the Reilly girls, but they were kind. I would later adopt them as my pretend grandparents, although I wouldn't tell anyone about it, including them.

On our first day in the new flat, my mother told me to stay outside, out of the movers' way, but remain close so I could help her unpack when the burly men were done carting our furniture. First, I stood by the side of the steep driveway and watched the movers' progress with carrying our things from the truck in through the back door. After I made sure that the television and my favorite chair, the black one with the large pink flowers, were safely off the truck and on their way to the new flat, I walked around to the front of the house where I surveyed the neighboring houses. I saw no children out. This was unusual in Brighton, where virtually all houses had two or three flats, each of which housed an Irish-American family with at least five children. But maybe it was too chilly for them to be out this morning. I pulled my navy blue car coat tighter.

Suddenly, a shadow covered me. I looked up and saw a girl with a big grin on her face. She had short, thick, blond hair.

"Hi," said the girl. "My name is Debbie. I live on Upcrest Road." She pointed past a neighboring house to a street parallel to my new long driveway.

"Hi," I said. "I'm Anne." I hoped I sounded okay. At age six, I didn't have the social graces for making new friends.

"Do you go to St. Columbkille?"

"Yeah."

"What grade are you in?"

"Second."

"I'm in fourth grade. Who's your teacher?"

"Sister Sophia."

"Oh, yeah, I had her in second grade. She's sooo nice!"

"Yeah," I said, hoping this girl wouldn't think I was a baby with all these one-word answers. But even finding single words was a stretch for me.

"Do you want to play with me some time?" she asked.

"Sure!"

"Okay, I'll ask my mom if you can come over this afternoon. And you should ask your mom, too."

"Okay," I said, knowing the answer would be "no." My mother had already told me she needed my help unpacking. But I didn't want this girl to know that my mother didn't let me do things with friends. She'd find out soon enough.

"Okay, see you later!" Debbie called as she scampered off. She ran between two houses instead of going down our driveway. I watched as she went into a dark brown house.

Sure enough, my mother didn't let me out to play that day with Debbie, nor the next. There was too much work to do with unpacking and settling in. But Debbie was not deterred, and she and I played together most days after school. On nice days, we'd walk the neighborhood or sit on my lawn. If Mr. Johnson was outside, the two of us would hang around him, hoping for stories of his early life in the Midwest. On cold or stormy days, we'd play at either of our houses with our Barbie dolls.

"Where are all the oranges I bought?" my mother asked one Saturday.

"I ate some," I said.

"There were three there Thursday night. Did you eat three oranges yesterday?"

"I gave some to Debbie."

"Jesus H. Christ, I don't have enough money to feed the neighbor kids. Why did you give her food?"

"We were playing here. She said she was hungry."

"If you're going to have her over here, don't give her any more food. I can't afford it."

I didn't know how I'd tell Debbie that she couldn't eat at my house. Instead, I learned how to choose foods that my mother would not likely notice were missing. Like saltine crackers with peanut butter or cereal with milk. Anything that she'd be less likely to count. So I could still be a little hostess with my friend but avoid my mother's ire. Debbie did think it a little odd when I said we couldn't have any fruit because it was all for my mother. She said her mother was always trying to get her and her brother to eat more fruit.

In late December, we stood at the kitchen table, admiring the Christmas cupcakes that Margie and I had just sprinkled with red and green sugar crystals. The kitchen was warm from the oven, which was emitting delightful smells of Toll House cookies. We were making enough Christmas goodies to feed a dozen people, but only the three of us would eat them.

Through the door I could see our tree in the living room, blinking lights sparkling off the tinsel, faded antique glass ornaments mixed with newer ones from the five-and-dime store. Some wrapped presents lay underneath, but the ones for me were still hidden away because I couldn't resist stealthily opening them before the big day.

"Santa's not real," I announced.

The two women's head swiveled sharply to look at me. My mother had a broad grin on her face. Margie's face was drained of color, and her hand shook as she lifted her cigarette to her lips.

"Where did you hear that?" my mother asked.

"Debbie told me."

"Well, what do you think?"

"I know he's make-believe."

"That's ridiculous. Of course there's a Santa," Margie reassured me.

"All the kids say he's not real."

"How can you do this to me?" Margie asked. There were tears in her eyes.

"Do what to you?"

"How can you take Christmas away from me?"

"Christ, Margie, no one is taking Christmas away from you," my mother replied.

"But she's taking all the fun out of it now."

"It will still be fun, Margie," I said. I wanted to touch her arm, to let her know everything would be okay.

"I might as well return all the presents I bought for her," Margie said to my mother.

"No, don't do that!" I sobbed.

Margie grabbed her mug of black coffee and ashtray, cigarette dangling from her lips, and walked off to her room behind the kitchen. We could hear her crying through the walls.

My mother sighed. She looked at me.

"Jesus, she's like a little kid sometimes."

"Will she really take back all my presents?"

"I don't know. I hope she doesn't take mine back."

I wanted to erase everything I'd said. I couldn't understand why Margie was so upset, but clearly it was because I said Santa wasn't real. I didn't want to hurt her, didn't want to make her cry. And I certainly didn't want her to take back all my presents. I knew from sneaking into her closet that she bought the presents that were labelled from Santa. If she returned all my presents, I'd have only the one present from my mother. That was how it always was. My mother's gift to me was usually something like a bathrobe or sweater. It would be wrapped in Christmas paper with a tag that read, "To Anne. Love, Mom." After ripping off the paper, I'd see the Filene's or Jordan Marsh box logo and I'd know it would not be a toy or doll.

From the perspective of years, I now know that Margie needed the magic of Christmas. In many ways, she remained the twelve-year-old girl who lost her mother to an untimely death from stomach cancer. Margie then lived alone with her belligerent, alcoholic father for six years until she could escape. She wanted a Santa, a loving father figure who never yelled, never belittled, never threatened. And she wanted me to remain a little girl so that I could keep the childlike spirit of Christmas alive in our home.

My mother, on the other hand, was in a hurry for me to grow up. The older I became, the less work and responsibility she would have until finally I'd be of an age when I could take care of her. Plus there would be less immediate work: no filling stockings with Santa presents, no setting out cookies and milk, and no toys to lay under the tree. Although Margie did most of these duties, my mother didn't particularly like the special attention I received as recipient of Santa-largesse. She preferred to have the most and best gifts under the Christmas tree.

I wanted to please both of them, always thinking that if I was a good girl they wouldn't send me away again. My dilemma was in choosing whether to grow up quickly, as my mother wanted, or stay childlike for my aunt. I chose the former. My mother had greater power over me and could decide on a whim to have me committed to an institution. I would become an adult in a little girl's body.

I discovered the piano that winter. I stayed late after school one day to help my teacher clean blackboards, aiming for teacher's pet status. The sound of music drifted from the end of a darkened hallway. I tiptoed over the black and white tiled floor until I was a few feet from the source. A girl, another second grader, was playing an immense upright piano. This girl was very popular—all the girls wanted to hold her hand as we stood in one of the many lines going into and out of our classes. *Maybe the kids would all love me too*, I thought, *if I could play piano*. The girl's brown penny loafers swung in the air beneath her, her green gabardine uniform shiny from many years of hand-me-down wear. She stopped playing and quickly looked around. Maybe I had made a noise of appreciation.

"What are you doing?" She frowned.

"Just listening," I said. "It sounded nice."

She smiled quickly at this. "I take lessons every week with Sister Frances. She lets me use this piano. I have to practice *every* day."

It sounded wonderful to me. I wanted to be able to play piano, to make lovely sounds like this.

"How much are the lessons?" Even at seven years of age, I knew that cost could be a major barrier.

"A dollar a lesson."

I thought through the math. My mother gave me five cents a day for milk at recess. Another dollar a week would be a lot of money to ask for.

That night, after my mother paid the teenage girl who babysat me after school, I broached the topic.

"Ma, can I take piano lessons?"

"Where did this come from?" she asked. "We don't even have a piano."

"Please, Ma," I said. "Sister Frances lets the kids practice on one at school."

"Well, I can't afford it."

"It's only a dollar a lesson," I told her.

"The answer is no."

When Margie arrived home, I heard her ask my mother why I was crying.

"She wants to take piano lessons. I can't even afford my half of the food we put on the table. How can I pay for the lessons?"

"How much are they?" Margie asked.

"A dollar each."

"Wouldn't she need a piano to practice on?"

"Anne said that she can use one at school."

"Well, maybe I can help with the cost," Margie said. "I always wished I could play piano, but it's too late for me."

At supper that night, my mother surprised me with the news that I could indeed take lessons. I ran over to her and gave her a hug.

"Thanks, Ma. I promise I'll practice really hard."

Soon after this, I overheard my mother talking with Margie about hiring a new babysitter. The current one had quit suddenly, and my mother didn't know who else to ask. She sounded desperate. I walked over to the kitchen table. Cigarette smoke and coffee steam mingled a foot above its surface.

"I don't need a babysitter," I announced.

"Yes you do," said my mother. "You're only seven years old."

"But Babs never did anything," I said. "She just sat on the couch and did her homework. I did all the chores, I made my own snacks, and I did my homework by myself. She never even talked to me." Unfortunately this was all true.

"I'll think about it."

The next day my mother said I could stay by myself after school. I'd have to call her every afternoon when I got home. The landlady, Mrs. Johnson, would usually be upstairs if I needed anything. I'd have to keep my key with me at all times and couldn't lose it.

"Don't worry, Ma," I said. "I'll be fine."

I even believed this myself.

And that's how I solved the problem of money for the piano lessons. The babysitter had cost my mother ten dollars a week, so with my initiative my mother was coming out significantly ahead. At age seven, I became a latchkey kid, long before I even knew the term or what it meant.

To say I adored the lessons, the tedium of scales, the details of reading music, would be an understatement. Who knew a wooden box with strings and hammers could give a seven-year-old girl such pleasure, boost her self-confidence if only a smidgeon, and provide a means of connecting with a good teacher? Sister Frances told me I played my pieces beautifully. Each week she placed gold stars on my music book pages. I could have kissed the hem of Sister Frances's habit for each of those little stars.

My passion would eventually drive me to provoke my mother's anger by lobbying for my own piano. We bought a huge, used upright for thirty-five dollars from an old lady whose arthritic fingers could no longer play. Perhaps she hated the daily reminder of what she could no longer do, so she let it go for a song.

Music became my refuge. I'd play when I'd had a frustrating day at school. Maybe a girl snubbed me, or a boy called me fatso. Maybe I felt lonely walking home alone. But when I sat at the piano, I was the queen. When my mother wasn't home I could bang on the instrument as loud as I wanted. *Take that, Kathy Murphy! Take that, Tommy McDonald!*

My mother's patience for my musical education was short-lived, and she soon found other things for me to do when I sat down to practice. It came to a head one evening when she came home from work with a scowl on her face.

I had just climbed onto the wide, dark mahogany bench. *Maybe she won't notice that I'm not in the kitchen*, I thought. *Maybe she'll be thinking so hard about peeling the potatoes and she'll forget about me.* I craned my head to look at the brand new music book, *Grade 2 Exercises*, I'd bought from Sister Frances. Slowly, I opened to the piece Sister Frances had assigned me that week. I pressed the book open with the flat of my right hand. I hovered my hands palm down over the piano keys. Sister Frances told me to always start in this position. I concentrated on the music in front of me, and I began to play. I'm not sure why I was so careful not to make noise with the page turning, given that I was about to play this monster upright that echoed through our apartment. Maybe I thought my mother wouldn't stop me after I'd started playing. She'd enjoy hearing the music so much that it would calm and soothe her, and she wouldn't want to interfere with the beautiful flow of notes.

"Anne," I heard her call. My heart sank.

"What?" I asked.

"Come out here. I need you to help me."

"But I'm playing piano," I said. "Sister said I have to practice every day."

"Come out here now."

With cheeks burning, I slid off the bench and walked out through the dining room and stopped in the kitchen doorway.

"Wipe that sullen look off your face," my mother demanded.

There was nothing I could do to stop the anger flashing out of my eyes. Before I knew it my mother crossed the kitchen to where I stood. The sting jolted me as the palm of her hand hit my left cheek. Slimy potato water dripped down my face. The back of her hand connected with the right side of my head as her arm swung back. I felt a scratch from her diamond cocktail ring, the one she'd had made from her engagement ring and that of her mother-in-law. I held my breath. I knew if I stood very still and didn't look at her, she might only hit my face a couple of times. Stepping back would anger her more. Then the hitting would get harder and faster, and she'd start screaming. I think I hated the screaming almost as much as the hitting. Then, she did something worse.

"I wish I'd put you up for adoption when I had the chance," she blurted.

Oh, I really wish she had, I thought. She must have read my mind, or maybe she wanted me to say that I was happy she kept me. But she seemed to get angrier at my lack of reaction.

"Well, maybe I should just send you away right now. I'm sick of the sight of you."

This had her desired effect and made me cry. My greatest fear continued to be my mother sending me away again.

It was almost six o'clock, and Margie would be home from work soon. She'd step off her bus at the end of Brooks Street at 5:51 P.M.

and slowly walk home, feet sore from being squeezed into black high-heeled pumps all day. At 5:59 P.M., her keys would jingle in the back door lock; I'd be safe if I could just hold out for a few more minutes. When my mother hit me while Margie was at home, she rarely gave me more than one quick slap to the cheek. Maybe Margie could talk my mother out of sending me away. After all, I'd been allowed to live with them for the past two years, so Margie must have been having some influence on my mother.

When Margie was away, my face became a target, my cheeks like dual bull's-eyes as my mother's hand aimed and struck. Injuries to the middle of my face were collateral damage as my mother slapped my face from side to side—palm to one cheek, back of hand to the other. The physical injuries—cuts and scratches and small bruises—came from her nails or her jewelry. The logic skills I used to solve tricky math word problems at school failed me with my mother. I usually couldn't figure out what I'd done to precipitate a beating. So I sought refuge. Margie was my best shelter; she shielded me from my mother like a seawall protecting against storm damage. She couldn't hold back the worst tempest, but she could lessen the impact. Maybe the weight of single motherhood felt a little lighter to my mother with her sister to share the load. Or maybe my mother was ashamed of her actions.

Perhaps by hitting me, my mother purged some deep anger that simmered all day like an active volcano, the heat getting more unbearable as her day went along, until she erupted at home more from the pressure building within than from any external forces, such as her child. She might have interrupted my piano play so that she could have some help in the tedious supper preparations. Maybe she was lonely and wanted some company or needed to feel that her child loved her.

While in medical school, I learned about a pediatric disease called *slapped cheek syndrome*, so-called because a hallmark sign is a bright red rash on the cheeks that looks as if the child had just been slapped. I learned that it is usually a benign, self-limited illness, caused by a virus. In contrast, my mother's slaps felt malignant, and their effects were lasting. Hitting a child is like a virus that spreads insidiously. Parents strike children, who smack their children, and the behavior passes down through the generations. My grandmother hit my mother, and my mother hit me. I made it stop there. My husband and I never struck our children, and we hope that our legacy of peaceful, loving childrearing will endure.

Being a latchkey kid had its pluses and minuses. I'd let myself into the apartment after school. On bad days, there'd be no sign or sound of either of the landlords. No one would save me from the bogeymen. On a good day, Mr. Johnson would be working in the yard or in the garage, so I'd know he'd hear me if I screamed.

After quietly closing and locking the door, I'd slowly and stealthily move from one room to the next, checking behind doors, under beds, and inside closets for the scary man I knew must be lying in wait. After I'd completed my rounds and checked all locks, I'd get myself settled with a snack and television. This was the part I liked—no adult around to tell me what to eat or not eat, or to make me turn off the television.

When only soap operas were on, I explored our flat. Nosing into things gave me a feeling of power. No drawer or cabinet was off limits. One day, I rifled through the contents of my mother's desk. The bottom drawer contained dozens of photographs, some faded and curled at the edges. A few were professional, eight-by-ten-inch portraits set into cardboard frames. A Hollywood-handsome man caught my attention. He appeared to be in his mid-twenties. His slicked-back hair looked to be dark blond or light brown. His eyes were small and pale. Even straight on, his ski-slope Irish nose was noticeable. His lips parted in a slight smile, as if he knew some secret he wasn't sharing. He wore a pinstripe suit jacket, button-down shirt, and tie. I inched the portrait out from its sleeve, turned it over, and read, "James Hugh McTiernan, 1946."

That's my father, I realized with a shock. I knew his name because that's what was on my birth certificate, a copy of which I'd brought to school to register for First Communion. I held the picture aloft, as if to feel the effect of him standing over me and looking down. I pressed it to my chest. I smelled it. I kissed his forehead. But none of this produced any change in the small eyes and slightly smiling mouth. I didn't calculate the passage of years, didn't realize that fourteen years had passed since that photograph was taken, and he'd now be a man approaching middle age.

Carefully, I placed the photo to the side and looked around for more of him. I found about a dozen, laid them out in a circle. In some, he stood with his arm around a beautiful, smiling brown-haired woman. Although I soon realized this was my mother, she looked too happy to be real. In one picture, my father held an infant in his arms, a big smile on his face. I turned it over. "Anne McTiernan," it read, "March 22, 1953." He held me once, I realized. I wanted him to hold me again. I put the photo next to his portrait. There were pictures of me at various ages: a fat baby in a pretty dress clutching a stuffed bunny; a toddler at the beach; a kindergartner playing in snow outside the Watertown house near Rosary; a first-grader in a new school uniform. There was no dad in these pictures, literally or figuratively.

I wanted a father so badly. I thought that if I had a father, my mother wouldn't have to work, and she'd be happy. There would be someone to take the burden of decisions off her shoulders, someone to take care of finances, someone to handle manly things like fixing the car and changing light bulbs. I learned from television that dads taught kids that they can take risks and be okay. In the exercise studies I've led as a physician, I hired exercise trainers to work with our study participants—to spot for them. A good spotter knows when to intervene to prevent an injury and when to push a client to do more. I needed a dad to spot for me.

I also wanted brothers and sisters. My friends often complained about their siblings and told me I wasn't missing anything by not having sisters or brothers to pick on me. It didn't help. I could see they had someone to share their life experiences with, someone else to take the rap if their mother or father was in a bad mood. I knew if I had a sister or brother I wouldn't be so lonely. If I had a dad, I'd have a chance for a complete family.

One evening, soon after I found my dad's photos, my mother called me into the living room.

"Have you been looking through my desk?"

"Yes," I whispered, afraid of her wrath if I lied or if I told the truth. "I was looking at the pictures in the bottom drawer."

She stared at me. My heart was racing.

"I saw the pictures of my father."

"Jesus."

"How come he never comes to see me?"

"It's because your father is a no-good bum and a drunk. He doesn't care about you at all."

"But there was a picture of him holding me."

"Grandpa McTiernan made him come see you. Your father would arrange a visit. I'd get you all dressed up in your best outfit. Then you'd wait by the window, looking for him, but half the time he wouldn't come. It was heartbreaking, watching you wait for him."

"Why did he stop coming?"

"Grandpa McTiernan died when you were three years old. After that, there was no one to tell your father to see you. So he stopped."

I bit my lip. I realized I must be a terrible little girl, if my own father wouldn't see me unless someone made him do it.

"He also stopped paying child support. So I had to take him to court, and still he only pays half what he owes me. He's supposed to send twenty dollars a week, but it's never more than every other week."

Over the years, I would return to those photographs of my father. I'd wish I could be pretty, and more interesting, so he'd want to see me. The photos faded over time, but my desire for a dad to love me never waned.

During my residency training, I worked at one of Seattle's clinics for low-income patients. It was routine to ask patients about their social situations and connections to determine whether they had strong enough relationships to help them through their illnesses or whether they needed extra support from our social workers. I had several divorced male patients who complained that their children had nothing to do with them. I'd stay quiet, not wanting to know why their families were fractured. Some of them added that they hadn't been part of their children's lives and blamed the mothers. I hoped my face didn't reveal my lack of respect for these men. I never could understand how a man could allow a bad relationship with a woman to drive him away from his children.

CHAPTER 4

Changing the Menu

At nine o'clock on a humid August Saturday morning in 1960, Debbie knocked on our back door.

"Hi, Anne. Can you come out to play?" she asked through the screen with her usual huge grin.

"Ma," I called over my shoulder. She hunched over the breakfast table in her pale peach summer nightgown, her back curved forward in her premature dowager's hump. Her black coffee grew cold as she read the morning newspaper. She hated me calling her "Ma," the name all the Brighton kids called their mothers. I did it anyway, especially when other kids were within earshot.

"Ma, can I go play with Debbie?"

"Okay, but stay in our yard or Debbie's."

"I will," I shouted as I ran out the door, eager to find out what exciting things were in store. I still couldn't believe my luck that this fourth grader had befriended me, a nerdy little second grader. Sounds of kids playing surrounded us as we walked down my driveway. Gradually, it would quiet down after dark, after a few calls from mothers to "get in the house this instant or else."

Over the summer, Debbie and I spent almost every day together. We'd lie on our backs on the sloping lawn in front of my house and stare at the clouds, holding stalks of grass straight up in our mouths.

Sometimes we'd pluck plums from the trees next door, being quick so the crabby old lady couldn't see who was thieving from her. On this Saturday we idly threw a pink ball back and forth in the shade of Debbie's front yard until her mother called her in to lunch.

Not knowing what else to do, I trudged back up the long driveway to the back door of my house. I reached up and pulled the handle of the screen door with its peeling green paint, expecting it to fly open as usual. It didn't move. The little silver hook on the inside must have gotten latched by mistake.

"Ma, Margie," I called. "The door won't open. Let me in."

My aunt appeared behind the screen door. Behind her, the washing machine swung into its spin cycle. Barely visible through the dark screen, Margie clutched a wad of Kleenex in her hand. "Your mother said I'm not to let you in." Her voice caught.

"Why?" I wailed, terrified. "Why can't I come in?"

"She knows what she did wrong," I could hear my mother say in the background.

I had no idea what I'd done wrong. I stood sobbing. Margie was also crying by this time. An eternity passed, maybe five minutes. Finally, my mother appeared behind the screen.

"You were out all morning instead of staying home to help me clean the house," she said, "so you can just stay out. I'm not going to let you in."

"Mary, please let her in," Margie said.

"No, I don't want that ungrateful brat in my house." With that, she went back into the kitchen.

I stood outside the screen, Margie inside. Mr. Johnson's lawn mower roared nearby. Someone listening from the outside would have heard a toneless symphony: washing machine spinning, Margie crying, me sobbing, lawn mower growling.

I sat on the Johnsons' stairway. I was terrified that my mother would never let me in the house again, that she'd banished me for good. It was finally happening—that thing I'd feared all my life—my mother was sending me away again. Only this time I didn't know where. Or maybe she was just kicking me out, and it would be up to me to find a place to go. But I had no other place. My mother and Margie were all I knew, my only connections in the world. Sure, there was school, but the nuns kept us at arm's length. They took care of their own in their cloistered nunnery. There would be no room for me there.

I'd seen child actors on television get mad at their on-screen parents and threaten to run away. The child would pack his or her things into a large handkerchief and tie it to the end of a stick. The kid then marched out after announcing to the mom and dad that he's never coming back. I could never relate to these scenarios. Running away was the last thing I wanted to do. I spent all my energy thinking of how I could be a better little girl to make my mother love me, make her less angry with me, so that she'd want to keep me living with her and Margie. And now my nightmare was coming true.

After what felt like hours, the landlady Mrs. Johnson came down the stairs, her lilies-of-the valley cologne preceding her. I felt her cool hand on my shoulder as she stepped onto the landing.

"What's wrong, dear?" she asked. "I could hear you all the way upstairs."

Her soft brown eyes gazed down at me, her slight smile showing the gap in her front teeth. She wore a yellow gingham housedress with a ruffled apron. Her short white hair stood out like a halo around her face.

"My mother won't let me in the house," I said.

"Why ever not?" She had remnants of a Southern accent.

"I don't know," I got out between gulps of air.

She moved around me. "Mary," she called. "Mary, can you come here, please?"

My mother appeared behind the screen. "Hello, Mrs. Johnson."

"Mary, let your daughter in."

"No. She's being punished. She's been very bad."

"Now come on, Mary. Be reasonable. Anne's a good girl. You let her in right now."

Reluctantly, my mother undid the latch and opened the door. Head down, I squeezed past my mother quickly. While I was relieved to be allowed into my home, I felt so ashamed that Mrs. Johnson had heard my mother talk about me and worried about future repercussions from my mother being chided by Mrs. Johnson. I didn't know what I'd done wrong but vowed to myself never to do it again. Otherwise, I was sure my mother would banish me for good.

Looking back today, I can see the power my mother yielded over me. She'd sent me to various boarding homes and institutions as a young child, the last one almost killing me. Being abandoned was my greatest fear. All she had to do was to make a threat, veiled or overt, and she had me quaking in my shoes, anxious to do whatever it took to make her happy with me. I also see that there wasn't anything I could do to assuage her anger. Her rage was her own, and it had nothing to do with me other than providing her the means of feeling some control over her own life. It didn't take me long to realize in medical school that I could never be a pediatrician—I couldn't bear to watch children suffer.

"Ma!" I called as I slammed the door behind me. A couple of weeks had passed since my mother locked me out. There'd been no mention of it in the meantime. Still, I felt uneasy every time I left the house.

"For Christ's sake, I've told you a hundred times not to slam that door."

I slowed my pace, red Keds squeaking on the linoleum. When I rounded the corner from the back hall, I could see her clearly. She sat at her usual place at the kitchen table, sleeveless cotton blouse sticking to her back. The heat bothered her terribly, which made me wonder why she was drinking black coffee and smoking a cigarette. I watched her as I softly approached, trying to gauge her mood.

She looked up. "How can you not be sweating?"

"I dunno."

"Where have you been?"

"At Debbie's."

"What were you doing?"

"Playing Barbies."

"What's that thing in your hand?"

"It's a fur stole for my Barbie. Debbie's dad works for a fur company, and he brings home scraps for Debbie's dolls. Debbie gave me one."

"Let me look at that." She felt the soft fur pelt and turned it over. "Humph, pretty fancy. You'll have the best-dressed Barbie in Boston."

In 1960, fur was a status symbol, one of the first things a woman bought if she landed a rich husband. Neither my mother nor aunt owned a fur coat or stole. This had nothing to do with feelings about animals, and everything to do with lack of money. My mother did have a small fur pelt that she sometimes wore over her wool coat. I used to sneak it out of her closet and drape it around my shoulders. The little head and feet were still attached and made it seem more real. It didn't occur to me that an animal had suffered for this fashion statement and it didn't bother me that my Barbie would be draped with something that had once had a life. Style was everything.

"Debbie invited me for a sleepover," I blurted out. I waited for my mother to say "no," hoping that she wouldn't be mad at me for asking.

"For when?"

"Next Saturday."

"Who will be watching you?"

"Her mom. Her mom's always home. Maybe her dad, too."

"What if you wet the bed?"

There it was. My mark of shame. Well, one of my marks of shame. There was no predicting when the floods would come at night, and there was no way to stop them. I felt my eyes well with tears. I'd never had a sleepover before, unless you count the institutions I'd lived in before first grade. I'd probably wet the bed at those places, but thankfully I didn't remember.

"I don't know," I mumbled.

"You could wear the plastic pants."

"Okay." I hated the plastic pants. They made my skin hot and clammy, and the elastic dug into the top of my thigh. Still, if they would allow me to have a sleepover, I'd use them.

She sighed. "I suppose I'll have to talk to Debbie's mother. So she knows what might happen. And you'll need to bring extra underpants and pajamas."

My cheeks burned. The only people who knew about my bedwetting were my mother, Margie, and our family doctor. Although, come to think of it, my mother must have told some people at her office because she kept coming up with new "treatments" that they told her about. Like the horrible plastic pants, the rubber sheet I slept on every night, and the adult-size diapers that a coworker's aged mother had been in before she died.

I arrived at Debbie's house full of anticipation. I carried a change of clothes, including my "in case of bedwetting things" in an old hat box my mother let me dig up from the back of her closet. I couldn't quite relax until Debbie's door closed on my mother's retreating figure. She had walked me there, probably to reassure herself that Debbie's mother was indeed home.

We two girls concentrated so hard on our Barbie play that we were surprised when Debbie's mom called us to dinner. It felt strange to sit across the kitchen table from Debbie's dad and brother. Her dad joked and teased Debbie and me, making me blush while everyone else laughed. Her mom beamed with pleasure when her dad said this was the best spaghetti and meatballs he ever had. I had no idea how to talk with a man or boy and was surprised at how relaxed Debbie and her mom were with these strange male creatures. Other than bringing our plates over to the sink, we didn't have to do any chores for dinner. Instead, Debbie's mom told us to go play until bedtime.

Lying wide-awake next to Debbie on sleeping bags laid out on the floor, I listened to her quiet snores. About an hour after we'd turned out the lights, I saw the door open a few inches. Her mom was silhouetted against the hallway light. She saw me raise my head.

"Are you still awake?" she asked.

"I can't sleep," I said. I didn't want to tell her that I was afraid that I'd wet the bed—in this case Debbie's sleeping bag—if I fell asleep.

"Are you okay?" she asked.

"I just can't sleep. Do you have a sleeping pill I could have?" I don't know why I asked for a sleeping pill. My mother and aunt never used them. I'd seen characters on television pop pills to sleep and assumed that's what all people did.

She laughed gently and said, "Sorry, honey, I don't. Why don't you just put your head down, close your eyes, and think nice thoughts."

Her words must have worked because the next thing I knew Debbie was shaking me awake.

After another day full of Barbie play, it was time to go home. I didn't want to leave. I wanted Debbie to be my sister and to have a dad bring me furs for my Barbies and laugh with me. But Debbie and I made plans to see each other the following afternoon after school, so I knew I could continue to experience Debbie's family secondhand.

As my mother and I walked down the street toward our house, I felt so proud to have a best friend, to have stayed with a normal family, and to have slept through the night without wetting the bed.

Then a sharp sting to the back of my head brought me out of my happy reverie.

"You little brat," my mother hissed.

"Huh?"

I turned toward her, making my face a perfect target. Back and forth her hand flew, slapping one cheek and then the other. I knew enough not to say anything, but I was more shocked than usual. Once again I had no idea why she was hitting me.

"I was mortified when Debbie's mother said you asked for a sleeping pill. What the hell's the matter with you?"

I shrugged my shoulders.

"Answer me, you little shit."

"I couldn't sleep."

"Now she's going to think I'm a pill popper. And that I give my daughter drugs."

I wanted to hide in the thorny bushes next to us. Until now, my mother's strikes had been at home, behind closed doors. Margie knew, but no one else. I felt so exposed there on the street opposite Debbie's house. I prayed that no one would look out of the window or walk by. I hoped she would let me start walking again so we could get home. My cheeks burned as much from shame as from the slaps.

My only knowledge of a real family came from television, where fathers put family first, children could be naughty without taking a beating, and single parents like Andy Griffith could take care of their children. But television couldn't show me a Brighton factory worker in 1960 who'd stoop to pick up fur scraps under the cutting table for his little girl's doll.

I saw no way that I could have such a family. I believed my mother; I was a little shit, therefore, didn't deserve the home life I had, let alone the one I craved.

Something pinned me down in a cold puddle of water. I couldn't move. I woke up and realized the cold liquid was urine-soaked sheets. I'd wet the bed again. I was mortified to still have this problem at seven years of age, but I had no idea how to stop it from happening. It had been a week since my overnight with Debbie, and almost two weeks since my last bedwetting episode. I'd hoped I'd outgrown it, but clearly it still plagued me.

"Ma," I called out. "I wet the bed."

"Wha . . ."

"I wet the bed," I called louder. Her bed was right next to mine, but she was hard to wake at night.

"Jesus Christ, Anne, not again."

"Sorry, I couldn't help it." I was crying now. So far we were playing our parts exactly, without any cues needed. Every time I wet the bed, we said the same things. My mother yelled, and I cried.

"Go change your pajamas."

Margie appeared in the doorway, her pastel flower-printed flannel nightgown flowing around her. "C'mon, Anne," she said. "I'll help you. Let's go quickly."

I grabbed some clean pajamas from my bureau and followed Margie to the bathroom. She helped me take a quick bath and change into clean nightclothes. Then she gave me a hug and led me back to the bedroom.

My mother had stripped the bed. Everything, including the top sheet and blanket, seemed to be involved.

"You little shit," she screamed. "Look what you've done. There's piss everywhere! I'm so sick of having to clean up after you."

I didn't see it coming. Suddenly my face was being smothered by wet sheets and the smell of my own urine. I didn't dare step back to shield myself, so the urine soaked into my eyes, nose, mouth, and hair until she finally tired from the exertion.

"How do you like that?" she screamed. "Maybe if you have to smell it you'll stop peeing in the bed."

"Come on now, Mary," Margie said quietly. "Let's just get the sheets changed, and everyone can go back to bed."

I stood there, face wet, not knowing what to do. Would she yell at me if I came near her reeking of piss? Would she be madder if I ran to the bathroom to wash my face and hair? I felt so ashamed of myself for wetting the bed like a baby, being covered in pee, sleeping in it, waking up my mother and aunt, and the extra work of cleaning my sheets and pajamas. Now my shame was even greater looking at the room through urine-soaked eyes. I felt nauseous from the smell but petrified that if I was sick to my stomach it would make her even angrier. The thought of having my face rubbed in vomit made me want to retch.

Finally she said, "Go wash yourself, Anne."

Gratefully I went to the bathroom, cleaned my face with Ivory soap, and tried to rinse out the strands of wet hair. It was too late to wash my hair. Back in 1960, hair washing was a major chore that involved two Breck shampoo washes and rinses, followed by time-intensive setting on pink plastic curlers using green or pink Dippity-Do setting gel. With luck your hair would dry overnight, but your sleep would not be restful on those hard little curlers that dug into your scalp. So I went back to bed smelling of urine, and I'm guessing the smell of stale piss was with me the next day at school.

I must have also wet my bed at Rosary Academy since I was only four years old when my mother sent me there. I wonder if I just stayed on the urine-soaked sheets through the night, then made up the bed in the morning and slept on them, damp or not, the next night. Maybe some of my nausea there was from the constant smell of urine.

Until I was eight years old, I wet the bed several times a week. Adult diapers and plastic pants failed. The urine-soaked-sheets-rubbed-in-the-face treatment also didn't work. My mother's final solutions were to restrict liquids—none after dinner—and to have me sleep on a rubber sheet. These didn't work very well either.

I was convinced that my bedwetting was a sign of my pure evil nature. There was a devil in me, and he did whatever he could to make my mother's life miserable. Making me wet the bed did a very good job of this. It required me to wake up my mother—almost a mortal sin because sleep was the most important thing to her, second only to food. It gave my mother more work to do, disgusting work at that, and it required contact with one of my excretions—urine—which she'd tried to bypass in my infancy. Most of my diapers were changed at the various institutions she sent me to, and when I was at home, Margie took care of most of the diapering. My bedwetting necessitated some thought and planning time for her to consult with doctors and figure out how to get me to stop wetting the bed. And since none of the remedies worked, it frustrated the hell out of her.

Looking back, I see that my mother was in a rush for me to grow up. Wetting the bed was an infantile thing for me to do. I'd later learn that she wanted an adult daughter to take care of her, but at the time, I could see that she was sick and tired of parenting me. And since I wanted to please her, I became a mature-acting kid.

My body, as if sensing my mother's urgency, grew early and fast. I was one of the tallest girls in the class. My early growth spurts were a cause of embarrassment. I wanted to be average, to fit in with the other girls—I didn't want to stick out at the end of the line. My girth was also unusual in our school. Families, especially the large Irish-Catholic ones, could barely afford to provide the basic food needs for their children, let alone enough excess food to make a kid overweight. When a nun taught us that gluttony is a sin, fifty kids swiveled their heads to stare at me, which made me want to eat more when I came home to our empty apartment.

My mother didn't seem to have a problem with my excess size, other than to say she couldn't afford to buy me new clothes all the time. I think she must have liked my being larger because I looked older, therefore, less like a needy little girl.

One benefit of a mature daughter is that she can do more housework than a kid. My responsibilities moved quickly from setting the kitchen table and sweeping the floor to peeling potatoes and cutting vegetables. By the end of second grade, I was responsible for cooking supper every night. Margie and I shared the dishwashing responsibilities.

My breasts developed before I entered third grade. My mother must have noticed because one Saturday in August she announced that she was taking me shopping. This was very unusual. Margie occasionally supplied me with bargain clothes she bought in Filene's basement, but my mother rarely took me to a store. With a beaming face, my mother told the saleslady that her daughter was becoming a woman. I wasn't crazy about the saleslady touching my chest, or my mother watching the proceedings, but I was proud of my two new Teenform bras.

Margie didn't share my mother's excitement. I overheard them talking that night after I'd gone to bed.

"She's too young to have a bra. She's just a kid, for God's sake," Margie said.

"Jesus Christ, what was I supposed to do? Her boobs were hanging out from her undershirt."

"I didn't notice anything."

"You don't want to see it, Margaret," my mother said. "You want her to stay a little girl forever."

"But she's only seven years old!"

Six months later, just after I'd turned eight, I woke up with blood on my pajama bottoms. I jumped to the only logical conclusion—I was dying. It was a workday, and my mother and aunt were competing against the cruel workingwoman's clock. Usually, we all did our own things in the morning, three runners on our own tracks. I dressed myself, made my breakfast, and left for school at 7:30 A.M. Margie sprinted to catch her 7:45 A.M. bus, stopping only for slugs of coffee and drags of her cigarette. My mother sat at the kitchen table with black coffee, the *Boston Globe*, and a cigarette. She'd leave the house at 8:15 A.M. for her job as executive secretary at the regional Chevron office. A change in one person's routine could bring our morning program to a screeching halt.

So it was with a great deal of trepidation that I told my mother what I had found. To my surprise she didn't act angry but told me I had become a woman that day. She opened the bathroom cupboard, took out a package marked "Modess," said these were sanitary pads, and showed me what to do. I was not happy. While I did want to grow up fast to please my mother, I didn't like this turn of events at all. Now it all seemed too sudden. Did this mean I'd have to dress in nylons and heels like my mother and aunt? Would I have to get a job now? Was I supposed to smoke and drink black coffee? Could I still play with my Barbies? Could I still watch cartoons? Well, maybe being a woman, I could stay up as late as I wanted. Now that would be fun.

My mother let me stay home from school. I spent the day going in and out of the bathroom and went through most of that Modess package by the end of the day. On each trip to the bathroom, I prayed that the blood would stop, that it was a terrible mistake. But no, there it was again. I wondered if it would be gone by the next day, and I could go back to being a girl. *Maybe it won't happen again,* I thought. Then one question after another popped in my mind: How will I change these pads at school? Should I take a big package of them in my green book bag? What will I do at school with the dirty ones? What if the nuns won't let me go to the bathroom? Will the other kids laugh at me? What if the blood leaks onto my uniform, or worse, down my leg and onto my third grade classroom floor? Oh dear God, what if I never stop bleeding? Will I have to wear these diaper-like things for the rest of my life?

When my mother arrived home that night, she came into my bedroom, sat on the side of my bed, and asked me how I was doing. She said that all girls eventually get their periods, and I was special and probably the first girl in my class to do so. As disturbing as my day had been, I was surprised and pleased at my mother's behavior toward me. It made me forget all the questions that had been circling in my head that day. I can see now that she found me more acceptable as a "woman" than as a child. It was one more indication of the end of the tunnel when she would no longer have to take care of me.

As a physician, I know that my early maturation was likely due to being overweight: a hormone made by fat cells, called *leptin*, may be a catalyst in the biological cascade that starts girls on their way to fertility by stimulating the ovaries to make hormones and eggs. But for an eight-year-old girl, it was another thing that set me apart as a freak when all I wanted was to be normal and loveable.

I was a smart kid. Too shy to raise my hand to answer questions, I nevertheless impressed the nuns with my perfect homework and test papers and by always knowing the answer when they called on me. I was also quiet and obedient. The nuns loved me.

Being smart had some advantages in school. Within the confines of the classroom, I was a superstar. The nuns were not particularly interested in helping all the kids feel good about themselves. Instead they let the whole class know who received the best grades and who were the good girls and boys. I was often singled out as a student the other kids should emulate.

My credentials changed when we left the classroom. Out in the schoolyard, I was a major nerd—too fat and uncoordinated to play games. I'd hang around the girls who skipped rope, hoping to be allowed to join. Sometimes they'd let me swing the rope—at least I didn't bungle that too much. But if they let me skip I'd be out after one or two jumps. So I was no good to a team.

One day in the spring of third grade, I lined up to jump.

"No fatsoes allowed," yelled one of the swinging girls as I approached the rope.

Hoping she didn't mean me, I didn't move. But when it was my turn, the girl stopped swinging.

"I said, no fatsoes allowed!"

"Yeah," said another girl. "No smart fatsoes!"

Head down to hide the tears, I walked away. I never tried to jump rope again.

This wasn't the first time I'd been called something derogatory about my size. "Fatso" was a favorite taunt from kids on the playground. "Lard ass" was hurled by Margie in her rare moments of anger. A particularly creative kid thought up "Annie, Annie, with the big, fat fanny." To her credit, my mother never taunted me about my fatness. She picked other things to call me—"little shit" was a favorite—but she never put me down for being overweight. Rather, she'd say I had a big frame or big bones. She herself had always been overweight or obese and seemed to empathize with my plight.

With no friends to play with in the schoolyard, I found ways to stay away. I'd eat my lunch in the classroom as slowly as possible. Then when the teacher shooed us out, I'd hide in the girls' bathroom as long as possible. Finally if a nun kicked me out of the bathroom, I'd walk around the schoolyard alone. Sometimes a kind nun would strike up a conversation with me, but mostly I'd be alone. After third grade, I talked my mother into letting me come home for lunch. She had to lie to the school and say someone would be there to feed me. While I was alone at home, I didn't have the mortifying experience of all the other kids seeing me friendless. I could read a book in peace for a few minutes. It never occurred to me not to return to school after lunch—I was too afraid of my mother and the nuns.

Debbie broke up with me that year, or whatever you call it when one girl decides the other is too young and uninteresting to hang out with anymore. It happened after she brought me to a fifth grade girl's birthday party. I was the only third grader there. The girls talked about which boys they liked and which boys liked them. They played rock-and-roll albums on a portable record player. They danced the twist, the mashed potato, and the lindy. I just sat and watched, moving only to pick up my plate of cake and ice cream. Debbie was unusually quiet on the way home. When we parted, I said our usual, "See ya tomorrow," but she didn't answer. She never called me again, never came to my door to ask me to play. When I called her house, her mom said in a kind voice that Debbie was busy.

Without Debbie, and with no real school friends to speak of, I withdrew more and more from the world of children. My circle became novels from the library, afternoon television shows, and my abbreviated family. I dealt with other kids only as much as was required during school hours. While I was no longer starving for food, I still was failing to thrive.

Chapter 5

Binging

"Anne, could you come here?" my mother called out.

We were getting ready for Sunday Mass. The year was 1961, and the temperature that July was already 80 degrees with 90 percent humidity at eight o'clock in the morning. Fans whipped up sticky air in every room. My dress, snug on my chubby frame, clung to my back. I had just buckled my black patent leather Mary Janes.

I walked over to the bedroom we shared and saw my mother, naked except for the girdle stuck midway up her thighs. She was bent over in front of the window fan, which groaned at top speed. Sweat dripped off her face onto the unpolished wooden floor. Her short black hair lay limp. She looked up at me, her features scrunched together like she was trying to move eyebrows and mouth to meet in the middle of her face.

"I can't get my girdle on with this damn heat."

Not knowing what to do, I stood there. I hoped she wouldn't ask me to help her.

"I need you to help me."

I moved over to her as slowly as an eight-year-old could, as if the fan were creating a wind tunnel in my direction.

"Here," she said. "Grab that side of the girdle and pull up when I tell you. Okay, now pull."

My mother's girdle was like a straightjacket to keep fat cells from going berserk. She wore a particularly rigid one with vertical stays around it. She'd step into it, cross her legs at the ankles, then hoist it up her legs. Going over the calves went smoothly, but things got rougher at thigh level. That's when she had to pull inch by inch, alternating the left and right sides, to advance it. I'm sure her biceps were flexing like crazy under her arms' layers of fat.

We yanked, but the girdle didn't move. Sweat rolled down her chest, over her downward-facing nipples, onto her belly. My hands, soaked, slipped as I grabbed the girdle's edge.

"Oh good Mother of God," she said, "I don't think I can get this thing up or down."

She grunted. "Anne, go get the powder from the bathroom."

I practically skipped out, happy to get away, but knew I had to return quickly. She took the Jean Naté talcum from my outstretched hand and sprinkled powder onto her thighs and lower body. The fan blew much of it around the room, as though we were in a snow globe. It tickled my nose and spotted my black patent leather shoes. My mother's body now looked like the cake pan Margie prepared with Crisco and a coating of flour.

"Okay, let's try again."

Another few minutes of pulling and grunting produced the desired result. She had me hold the opening in place while she pulled the zipper up. I stood back, worried that it would pop open and release all that powder and sweat with a rush. The zipper held, my mother finished dressing, and we made it to Mass only a few minutes late with just one dirty look from the Monsignor.

I couldn't wait to have my own girdle. A girdle would mark me as a real grown-up lady. And it would hide some of my corpulence. I hated being fat, hated being twice as thick at any point on my body as the other girls in the class. I was ashamed of my size, of how my school uniform fit me so snugly that I couldn't take a deep breath. I envied the skinny girls whose uniforms draped so loosely they could put a thick wool sweater underneath and still have room. I also despaired at having a similar body shape to my mother. I was on a trajectory to look like her when I grew up and I wasn't looking forward to it.

I hated the closeness of my mother, her intrusion like this into my physical space. On television, moms always shared bedrooms with the dads, never with their children. If only I had a dad living with us—I could have my own room and distance from my mother. A father would be someone stronger than my mother, someone who could protect me. I'd sometimes take my father's picture out from the bottom drawer of my mother's desk. I'd press it flat, hold it by the corners, and stare at it as if wishing him to come to life.

My mother stressed what a jerk he was, that he was an alcoholic, a womanizer, a liar, and a cheat. He once spent an entire month's rent money buying drinks for everyone at a bar. She said that he had no interest in me from the beginning and never asked about me on the few occasions they communicated about child support. Maybe she thought she was helping me realize how lucky I was not to have him around. What I took away, however, was the certainty that I was not worth a father's interest and love.

Still, I fantasized that someday my daddy would come back to the family. He'd sweep me up into his strong arms, hold me close, say how sorry he was that he had left me, promise to never leave again, and take care of me forever. In my fantasy I could feel his scratchy cheek on mine and smell a mix of Old Spice aftershave and cigarette smoke. I picked Old Spice because it was the only men's aftershave the local pharmacy had on display. I'd lift the top of the tester, put a dab on the inside of my wrist, and pretend I was close enough to my dad to smell him.

My mother did tell me some positive things about my father. He was friendly and talkative, the life of the party. This surprised me; how could bashful little me have come from a talker? He was very handsome; women were attracted to him like flies. He was also athletic and a wonderful dancer. Clearly I hadn't inherited these traits. My feeble attempts at roller skating, tap dancing, and ice-skating resulted in skinned knees, sprained limbs, and a bruised ego.

In spite of the mostly evil picture my mother drew of my father, I still hoped my parents would fall in love again and make a lot of babies. I dreamed of my mother marrying other men, too, like John F. Kennedy when he was alive. In my fantasy, the married president was conveniently single when he fell in love with my mother.

I imagined that my father would look like he did in his photographs, a two-dimensional dad. But children have three-dimensional needs. A real dad hugs, lifts, and soothes his child. He rubs his child's back while whispering in her ear that everything will be okay, baby, everything will be okay. The photos' arms would never hold me, touch me, or protect me. That flat, smiling face would never tell me I'm beautiful, never utter the words, "I love you."

I could not understand what I had done to make him leave me and why he wanted nothing to do with me. I assumed I had been a bad girl or I was too ugly for him to tolerate. Or I was just unlovable.

So I looked for a love substitute and settled on food. This wasn't a conscious decision, but I was following in my mother's and aunt's footsteps. The Irish love their sweets, and what are you supposed to eat with your cup of tea if not a few cookies or a slice of cake? My mother was obese, and my aunt never met a sweet she didn't love.

Food greeted me when I came home to an empty apartment after school. It was my playmate during recess when I was too shy to make friends. Eating gave me something to do during dinner when my mother and aunt complained about their bosses and coworkers but didn't want to hear about my day at school. They told me children should be seen but not heard. Food was my comfort, my companion, and my constant security.

My favorite food was chocolate. I adored all kinds: Reese's Peanut Butter Cups, Mallomars, Nestlé Crunch, Mr. Goodbar, Mounds, and sometimes a plain Hershey's Milk Chocolate bar. The nuns sold five-cent candy bars at snack time. I didn't get an allowance, but I could earn two dollars a week setting my mother's and aunt's hair. Those two dollars bought me a lot of candy. Each morning at snack time, I would hand the nun my quarter and snatch up five candy bars. Too embarrassed to let the other kids see me gorge myself, I'd eat only one during snack time and carefully put the remaining four into my book bag.

At 2:30 P.M., I'd let myself into our flat with the key I kept at the bottom of my bag, close and lock the door quietly, and do my quick bogeymen scan. My mother would call at 2:45 P.M., and the conversations were always the same.

"Hello," I'd say.

"It's me," she'd say. "Did you start your homework yet?"

"Yes," I'd lie.

"Don't forget to do your chores and put the potatoes on to boil at quarter to five."

Throughout the call I tried to keep my voice mellow for fear that my mother would get angry about something I said or didn't say. I didn't dare tell her I was afraid to be home alone, or I was desperately lonely, or I felt like a freak for having no siblings or friends to play with after school. Complaints of that sort could earn me a beating, or screaming, or even worse, the silent treatment.

After that strained call, I'd settle down in the living room with a big glass of milk in front of our black-and-white television. I'd lay my candy out on the dusky pink leather ottoman in front of the black chair with pink flowers. I'd unwrap and slowly eat each one of the bars, leaving the Mallomars for last. My favorite after-school shows were *The Loretta Young Show* and *Adventures in Paradise*, which were about grown-up, romantic relationships. These shows taught me most of what I knew about how men and women communicate with each other. And it was comforting to know that everything turns out okay in the end.

The candy was the appetizer to my afternoon-long meal. I would hunt through the kitchen for anything edible. We didn't have much junk food in the house—sodas, chips, and other snacks were expensive and purchased only for special occasions. So I would gather up Wonder Bread or saltine crackers, Marshmallow Fluff, and Skippy creamy peanut butter—sometimes grape jam—and settle in front of the television again, only this time I'd do my homework so that I'd have it done by the time my mother got home. I ate to fill my emptiness, and the food in turn filled me out. Occasionally, I'd eat enough to make me throw up.

I've seen many patients struggle with their weight. From weight loss studies with hundreds of women, I've learned diet tricks that can make a person feel full and less likely to overeat: reduce sugary drinks, replace high calorie foods with lower calorie foods, prepare meals at home, keep calorie content of snacks low, journal food intake. These tricks will work well if you're eating to fill an empty stomach, but if you're eating to satisfy a hollow heart, they won't help. And when I was a kid, all the chocolate in the world wasn't going to fill my void.

My mother was in charge of cooking and supplies in our household, and she ran a tight ship. She chose the menu, did the shopping, and prepared most of the meals. I was her reluctant sous chef and had specific cooking tasks to complete before she came home.

I learned early the consequences of not paying attention to my kitchen jobs. Shortly after beginning third grade, I found a note in the kitchen one day after my bogeyman search. In my mother's handwriting, the note listed my chores: set table, sweep kitchen floor, boil potatoes. With two and a half hours until my mother arrived home, I knew I had plenty of time to do the chores later. After setting up my after-school feast, I turned on the *Queen for the Day* game show. I fiddled with the television antenna for a few minutes to get the picture right. At 2:55 P.M., the phone rang. My mother was ten minutes late calling. *She must be having a busy day*, I thought.

"Hi, it's me," she said.

"Hi," I said.

"Are you doing your homework?"

"Yes," I lied.

"Don't forget to do your chores and put the potatoes on."

"I won't forget," annoyed that she didn't think I could remember.

After *Queen for the Day*, I did my homework with the television on for company. By now it was four o'clock. I practiced piano for thirty minutes—Sister Frances's instructions. I'd try to practice more after my mother came home as a way to avoid her. Then, I settled into one of the ten or so library books I'd schlepped home the previous day. Suddenly I heard my mother's voice talking with the landlord outside. Panicked, I jumped up, dropped my book, and raced to the kitchen. I had time to throw plates and silverware on the table and do a quick job with the broom, sweeping the dirt under the stove. As I stood near the stove, I remembered with horror that I had forgotten to boil the potatoes. I heard a key in the back door. I moved back over to the table and held on to the back of a chair. I felt faint.

"Did you put on the potatoes?" my mother asked.

"I forgot," I mumbled, looking down at the floor that wasn't completely clean from my sweep.

She crossed the room in one stride, hand striking my face with her handbag still in the crook of her arm. The handbag swung as she slapped me over and over.

"Jesus, you're so lazy," she said. "Why couldn't you do just this one thing for me? What the hell did you do all afternoon?"

I didn't answer, didn't look up from the floor.

"Fill the large pot with water," she said as she shrugged off her purse and headed to the bedroom we shared. A minute later she emerged in slippers.

"Did you wash some potatoes?" she asked.

"No."

"Oh, for Christ's sake. What's wrong with you? Get out six potatoes and wash them with the scrubber."

I did as told. My tears dripped into the sink as I ran water over the potatoes. I kept glancing up at the clock. It was 5:30 P.M. Margie would be home at 5:59 P.M.

My mother looked in the pot after I dropped the potatoes into the now-boiling water.

"These are still filthy," she said. "Take them out and really wash them."

Without thinking, I started to put my hand toward the water.

"Don't put your hand in there. How stupid can you be? Go get the slotted spoon to take them out."

I fished out the potatoes and brought them back to the sink. I filled the sink with cold water and started scrubbing. My mother came over to check the ones I'd cleaned and put into the drainer.

"These are still dirty. Can't you see? Oh, Christ, I'll have to do it myself."

She grabbed the scrub brush from my hand and shoved me away from the sink, but not before swatting me with the scrubber. Potato water dripped down my arm. I stood near her, not knowing what to do. I didn't watch what she was doing, though. I had no interest in learning how to properly wash potatoes. It was now 5:40 P.M. Nineteen more minutes.

"I have to go to the bathroom," I blurted and ran off. This would give me a few minutes reprieve before she came to collect me. The bathroom was next to the kitchen so I could hear cabinet doors and pots slamming.

After thirty seconds I heard, "Anne Marie McTiernan, get out here this instant." Her use of my full name was a sign that she was really mad. I emerged as quickly as I could.

"Get out the frozen peas."

I took the box of Birds Eye peas from the freezer. My fingers tingled from the cold while I waited for more instructions.

"Don't just stand there. Put them in the copper-bottom pot and put water on them."

I filled it to the brim, not daring to ask how much water to use. She grabbed the pot and dumped half the water in the sink, sighing.

A footstep outside the back door told me Margie was home. The sound of her key in the lock sounded like music. Things would be better now.

Often, I only remembered to do my daily chores shortly before my mother was due home. I became expert in cooking frozen hamburger in our cast-iron frying pan when I'd forgotten to defrost the meat. I would crank the gas burner up to the highest flame, throw in the solid block of meat, and add onion and peppers as I scraped the cooked meat off the edges. I learned that if I cut up potatoes into small cubes, I could boil them in seven minutes. My mother didn't seem to mind my dicing the potatoes—she probably thought I was doing some creative cooking. I became the ultimate short-order cook.

The Mary McTiernan Cooking School method, which had only one pupil, produced life-long results. I learned the basics of cooking. I could cook a roast, cut and boil vegetables, and mash potatoes. I made gravies and cream sauces. I learned to make a moist and tender meatloaf. My daughters say I make the best macaroni and cheese—the trick is to use full-fat cheddar cheese. But the main legacy my mother's lessons left me is that I hate to cook. I admire people, including my husband, who find working with food enjoyable. But I can't for the life of me understand it. On my nights to cook when our children were young, I frequently ordered take-out pizza and then danced around the kitchen with my girls.

A major finding from one of my weight loss studies was that women who cooked their own meals at home lost the most weight. Based on these results, I encourage people to prepare more of their food at home, but I hope they forgive my own dislike of cooking.

Real women cook, and righteous women love to cook. I envy their culinary classes in the taste *du jour*. My eyes narrow when they discuss the relative benefits of sautéing with nut oils versus olive oil. I'm fiercely jealous when they receive words of praise for pulling off holiday feasts. These women make me feel inferior, like I'm not a real woman.

With only my mother and aunt to call family, I adopted people as honorary relatives but never told them of their new status. It was like unrequited love but not the romantic kind. Our Brooks Street landlord, Mr. Johnson, became my surrogate grandfather. He had emigrated from Kentucky and retired from the long-closed Brighton stockyards. White-haired and stooped, he wore the same outfit every day—green canvas pants, suspenders, and sturdy shoes. Working in his garden in the summer, he wore a sleeveless white undershirt and straw hat. In winter, he'd add a flannel shirt, but I could still see old-man hairs sticking out from the neckline of his undershirt. He kept a vegetable garden—he was particularly proud of his onions—and a worm patch from which he'd harvest bait into an old Maxwell House coffee can for catfish fishing on a river west of Boston. He burned leaves and paper trash in an old large metal barrel behind his garage. When he wasn't gardening or doing some repair ordered by Mrs. Johnson, he tinkered with his green and white Oldsmobile sedan. Except for the automobile repairs, these activities were unusual for that part of Brighton, as most men had lost their rural roots a few generations back.

I was allowed to follow Mr. Johnson around on some of these outdoor activities. I could help him weed the garden, pick up leaves and trash for burning, and find worms. I didn't like the latter but did it anyway in order to be with him. But he wouldn't let me hang around his Oldsmobile. I'm not sure if he was concerned for the safety of the car or me. I especially loved the extremely hot, humid, summer days because Mr. Johnson took a lot of ice tea breaks in the shade. He'd let me sit with him and tell me stories about Kentucky and the stockyards.

"Mrs. Johnson was so little when I married her that I could wrap my fingers around her waist and still have room."

He seemed proud of this fact. No man would ever say this about me. My middle was already so thick that a man would have trouble getting his arms around me. Oh, how I wanted to have a tiny waist like the young Mrs. Johnson. It made me envy her quite a lot, but it helped that her waist was old-lady thick now.

One summer day, the landlord's grandson, a year younger than my eight years, was visiting his grandparents. Not knowing me from school, he didn't realize what a horrible nerd I was, and he even seemed to think I was a little cool. The extra year I had on him probably helped. Given that I'd unofficially adopted his grandfather as my own, this boy could be my surrogate cousin.

We took a hike into the woods behind our house. It was unusual to have greenery in this section of Boston. Gardens tended to consist of thorny hedges and mud from all the kids' tramping. Our woods were smaller than a house plot, but to me they felt as deep and mysterious as Robin Hood's Sherwood Forest. There were real trees that shaded you on a hot day, underbrush that scratched your bare legs, and the most wonderful Concord grapes, whose skins were so sour you had to spit them out quick, in order to get to the clear, sweet grape inside. There was even a little poison ivy that my aunt warned me not to touch. The grandson and I walked deep into the woods, about five feet from Mr. Johnson's garage.

"Want me to show you how boys pee?" he asked.

"Okay," I said.

"I know that girls do it different," he said. "My sister showed me how girls do it."

He unzipped his pants and took out a small flesh-colored appendage that was shorter than the width of his hand. He aimed it at some low bushes. Out came an impressive yellow stream. I wished I could pee that way. I didn't feel uncomfortable. It seemed as natural as when the girls at school pulled up their uniform blouse sleeves to compare smallpox vaccination scars.

"Do you have any money?" the boy asked after he zipped up.

"I have two dollars I made from setting my mother's and aunt's hair."

He thought for a minute. "Let's go buy some candy."

The drugstore had the best candy selection in Brighton. Our route took us by three- and four-flat apartment buildings, then up Arlington Street with its one-family homes, and past St. Columbkille Church that sent my heart racing as I remembered God would probably punish me for looking at this boy's thing. We turned right on Market Street with its bars so dark the patrons must have lost track of time. After we passed derelict houses with rubbish piled in front yards, we finally came to brick storefronts with dusty merchandise in the windows.

In front of Woolworth's, my friend stopped and cried out, "Look, Anne. There's a scale. Let's weigh ourselves. It only costs a penny."

Oh, Jesus, I thought. *Don't let this happen. Please make one of those passing cars lose control and plow into me.*

My friend might as well have said, "Look there's a surgeon's table—let's get him to cut off our arms." I was that terrified at the thought of this boy knowing my weight. It didn't matter that he was younger and shorter than me. He was still a kid, a boy, who could point and make fun of my fatness—although he'd never done that even though my girth was well evident. My weight was a source of shame, and now someone other than the school nurse and my doctor would know my secret. Still, I didn't know how to say no to his enthusiasm and gave him a penny. He stepped onto the silver platform and craned his neck up.

"Oh, good," he said. "I've gained a couple of pounds." The needle pointed to sixty-five.

"C'mon, Anne, your turn," he said.

Oh Dear God, I prayed. *Please deliver me from this horrible fate. I promise I'll never say a swear word again in my life if you can only help me.*

Even as an adult, I feel the shame of my obese childhood. Research shows that overweight and obese women in this country regularly under-report their weight. Some refuse to tell. In medical terms, it's just a number, like blood pressure, that indicates risk for some health conditions. But many people with obesity are embarrassed about that number. And at eight years of age, I already wore that disgrace and didn't shed it for many years.

When no rescue appeared from above, I pushed a penny into the slot, stepped on the scale, and waited for the answer of doom. Nothing happened. The indicator didn't move. I weighed exactly zero pounds.

"Hey," said the boy. "It's broken."

He slapped the scale hard, then kicked it a few times. Still there was no movement. I remained weightless.

I made this boy my honorary little brother. He could work miracles with a scale.

Besides my honorary male relatives, I also had female relative stand-ins. Mrs. Johnson took care of me when I was too sick to stay alone, which meant I had to be deliriously feverish because usually I was on my own in sickness and in health. She'd give me glasses of ginger ale with a straw and tell me, "Lie still now, honey, while I do my housework." Mrs. Johnson made strange food, such as upside-down cakes and fried catfish, and she added little marshmallows to her casserole dishes.

I had a series of teenage babysitters in first and second grade. One of them, so Irish with her red hair and freckles that she could have just gotten off the boat, played games with me and helped me do my chores. She made a perfect big sister. She only stayed for a year, unfortunately. After that, I didn't adopt babysitters as relatives—they moved in and out of my life too quickly. It was too much like my real relatives who disappeared on me.

The Catholic Church provided surrogates of sorts—they even called their deities Father, Mother, or Son. So even when I was convinced that none of my relatives loved me, I basked in the knowledge that God the Father and Jesus loved me. I didn't become close to many of the nuns, and they weren't particularly motherly, which is not surprising given that most of these women entered the cloistered life without the chance to develop maternal skills. Some were vicious terrors, people who should have been kept away from vulnerable populations like children. But some were kind. I grew to love my piano teacher, Sister Frances, basking in the praise she'd bestow along with the gold star she'd award. The pleasure of her compliments sustained my interest in piano, more than any intrinsic musical talent.

This interest in subjects based on quality of mentoring would become a lifelong trait of mine. I chose internal medicine as my medical field for the simple reason that the two attending doctors on my internal medicine rotation were kind, patient, and brilliant men. Poor mentoring prevented me from considering certain specialties. The head physician on my psychiatry rotation was bitter, and some attendings in other fields were mean. I'd had enough bitter and nasty during my early years to last a lifetime, so in my adult years, I searched out compassionate, loving, and joyful people—just like I did with my surrogate family.

Chapter 6

Irish Stew

Our lives changed radically in 1961. First, my mother took and passed her driving test and bought a brand new white Rambler American sedan on a three-year credit plan. No longer were we limited to the Boston public transportation system. We could now travel ten miles to far-off places like Mattapan, Hingham, and Cambridge to visit my mother's and Margie's small circle of friends. We even took a trip to the White Mountains of New Hampshire, our first vacation ever.

In December, our travels then precipitously turned to the south shore of Massachusetts, to what my mother and aunt called "the country." There, I learned with surprise that I had an extended family, real blood relatives. I would meet a granduncle and several second and third cousins. I would learn about my mother and aunt's history.

A few weeks before Christmas, my mother had told me to get ready for bed when the phone rang. She answered the phone, then took a quick breath.

"Oh, dear God," she said.

"What?" Margie asked.

My mother listened intently, saying "yes" or "uh-huh" every once in a while. Margie frowned at her, clearly annoyed that my mother had not yet let her in on the bad news. Finally, my mother hung up and looked at Margie.

"It's GFS," she said. "He's had a stroke."

"Oh, Christ."

"He's in the Jordan Hospital. He's in a coma."

"Oh, dear God."

They noticed me watching them and sent me off to bed. As I lay under the covers, I could hear them talking quietly. *Who is GFS?* I wondered. *What's a stroke? And how could GFS, whoever he is, fit inside a comb?* My mother and aunt were clearly shocked by the news, and all kinds of hustle and bustle began. My mother made several phone calls. I heard Margie moving back and forth from the kitchen to her bedroom.

Soon, the door to the bedroom I shared with my mother opened, and a sliver of light showed Margie looking at me. I pretended to be asleep. She entered the room quietly then opened several of my bureau drawers and took clothes out until she had quite a high pile. *Oh, no,* I thought, *are they sending me away again?* Soon afterward, my mother came into the room and repeated the drawer-opening exercise, this time with her bureau. I was relieved to see that her clothes were also being piled up. My aunt dragged two suitcases out from under the twin beds.

I sat up, no longer able to bear the burden of feigning sleep.

"Close your eyes, Anne," said my mother. At her sharp tone, I fell back onto my pillow as if she'd shot me. I lay awake for what seemed like hours until I heard her get into bed.

The next morning, I learned that the three of us would be taking a trip after my mother and aunt finished work that day.

"We're going to the country," my mother said. "We have to see a man there who is very sick. He's in the hospital."

"Who's the man?" I asked.

They looked at each other. My mother took a big breath. "He's your grandfather. George Smith."

"I have a grandfather?"

"You'd be better off without a grandfather, for all the good he's done you," my mother said. "He's a drunk. And he never did anything for you, never cared about you."

With the surprise of it all, I reeled as much as an eight-year-old can, although this grandfather's not caring about me wasn't a surprise. My mother had made it clear that my father didn't care about me, so why should this other man?

"After school, make sure you do your homework and your chores," my mother said. "But don't set the table. We'll eat supper on the way to the country. You'll need to change clothes for the drive. Wear your navy wool slacks and blue sweater. Don't get them dirty. We've packed a suitcase for you. Here's a letter to give to the nuns."

"What's in the letter?"

"It says that we have to take you out of school for at least a week. You'll need to get your homework assignments for the week so you can keep up with schoolwork."

We drove that evening to Kingston, which lay just north of Plymouth. We ate dinner at Leland's restaurant on Route 3A. I ate a hamburger with a pickle and French fries, the first time I'd ever had a hamburger. My mother and Margie drank a pot of black coffee with their dinner.

After a restless night crowded into one room at a nearby motel, we drove to Jordan hospital in Plymouth. I wasn't allowed into my grandfather's room, so I sat on a hard chair in the hall while my mother and aunt took brief turns in his room. Neither of them seemed to want to spend much time with their father.

We passed most of the weekend visiting with strangers my mother and aunt said were relatives or old friends. Late Sunday afternoon, we visited St. Joseph's Church rectory in Kingston, the first time I'd seen a priest's residence. While there, my mother and aunt spoke in low and serious voices with the monsignor, using words like "funeral," "wake," "requiem," and "perpetual care." We returned to the hospital that night. Again, my mother and aunt in turn quickly visited my grandfather's room. Then they told me he had died that evening.

They arranged a traditional Catholic wake for their father—three afternoons and three evenings with the body laid out in an open casket at the funeral home, relatives and acquaintances visiting briefly and talking in low voices. I'd been to wakes before, so I wasn't expecting my grandfather to sit up and stretch out his arms for a big grandpa hug. I looked at him in his open coffin and wondered who he was and why I didn't know him. I watched people mill around. The ladies wore various versions of black dresses, black hats with veils that covered their eyes but left their red lips exposed, pearl necklaces, and white gloves. The men all wore dark suits.

One old man who was only a few inches taller than me caught my attention. He had thick, wire-rimmed glasses that didn't hide his clear blue eyes and a bald head spattered with freckles. He wore a threadbare suit with a vest pocket from which he'd pull and glance at a gold watch that had a long chain attached to yet another pocket. With a gnarled hand, he leaned on an equally gnarled shillelagh, an Irish walking cane. Most of the other men were downstairs drinking whiskey—it was an Irish-American wake after all—that some male relatives had supplied. Margie whispered to me that this little man was her Uncle Jake, my grandfather's older brother. She said he had no wife or children of his own, but he'd always been kind to her and my mother.

Uncle Jake seemed to take an interest in me and asked me questions about my life in Boston, gave me a dollar bill, and told my mother to make sure that I got supper that night. I was smitten. No man had ever been so nice to me in such a short period of time.

~

After my grandfather's funeral, my mother, aunt, and I went to my grandfather's house. My mother said we had to clean it out so they could sell it. Frigid air rushed out as my mother unlocked the front door. The house smelled of flat beer, stale cigarette smoke, moldy food, and old wet wood. Yellowing, soot-stained paint covered the walls. As we walked toward the back of the house, wood floors creaked and dirt crunched under our boots. I pulled my coat tight as we walked through the rooms.

When we arrived in the kitchen, Margie looked out the window and gasped. Hand clasped to her mouth, her large brown eyes darted back and forth.

"Jesus, Mary, and Joseph," my mother said as she followed Margie's gaze. "What in the name of God is that?"

She led us out to the backyard. Close to the house stood several mounds of cans and bottles, ten feet in diameter and at least twelve feet high. They reached to the top of the first story windows.

"Mother of God," my aunt said. "He must have thrown every one of his beer cans and liquor bottles out here for years."

My grandfather had carefully built four piles: one each of beer cans, beer bottles, small liquor bottles, and larger liquor bottles. The cans at the bottom were mostly rusted. Margie warned me not to touch them. She said they were dirty and she didn't want me cutting myself. I could see the word "Schlitz" on several. The liquor bottles were different shapes and colors. Some were labeled "whiskey," others "gin."

"We have to get rid of these," my mother said. "We'll have to haul them to the dump ourselves."

My mother and aunt both looked at me.

"Anne," my mother said, "don't tell anyone about this. Do you understand?"

Silently I nodded yes. I didn't know why I couldn't tell anyone, but I knew from my mother's tone that I had better keep my mouth shut.

That day, we began our weekly trips to offload the detritus of my grandfather's drinking. My mother and Margie filled two galvanized steel waste cans with cans and bottles. They hoisted one into my mother's American Rambler trunk. The untied lid thumped against the can as my mother drove the two miles to the Kingston Town Dump. The other can sat next to me on the back seat. The smell was the worst I'd ever experienced, until we opened the car doors at the dump. The smell of garbage would stay with us all weekend until we returned to Boston and washed our scrubbing outfits.

Perhaps to distract themselves from the stench in the backseat, my mother and aunt talked about their father as we rode.

"He began drinking after Mama died," my mother said.

"He should have married again," Margie said. "Then maybe he wouldn't have turned to liquor."

"He was a mean drunk, too," said my mother. In the rearview mirror I saw her eyes squint with the memory.

"He still got up and went to work every day, but he'd start in with the booze as soon as he got home at night. He once threatened to shoot me with his hunting rifle." Margie's voice broke. "He aimed it at my face and told me he'd be doing the world a favor to rid it of my ugly puss."

I didn't know what to say to any of this, so I just listened intently. It helped me understand why Margie was a teetotaler and why she didn't want alcohol in our house, but it didn't explain why my grandfather had no interest in me. Grandparents on television doted on their grandchildren. I wished he'd been that kind of grandfather. He must have been very lonely, I imagined, in his dirty old house with his mountains of cans and bottles.

Most children in alcoholic families experience direct effects of the drug, as relatives become belligerent, absent, or lose jobs and financial stability. Alcohol abuse cost me a family. My father's alcohol abuse was a factor in my parents' break-up. My grandfather's alcoholism drove his daughters away from him, and as a result I lost the opportunity to know the only grandparent who survived past my toddler years.

My mother's and aunt's abstinence made me curious about alcohol. While I drank to excess at times in college and beyond, I found that it didn't help me feel better. If I was depressed, alcohol made me sadder. If I was anxious, alcohol made me panic. So I was never dependent on it and didn't use it to self-medicate. My drugs of choice were chocolate and sugar, just as they were for my mother and Margie.

We traveled to Kingston every weekend for the next year. We meandered along old Route 3A, each small town melting into the next, because Margie was afraid of the fast new highway linking Boston to Cape Cod. The long drive gave my mother and Margie ample opportunity to teach me about my family. They had nothing else to do other than smoke and drink the thermos of black coffee Margie made for the trips. Sitting in the back, I was a captive audience.

They seemed to enjoy telling stories about their past, sharing the hardships of their childhood. They'd tell me how lucky I was not to have had their struggles. Perhaps in the telling, they relieved themselves of some pain, putting me in the unwanted role of little therapist.

They spoke mostly about their mother, whom they revered so much she took on a saintly image in my mind that didn't quite match the stout, scowling, white-haired matron in the curled and faded photos they would occasionally drag out of an old shoe box tied with a broken string.

"Our aunts all said Mama was a ray of sunshine, always happy, always had a kind word to say," Margie told me.

"They said I was just like her," my mother said. "I always try to look at the bright side of things."

I almost gagged on the Toll House cookie I had sneaked out of the tin Margie packed for the journey. Sunshine was the last word I'd have picked for my mother. More like the lead-colored clouds that obscure the sun before a sudden downpour.

"Oh, but she could turn suddenly," my mother continued. "She'd hit me with a wet dishrag if I didn't do my chores to her liking."

Margie sat silently when my mother described their mother's anger.

Their mother emigrated from Ireland in her early twenties with three of her sisters. Irish families commonly sent their girls to America, where domestic jobs were plentiful, but kept their sons home to tend farms and support aging parents. Margaret Feeley never saw her parents again. Her position as cook to a wealthy family on Massachusetts' South Shore also took her far from her Boston-based sisters. Her life must have been lonely, which may explain why she married my dour grandfather, George Smith. She lied about her age to her husband, the priest who married them, and her in-laws because being older than George might have been a deal-breaker in those days, when most women married under the age of twenty-one, and their husbands were an average of five years older.

Her in-laws, the Smiths, were Irish-Americans descended from immigrants who fled the Great Famine in the mid-nineteenth century. They relinquished the Irish love-to-live culture in favor of the puritanical New England live-to-work ethic. Their Anglo-Saxon name helped them blend into the New England culture of Kingston, Massachusetts, a small town north of Plymouth. But the tentacles of their Catholic religion would not allow them to completely assimilate. As a result, they were always the farmers, gardeners, cooks, and factory workers, never members of the Kingston board of selectmen or the town elite. When jobs were scarce during the Great Depression, and few people hired Irish, the local Catholic Church provided work for several of the Smiths.

The family bought and farmed land along Elm Street in Kingston. When farming was no longer profitable, the patriarch divided the plots among sons and brothers, who built identical box-style houses set back from the road. Into this family enclave came my grandmother. She and her husband settled next door to her in-laws and within a stone's throw of several other Smith relatives, including Uncle Jake.

I can't picture Uncle Jake without the large wooden rocking chair he sat in by his kitchen window, which gave him full view of Elm Street so he could see whoever drove past. One foot away from his rocker was a ceramic spittoon. Margie said it was disgusting, which made me both want to look and not look into it. Brown tracks trailed down its side, giving a clue to the vile and murky contents within. His chair was wedged between the coal stove, which he used most of the year, and a kerosene cook stove used only in summer months. He'd tell me to draw up a kitchen chair next to him, and then he'd recite poetry and ballads to me—I remember him reciting all 130 lines of "Paul Revere's Ride" without pause. Sometimes he'd tell me stories about fairies, banshees, and leprechauns, tales that he must have learned from his Irish grandmother. Margie said that's how people used to entertain each other before television and radio.

We usually stayed with Uncle Jake on our weekend trips to clean my grandfather's house. The three of us slept in his extra bedroom in two twin-sized camp beds that were shoved together. I had to sleep in the middle on the crack. The floor slanted so much that we sometimes rolled into one another. With no central heat, the room was brutally cold in the winter. So we slept in coats, hats, and gloves.

Staying with Uncle Jake saved us money, but it meant that we had to clean his house, too, in order to make it habitable.

One Saturday morning, my mother was struggling to make pancakes on the coal stove while Margie did some cleaning. My mother told me to get her more coal from the basement.

"Mary, don't make the child get dirty," said Uncle Jake. "I'll go and fetch it for you. Here, Anne, come sit over here where it's warm."

The three of us stared at him open-mouthed as he rose and shuffled toward the basement stairs. No one stood up to my mother. Nobody had ever offered to do a chore for me. I wondered if she'd yell at him or give him the silent treatment. To my shock, she said nothing and continued mixing batter. Then I worried that she'd take it out on me instead. I resolved to try to be good for the rest of the day, to keep her happy.

We shared Uncle Jake with his many visitors, who dropped in if they saw the front door ajar or the kitchen curtain open. The ladies brought him boxes of cupcakes or turnovers from Poirier's bakery. People delivered other things: the *Old Colony Memorial* newspaper, fresh mackerel, and milk in glass bottles with the cream floating on top for his coffee. In summer months, they'd give him homegrown produce: corn, tomatoes, cucumbers, and squash. They'd sit and talk to him in loud voices to accommodate his reduced hearing, for which he couldn't afford treatment. None of the visitors were as interesting as my granduncle, and I'd have to sit politely until they finally stood up, talked a bunch more, and left.

Uncle Jake always gave me one of his precious pastries. My mother would glare with jealousy—he didn't offer any to her or Margie. He also gave me a dollar at each visit. I didn't realize at the time that these gifts were real hardships for this poor man who had most recently worked as a low-wage gardener for the local Catholic Church and was now living on a minuscule monthly Social Security check.

Just as Uncle Jake took care of them in their times of need when they were young, my mother and aunt took on more responsibility for their uncle. They never raised their voices to him, never struck him, and never gave him the silent treatment. They thought of him now as their dependent, although they had less power over him than over me. As an adult, he could make decisions. He was averse to change and for a long time refused to accept modern conveniences. He didn't want a telephone and didn't know how to use one. He was comfortable using an outhouse and taking sponge baths in his kitchen sinks. He heated his 200-year-old house with only two coal stoves—one in the kitchen that roared all winter, and one in the dining room that he only used when the temperatures dipped into single digits.

One bitterly cold Saturday morning in December, my mother suddenly pulled to the side of Route 3A in Kingston. She yanked open the door, leaned out, and vomited onto the sandy gravel. We were on the way to my grandmother's grave to pay respects on the twenty-eighth anniversary of her death from stomach cancer.

"Oh, Jesus," my mother said after she regained her composure. "This is how it started for Mama. She vomited all the time then started throwing up blood and black things that looked like coffee grounds. Oh, dear God, what if I start chucking up blood? Then I'll die of the cancer, too."

"Oh come on, Mary, you're fine," Margie said, turning around to me and saying, "They took our mother to the hospital."

"When they opened her up, there was cancer everywhere," my mother said. "So they just closed her up."

"We never saw her again," Margie said.

"Until the wake. The wake was in our living room," my mother said. "People used to lay the dead out in their own houses in those days. I couldn't stand to go into the living room after her funeral."

"Our father made us kiss her dead cheek during the wake," said Margie. "I was petrified."

"I remember the day of her funeral," my mother said. "I was so sick that Cousin Elizabeth had to walk me up and down the front walk. It was bitterly cold."

"And I was just twelve years old."

This deluge of information made my head spin. Did my mother really have cancer? Would she die? What would happen to me?

And why on Earth would someone make you kiss a dead body? I had an aversion to touching dead people and hated having to kneel beside the open caskets at deceased relatives' wakes. This aversion would later prove a problem for me in medical school, although latex gloves provided a helpful barrier in anatomy lab. I just had to power through it, like I powered through childhood.

At least weekly, my mother would remind me that she had only one kidney. "I don't know how much longer I'll be on God's green earth," she'd say. It would be twenty-five years before I'd learn that a person could live just fine with only one kidney. My mother proved this herself by surviving to the age of eighty-seven. Her bout of sickness and fear on that cold December day never repeated itself. I suspect the cause was the overwhelming sadness of remembering her mother's death, coupled with the realization of her own vulnerability.

On other car trips to the country, my mother and aunt told me about happier family times; most focused on their mother's kitchen.

"We worked hard when we were young," Margie said.

"We didn't have it easy like you," my mother added. "Mama was always cooking and cleaning. On wash day, we had to take turns scrubbing the clothes up and down the washboard."

"She made bread every week, and we'd have to help her knead it," Margie said. "Oh, how I wanted store-bought sliced bread like the other kids brought to school. But Mama said we were too poor for that. Now, I'd give anything to have her homemade bread again."

"And we'd have to feed the chickens," my mother said. "During the Depression, we survived because we raised chickens and grew our own vegetables. And our father hunted ducks."

"Those horrible chickens used to chase me around," Margie complained. "They'd peck at my feet, and my cardboard shoes wouldn't protect me."

"Mama always had something cooking on her kitchen coal stove," my mother recalled. "She'd put a pot of oatmeal and water on the back burner at night, and it would cook slowly until morning. It'd still be lumpy in the morning, though. She'd have a pot of tea sitting on the stove all day long. By the end of the day the tea would be so dark you could practically stand a spoon upright in it."

"Then in the morning she'd have to stoke the stove up again. That was our only source of heat most days. When we had company, she'd light the parlor stove. God, it was so cold at night in that house. The only warmth we'd have would be from the bed-warmer Mama would make up for us with the hot coals." Margie's voice trailed at the end.

"She'd have to run the warmer over the sheets quickly so they wouldn't scorch, and we had to get under the covers right away. But the heat never lasted. Remember that Margaret?" My aunt nodded silently.

I shivered in the back seat. I experienced that bone-chilling cold at Uncle Jake's house. In the winter, I'd stand as close to his kitchen coal stove as I could get without singeing myself. I'd postponed trips to his brutally unheated outhouse as long as possible.

My grandmother's rays of sunshine must have been dampened down by the rigors of New England life, her puritanical in-laws, and the distance from her own relatives. Still, she made a home for her husband

and two daughters and dealt creatively with the economic hardships of the Depression. Her resilience rubbed off on her daughters. From her, they learned to work hard and be frugal. Her untimely death forced them to keep house and earn a living earlier than they would have if she'd lived. And they had to deal with losing a mother.

Jake was what my kids today would call "the cool uncle." With no wife or children of his own, he welcomed his two nieces with open arms. A stop at his house on their walk home from school would always find some sort of sweet treat, depending on which gifts of food had been given to him by the many Catholic matrons who felt it their duty to feed the bachelor Church groundskeeper. After their mother's death, their uncle became a refuge for my mother and aunt. They escaped to his house when their father was on a drunken rage. He would feed them dinner, keep them warm by his old coal stove, and entertain them with stories and epic poetry. After a couple of hours passed, he'd walk them home to make sure his brother had fallen asleep.

The weekend country trips added a mountain of stress to our already pressured family. My mother and aunt hated their jobs, detested housework, and now the added work of cleaning out their father's house tipped them over the edge. Our weekends were filled with long drives, heavy lifting, scrubbing twenty years of filth, and hauling garbage to the town dump. As a result, my mother and aunt bickered constantly. The time away from Brighton also curtailed my ability to see the few friends I had. I was incredibly lonely, and the library books in which I buried myself provided my only solace.

The kindness of country neighbors lightened our burdens a bit. The woman next door scrubbed my grandfather's filthy kitchen floor. Others stopped by with food and thermoses of hot drinks. Some invited us in on bitter winter days for coffee, milk, and cookies. Relatives fed us numerous meals. We also witnessed the greed of people taking advantage of two women who had no man to fight for them: the plumber who claimed my grandfather owed him a thousand dollars even though no bill was produced and the pharmacist who refused to fill prescriptions for Uncle Jake until his late brother's tab was paid.

My mother and aunt had only one cousin on their father's side—the daughter of George Smith's long-widowed sister. By the time I met Elizabeth, she was a single mom raising five teenagers aged thirteen to nineteen years. Elizabeth laughed more in one half hour than my mother did in an entire year, and she always had open arms and smiles for the three of us. She talked a blue streak with no hint of my family's shyness. My mother and Margie said Elizabeth's house was dilapidated, dangerously so, but to my eyes that could see only the love and joy among the mother and five kids, their home looked solid. I envied their large family, the gentle ribbing they'd give each other, and the clothes sharing between sisters. I never heard a cross word among them. The youngest, Kitty, played Barbies with me, which made me adore her even more. The girls were Irish beauties, the boys scarily handsome. Elizabeth's five children had no first cousins, so they were as happy as I was to call each other "cousin." Over the next few years, they all drifted into their own marriages, leaving little time for their little cousin who only visited occasionally. Still, their house provided warmth and love from Elizabeth and whichever of her kids were around.

One Saturday in late March of 1962, my mother and Margie snarled at each other the entire two-hour drive to Kingston. I don't remember the cause of this particular tiff. We had just taken the Kingston exit from Route 3 and were coming down the hill on Route 3A.

"Jesus H. Christ, Margaret," my mother said in response to something Margie said.

Suddenly the car sped up.

"Oh, my God, Mary, stop. Please stop," Margie screamed as she braced both hands against the dashboard. There were no seatbelts—not a standard feature back then.

I remained silent in the back seat, clutching the tin of Toll House cookies Margie had made for the trip. The ride thrilled me—I'd never been in a speeding car before and had never seen my mother drive more than forty miles per hour. While upset at Margie's terror, I was excited to see my mother act so recklessly.

"Mary, stop the car now," Margie said.

My mother slammed on the brakes as she swerved the wheel to the right. The car came to a thudding stop with the right wheel smashed into the curb. My shoulder hit the back of the front seat. Margie sobbed. She was folded up under the front dashboard. She held the side of her head. Blood trickled under her fingers. My mother stared forward, silent, gripping the wheel. Finally, Margie maneuvered herself up onto her bench seat. My mother glanced at her.

"Do you need me to take you to the hospital?" she asked.

Margie didn't answer.

"Margaret, you're bleeding. Are you sure you don't need to see a doctor?"

By now Margie had pulled her large black handbag onto the seat. Miraculously it had remained closed. She opened it, fished out a rumpled Kleenex, and pressed it against her head. Blood seeped through.

"Are you okay, Anne?" Margie asked.

"I'm okay," I said, rubbing my shoulder. I thought if my mother had to bring me to the doctor she'd get even madder.

With her purse handles over her arm, tissue pressed to her head with bloody fingers, Margie got out of the car and began walking down the street. My mother started the engine and proceeded at her usual slow pace. I swiveled my head to watch Margie as we passed her.

My mother and Margie didn't speak for the rest of the weekend, or for the following two weeks. If they had something to say to the other, I had to be the go-between, as in, "Anne, tell Margie that we are leaving for Boston in an hour." Or, "Anne, tell your mother that I'm taking the bus."

They commonly used the "silent treatment" as a weapon. This wasn't just a matter of being quiet, nursing wounds, or taking time for introspection. No, these were active silences, carefully crafted and executed. When my mother was the instigator, which was usually the case, she drafted the neutral party into her scheme. In effect the target would be shunned. When I was the target, it felt like they'd abandoned me again. I was invisible, of no consequence, unwanted, and undesirable. I didn't know if my mother would ever speak to me again or if she'd make plans to send me away.

I was forced to take sides in battles between the two women, and it was clear they both expected me to side with my mother. My mother demanded filial devotion. Margie said daughters should honor their mothers, no matter what. Even if they hadn't forced this affiliation, I would have sided with my mother, out of fear. Margie's anger toward me was just anger—snide remarks and some doses of silent treatment—but she couldn't keep that up for too long.

It was always the three of us—my mother, Margie, and me. My mother and father separated when my mother was four months pregnant with me. Margie moved in to help during the pregnancy and stayed. The problem was that the two adults in my life were both female, sisters, and prone to fighting. Not having resolved their childhood issues, they replayed them with me as audience and arbitrator. Those issues included poverty, their mother's untimely death, verbal abuse by their alcoholic father, and fear of God's wrath.

My mother held the reins as the head of our household. Margie saw her older sister as a surrogate mother, in some ways making me a de facto little sister. But Margie played other roles. She changed my diapers in infancy and later kissed my knee when I scraped it roller skating on the sidewalk made treacherous from tree roots. She baked cookies. She did man-of-the-house chores like taking out the garbage and changing lightbulbs. There were limits to her masculine role taking, however. Despite taking driver's education and having plenty of practice, she failed her licensing test three times. "The guy said I was too nervous," she reported. She never did get a driver's license and spent her life being driven around like a child.

"The McGraws are giving away new kittens," Uncle Jake said when we arrived at his house one Friday evening. We were all miserable from a freak hot spell. The radio announcer said it reached 91 degrees in Boston. At least my mother and aunt were on speaking terms again.

My ears perked up at the mention of kittens.

"Mrs. McGraw stopped by yesterday to give me some cupcakes and told me her cat was about to whelp. She said they'll have to throw the unplaced ones into the Jones River. I said I couldn't take care of a cat. Besides, the damn thing would trip me up."

"Oh, no, they can't drown them!" I said.

Margie and I turned toward my mother.

"We're not getting a cat," my mother said. "I don't have time to take care of a cat."

"Anne and I will take care of it, Mary," Margie said.

Margie and I pleaded until my mother finally agreed to drive us over to look at the litter. Lucky was the only kitten left when we arrived, but that didn't matter to me—I fell in love with the little fur ball. My mother relented, and Lucky was ours. He turned out to be a terror, but

I liked that in a cat. Another creature could take the heat from my mother.

"I cut off our cat's whiskers when I was your age," my mother said when we were back in Brighton.

"Huh?" I asked. Lucky was curled up in a shoebox in the kitchen, asleep.

"We had a mean black cat when I was a girl. It was always chasing my feet, and it scratched me when I tried to pick it up."

"Why did you cut off its whiskers?"

"I don't know. I was mad that it kept biting and scratching me. Plus I wanted to see how long it took for them to grow back."

"How long did it take?"

"They didn't grow back. He was almost blind after that, always walking into the corners of walls."

"Did your mother get mad at you?"

"Yes, she was furious. She took her wet dishcloth from her shoulder where she always carried it. She rolled it up like this. Then she hit me with it like this."

My mother demonstrated several times, hitting my legs with the wet dishcloth that always rested on her own shoulder. As she did so, her mouth pursed and her eyes shrunk as small as two black peas. My grandmother came to life during this reenactment. I didn't dare tell my mother there was no need to show me what the wet dishcloth felt like—hearing the story would have sufficed. But she must have wanted me to feel her girlhood pain.

After a year of weekly trips to Kingston, we finished cleaning out my grandfather's house and sold it to a young couple for $11,000. After paying off the creditors, there were a few thousand dollars left. My mother and Margie decided to spend that money on Uncle Jake's house to make his existence less tenuous. They added an indoor bathroom, hot running water, and a telephone. He only agreed to these "newfangled" items when his nieces convinced him that it wasn't safe for us to stay at his house with its lack of hygiene and safety. He drew the line at central heating, however. He said it was much too expensive, and if we were that cold at night we should stay at a hotel or with another relative.

With the sale of the house, the weekly country excursions ended in September of 1962. I missed my granduncle but didn't miss the smoke-filled car rides, the bitter sniping or silence between my mother and aunt, and the bone-chilling cold and filthy smell of my grandfather's house. But our return to normalcy would be short-lived.

On an early November evening, the phone rang. My mother's face drained of color as she listened to the caller. It was Dr. Cronin reporting that Uncle Jake had had a heart attack at St. Joseph's Church that afternoon. The doctor said it was too soon to talk about prognosis. In the short term, he needed rest and good meals, and he could no longer work. Our weekend country excursions were back on.

Those trips took a toll again. After a month, my mother and aunt convinced Uncle Jake to come live with us. This would solve two problems—the trips would stop, and they wouldn't have to worry about him living alone during the week. I was ecstatic. We'd have another family member in our house, and a man at that!

We worked hard readying our apartment for a male inhabitant. Margie gave up her room for him and moved into the living room, where she'd sleep on the Castro convertible couch. I helped move some of her clothes to the front hall closet and to a small chest of drawers we'd placed in the living room. Margie said Uncle Jake had so few clothes that he'd only need one drawer of her large dresser.

"We won't be able to dry our lingerie in the bathroom anymore," said Margie.

"And no more prancing around the house in our nightgowns or underwear," my mother added.

"We'll have to make sure to close the bathroom door all the way when we go," Margie said.

"I suppose we'll have to make room in the bathroom for his things." They both sighed.

"I'll go work on that," Margie said. Soon, clinking sounds of bottles being moved around came from the bathroom, which opened right into the kitchen.

"Oh, Jesus," my mother said after Margie returned. "I hope Jake can get used to peeing in the toilet at night. I don't want to have to empty a bucket of urine every morning."

Neither woman looked happy. I hoped they wouldn't change their minds about letting him live with us. I didn't dare show my excitement about him coming, in case it annoyed my mother and aunt, who seemed to regret their generous gesture. But inside, I was doing jumping jacks. I would no longer have to come home to an empty apartment—I'd have a constant companion, someone who would talk with me and tell stories. My granduncle would also temper my mother's anger. She treated him with respect, was even subdued around him. Maybe she'd be embarrassed for him to see her yell at or hit me, or to threaten to send me away. Everything would be better now, I was sure of it.

We picked up Uncle Jake the weekend before Christmas. Before he left, he looked around his house then stood out front looking at his acre of land with its six gnarled apple trees that produced wormy fruit each fall. Slowly, he picked his way down the walkway toward our car. As we drove away, he kept his gaze to the side of the road, as if to say goodbye to every house and landmark. I wished he'd smile. My selfish excitement at bringing him home with us blinded me to his sorrow at having to leave the place he'd lived his entire life.

At home in Brighton, Uncle Jake and I took walks together every day. I felt proud to have the neighbors see me strolling arm and arm with this kindly older gentleman. We'd have to walk slowly going back up the steep driveway.

"My ticker's not up to snuff," he'd say.

On the first school morning after Christmas break, I ran into Uncle Jake's room to say goodbye. I leaned over the bed and hugged him quickly, thinking how funny he looked without his glasses. I turned and kicked the pail next to the bed. It fell over and a torrent of liquid spilled onto the wooden floor. Margie heard the commotion and poked her head in.

"Oh, Christ," she said. "The piss is all over the floor." She disappeared and ran back in with an armful of towels.

"I'll miss my bus," she said. "Anne, how could you be so clumsy?"

"Don't yell at the child," Uncle Jake said. "It's not her fault."

"Well if you'd use the toilet at night like a normal person this wouldn't have happened."

I inched out of the room, my face red with shame. I felt terrible that I was causing everyone so much trouble but wondered if all men peed into buckets by their bed at night.

Uncle Jake stayed with us for less than a month.

"I miss Kingston," he told my mother and aunt. "I want to go home. I'm just not a city man."

So Uncle Jake went back to Kingston. I knew my spilling the pee bucket must have made him decide to leave Boston and return to his house in the country. I'd ruined my one chance for living with a man, albeit an old and sick one. No wonder my father didn't want anything to do with me.

Chapter 7

Just a Taste

Carefully, my mother laid a present under the Christmas tree, leaning it at an angle against several other brightly-wrapped gifts. I sat near her, breathing in the smell of fresh pine. It was a few days before Christmas, and my mother had just arrived home from work. I looked at the tag on the new gift: "To Mary, From Mr. Stevens." I didn't need to look at the thirty or so other presents under the tree—they were all addressed to her. My mother was an executive secretary to the director at an oil company's regional office. The managers and office workers knew they had to be nice to my mother in order to get favors, such as easier access to the big boss and her discretion when they came back from lunch smelling of booze. Each day during the weeks leading up to Christmas, my mother brought home a few gifts and placed them artfully under the tree. Occasionally one of the men would send home a present for me, but not this year. There were no business gifts for Margie. Shortly before Christmas, our family gifts would be wrapped and placed on display.

Being a nine-year-old kid, I had little money of my own, but I had some resources. My mother and aunt each paid me one dollar a week for setting their hair, and Jake gave me a dollar each time we visited him. I'd saved thirty dollars for Christmas presents for my mother and Margie. I spent five dollars on a Woolworth's scarf for Margie—she always loved what I bought her. The remaining twenty-five dollars went to gifts for my mother—a blouse that Margie helped me pick out at Filene's basement, some Estée Lauder cologne, and a ceramic statue of the Blessed Mary. I was worried. If my mother thought I hadn't spent enough on her, she'd be angry.

We'd had several Christmas fights in the past. Sometimes my mother and aunt were worn out from all the holiday preparations added to their challenging work lives and commutes to Kingston. But my mother's anger, if she wasn't happy with her presents, was the scariest. If she and Margie had a blow-up about Margie's gifts to her, I'd have to be the go-between delivering messages as they gave each other the silent treatment. If she was angry with me, I could get a beating, or she might stop talking to me.

At supper that night my mother suddenly said, "Anne, I'm short of money this year. I'll only have one present for you."

"Okay," I mumbled. Margie drew in a sharp breath.

"There's nothing I can do," my mother said. "The bills keep piling up. The heater is taking more oil this year, and the cost of food is up. The gas and meals in Kingston are hurting, too."

True to her word, my mother bought me a bathrobe I didn't want. Margie gave me several games and a new Barbie with several outfits. I was getting a little old to play with Barbies, but I loved the dolls so much that I couldn't give them up.

I didn't mind that my mother received a lot of gifts from her office. What bothered me was that she displayed them to show how much everyone loved her and that she was so much more important than either Margie or me. Even worse, we had to sit by the tree while she opened all her presents. At least I was allowed to play with the toys I'd received. I sat stroking my new Barbie's long blond hair as my mother opened the last of her gifts.

"Well, at least the men at work appreciate me," she said.

"What do you mean, Mary?" Margie asked.

"Well, that brat Anne couldn't be bothered with buying something nice for me," she sneered.

My tears dripped onto Barbie's dress.

"She spent all her money on you, Mary," Margie said. "I know because I helped her with her shopping."

"Well, then, I'm not sure where her money goes. She must be spending it all on candy."

No one said anything.

"I'll go get started on dinner," my mother said. "We'll eat at one o'clock. Anne, I need you to come peel the potatoes."

It was another quiet Christmas. This time my mother was angry with both Margie and me. Her silence lasted for several days.

The grown Anne—wife, mother, doctor—wants to hug my younger self, tell her that presents are only one small manifestation of what you feel for another person. I want to say that her mother's issues with gifts were all about her own insecurities, not about anything being wrong with Anne. I'd like little Anne to enjoy the exchange of gifts on holidays, as my daughters and grandchildren do.

A man appeared in our lives the following summer—mysterious, faceless. Only one of us welcomed his visit.

It was the kind of hot summer night that made you sweat in your sleep. Now ten years old, I lay on top of the sheets in my baby doll pajamas. No amount of heat would make sleeping with fewer clothes acceptable in my family. I was in the middle of my recurring nightmare of walking naked around my fifth-grade classroom when Margie burst into the bedroom, raced over to the window, and slammed it shut.

"Anne, get up. Here put this robe on."

"Huh?"

"Come on, you have to get up."

Through my brain fog, I heard my mother yelling into the phone that there was a man outside. Margie put her arm around me and led me to the other side of the house, to her room. She told me I could lie down on her bed. After a minute, I heard a knock on the door and the landlord's voice. A blue light swirled outside Margie's bedroom window, followed by more knocking and male voices. Then I heard nothing else.

The next morning my mother told me that there had been a man peering into the window of the bedroom she and I shared. She said if I was home alone, I was not to open the door to anyone and I had to keep the windows shut and locked. I wasn't particularly worried about a man outside our window. I couldn't understand why someone would want to watch me lie in bed. No Sleeping Beauty here; I couldn't hold a male's attention while awake and thought I must be even more boring when asleep.

That night, over a dinner of American chop suey, my mother wondered aloud if it had been Jim McTiernan looking in my window. I jolted to attention, eardrums tensed, eyes riveted on her so I wouldn't miss a single nuance. She said the man next door went to high school with my father, and they were probably drinking buddies now. My father could have come over to our yard from that neighbor's house.

This speculation left me even more speechless than normal. I wanted to ask how we could know this for sure and whether he'd be back again. I wanted to suggest that we lay a trap outside my window so we could detain him long enough for me to get a good look at him, to touch him, to smell him. Neither my mother nor my aunt seemed to notice my stunned silence. They went on discussing Jim McTiernan as if the possibility of his being a Peeping Tom was of casual interest.

I sparkled with pleasure at the thought that my father had sneaked a look at me. He was definitely the voyeur, I decided. He's finally come back to me. Maybe he wants a little girl to bounce on his knee, read stories to, and play Parcheesi with. Maybe he'd teach me how to dance like Shirley Temple. Three years earlier, I'd quit tap dancing lessons after I mistakenly led twenty little girls, clad in multi-colored polka-dot satin costumes, in endless circles in our Good Ship Lollipop recital. Mortified, I refused to return to class. My mother didn't mind—she was happy to save the two dollars each week and the hassle of sewing recital costumes. Still, I always wished I could dance, wished I could feel the music move through my body and move my feet in time, one-two-three-four, one-two-three-four.

"Your father was a wonderful dancer," my mother once told me. "Women would line up for a few minutes in his arms."

I imagined him choosing to dance with me over a line of beautiful women. He'd lead me around to Frank Sinatra's "I've Got You Under My Skin," my white gossamer gown flowing behind, all eyes on me.

My dad would be like the television dads, I was sure. His voice would be deep and melodious. His eyes would twinkle as he gazed down at me, full of tender love for his little girl. He'd laugh as I twirled around like a ballerina. He'd listen to what I told him and say, "That's nice, Kitten." If I asked for something, he'd say, "Of course you can have that, Sweetheart," and hand me a twenty dollar bill from a wad he kept neatly folded in a silver money clip. My dad would let me stay up late to watch my favorite shows, maybe even until nine o'clock. We'd sit close together on the forest green sofa and watch the Flintstones at 8:30 P.M. on Friday nights.

My dad. I loved thinking those words, even though I'd never been able to say them aloud. He wouldn't notice how fat I was, and maybe I'd even become slim with him around. He'd make me so happy that I wouldn't need candy or cake or cookies to fill the emptiness.

And I'd finally be able to go to the St. Columbkille School father-daughter breakfast, which was held every spring. The principal announced it on the loudspeaker several weeks in a row, reminding the girls to tell their fathers. The nuns wrote the date and time on the classroom blackboards and sent us home with letters addressed to our dads. Mine was addressed to Mr. McTiernan. Each year, I read the letter several times, hoping it might hold some secret information about how I could find my dad and convince him to take me to the breakfast. I wished the nuns had promised him that his sins would be absolved if he'd just come back to his daughter for a day. Or maybe offer a raffle for a bottle of liquor that he couldn't resist the chance of winning. Of course this was all moot because I couldn't give him the letter. I didn't know where he was and had no idea how to reach him.

I didn't dare hide the letter from my mother, afraid I'd get a slapping if she found out. On television, kids hid teacher notes, letters, and even report cards from their parents. The Beav's parents didn't slap him around when they found out. They just said things like, "We're very disappointed in you, Son. Maybe you should go to your room for a while and think about what you've done." The Beav would hang his head in shame, shuffle off to his room, and lie on his bed juggling a baseball. No television kids were beaten or slapped. They weren't called "little shits."

My pleasure at the thought of my father trying to come back to my life was transient, as I remembered that I was an ugly ten-year-old who had no business wearing baby doll pajamas that showed my rolls of fat. I realized that my father would never want another thing to do with me, now that he'd seen the horrible creature his daughter had become.

Soon after the Peeping Tom incident, Margie installed special locks on the windows, which prevented them from being raised more than a few inches. I hated them. During the hot Boston summers, I wanted to throw the windows open to let in the little breeze available. But now our home became a stifling hot prison. While the Peeping Tom hadn't stolen my innocence—I still didn't believe he was really looking at me—he had taken something much worse. He'd sucked the air right out of our home.

We moved the following winter to a flat about a mile away. I was saddened to realize my father would not know where to look if he tried to find me again. The upside was that I'd have my own room—a converted porch—finally I'd have some physical separation from my mother. The immediate reason for the move was a broken furnace that the landlords refused to fix, even after they saw us sitting in our woolen coats and hats. It was uncharacteristic of them not to acknowledge a problem—they must have been short on money.

On a warm spring day, my mother clenched the American Rambler's wheel in the ten o'clock and two o'clock position. It was 1965. Now an awkward twelve-year-old, I wished myself older. Margie sat in the passenger seat, knuckles of her right hand white as she gripped the passenger door. Her left hand pressed up against the dashboard. She'd shift from her braced position only long enough to take a drag from her cigarette or to light another. I was engrossed in a book in the back seat but had one ear on their conversation.

We were on our way to my second cousin Kitty's wedding in Plymouth. I'd been surprised at the choice of March for a wedding—that month could be miserably cold, rainy, or stormy in Massachusetts. As I tried to concentrate on my library book, I realized my mother and aunt were talking about the bride.

"She's much too young to be getting married. She's only seventeen, for God's sake," said my mother.

"Her mother let those kids do whatever they wanted to do," Margie added. "They're all wild."

My brain swirled with this talk of my cousin. I loved Kitty, wished she were my sister. I was excited to be going to her wedding but wondered if I would see her much now that she would be moving out of her mother's house and starting her own family. I didn't know that seventeen years old was too young to marry; the heroines in the historical novels I devoured usually married by this age.

Ours was a virtuous home. There was no hint of sexuality, no candlelit dinners with a visiting beau, no sexy nightgowns or lingerie. I don't know how much of our puritanical view of sexuality stemmed from religion, how much from our Irish heritage, and how much from our particular family. The Church taught us that sex was for procreation; therefore, it was limited to a married couple, husband and wife. The Church didn't provide exact guidance on what was a venial sin, or a mortal sin, or no sin at all. Clearly, the full act of intercourse was grave unless it occurred within marriage, without contraceptive devices. Homosexuality was never discussed in my school, Church, or home, so I didn't learn the Catholic dogma on this until I reached my late teens. Other types of sexuality were less clear. This latitude allowed priests, nuns, and individuals to interpret the degree of sinning.

The Irish were especially sensitive about sexual sins, thinking that just about anything would send you to hell. For my mother and aunt, sex was something dirty, not to be referenced in any format. I grew up thinking that sex was something done behind a married couple's closed door, as quickly as possible, and hopefully on only a few occasions every ten or eleven months—the childbearing interval typical for Irish Catholics who were doing their duty to procreate. When I ventured to ask my mother what sex was all about, she said, "It's wham bam, thank you ma'am," and wouldn't explain further.

At my cousin's wedding, I was embarrassed yet excited at the garter removal ceremony—drums banging, people laughing and clapping, the groom reaching farther up her leg, the poor girl with more and more leg exposed. I'd never seen a man get that intimate with a woman, and now it was happening ten feet in front of me. I didn't dare look at my mother or Margie. They were neither laughing nor clapping. I wanted so badly for a man to touch my leg, for a man to want to be that close to me. But I knew that my fatness would repulse any male—there would be no wedding in my future. Later, I saw my cousin in tears. I couldn't understand why she could possibly be sad when she had a man committed to her, someone to love and take care of her. Perhaps they were tears of joy.

Still, my discomfort at the thoughts of sexuality didn't stop me from having my own infatuations. I was a serial, monogamous crusher. Each crush would last about a month, and each boy was my one true love. I fell hard for the boy whose lock of light brown hair fell so cutely onto his forehead and for the skinny boy whose knees couldn't fit under his desk. I loved the one with black hair, fair skin, and freckles. I longed for the tall, handsome Italian boy with his dark hair slicked back with Brylcreem. The one with dimples on each cheek made me swoon. All of these passions were secret—I was too shy to even look at boys. I was terrified they would notice how my cheeks turned beet-red and my armpits leaked whenever they walked past my school desk.

I had a rich fantasy life with each love. I was always thin with thick hair. I would laugh and smile with the boy. I'd be a brilliant conversationalist—he'd hang on my every word. The touch of his hand would electrify me. He'd bend down to kiss my lips, which would burn with pleasure. As I thought of this sensual detail, I'd touch my lips with my fingers or sometimes kiss my own arm, pairing a tactile sensation to the dream.

My friends had crushes too—I knew because they'd tell me. But when a friend went on and on about her latest love interest, I'd just listen, smile, and nod. I'd never share my own desires because I knew their response would be to tell me there's no way any of those boys could like me, so why waste time talking about my latest unrequited love.

The situation wasn't helped by hearing what the cool kids, the ones in the clique, were doing. Every Monday morning, we'd hear stories about that weekend's parties, the ones I was never invited to. We'd hear about spin-the-bottle games and who kissed whom in which closet. We'd see a girl sporting a new going-steady ring with tape wrapped around the back so it wouldn't fall off her delicate finger. We nerdy kids enjoyed some titillation in hearing about the cool kids' adventures, sort of like fans following movie stars.

But the reports mostly made me feel even more ugly, awkward, and unwanted than before. I wanted to be one of the cool girls, to be pretty, thin, and vivacious. I wanted boys to want me. I knew if only I could be attractive to boys and get a boyfriend, everything would be fine in my life. But I could see no way out of my dilemma. I was a fat nerd, and that was that. Those Monday afternoons, I'd eat even more than usual after school, subconsciously hoping the food could fill the deep, dark emptiness within me. It never worked.

My idea of what a family could be changed in the summer of 1965. It was a brief time—just a few days—but it set up my deep longing to create a family for myself. The experience would also cause an irreparable divide between my mother and me.

My mother's friend Kathy invited me to stay with her family for a few days. I dearly loved Kathy and her three children, aged eleven, nine, and six. And the dad seemed so kind that I wasn't very afraid of him. They lived in the top floor of a triple-decker house in Cambridge. I fit right into this younger group of kids like a gosling nestled deep in pond reeds, not visible to the outside world. Gone for the time being were my thoughts of boys. Instead I dove deeply into games of castles and dungeons and secret caves, all created with variations of blankets draped over furniture.

I barely noticed the parents during the visit, although I did feel a little embarrassed to see Kathy making breakfast in a flimsy pale green negligee. Granted it was August, and there was no air conditioning in their apartment. Still, I didn't want to see this woman's almost-nakedness, especially since her husband kept coming in and out of the kitchen, as he got ready for work. Men weren't supposed to see women with scanty clothing.

Kathy sipped a constantly full cup of tea all day into which she'd occasionally pour some clear liquid from a bottle. Lunchtime still found Kathy in her negligee. She didn't seem to mind the thick layer of dust that covered every surface. The threadbare furniture surprised me—I had thought if a dad was in the picture the family would have more money.

Those few days were idyllic in what they didn't include. No one got angry with me. No one yelled at me. I wasn't hit, and the children weren't spanked. I didn't have to cook dinner. The children were expected to help clear the table, make their beds, and keep their rooms tidy. Other than that, they were free to play all day. I wanted this to be my family. I wanted to preserve the warmth of the little six-year-old girl who snuggled onto my lap while I played Candy Land with her older sister. I wanted the sweet banter with their brother to never stop. He loved to show off his card tricks and his strength, but he displayed a great deal of restraint with his sisters even when they taunted him.

Much too soon for my liking the visit ended. Kathy reminded me on Friday that my mother would be picking me up at 5:30 that evening, so I needed to be packed and ready. My heart sank. I didn't want to leave. The girls voiced it better than I could have.

"Mooooom," they pleaded, "we don't want Anne to leave. Please, please, please, can she stay for a little bit longer?"

"Sorry girls, but her mother is coming today. They have to visit Anne's granduncle in the country this weekend. So she has to leave tonight."

"No fair," they said in unison, showing that they had practiced this duet before.

My mother was cheery when she picked me up. Out on the jagged sidewalk, she and her friend talked grown-up speak for a few minutes. Then, my mother said it was time to go. Kathy hugged me, while the girls threw their arms around my legs. Acute awareness of my mother's scrutiny kept my goodbyes short and eyes dry. We made a quick stop at home to pick up Margie and headed to Uncle Jake's house. Riding alone in back, I dove deeply into a *Little Women* sequel and the tin of Toll House cookies Margie had made for the trip.

Later that weekend, my mother and I stood on Uncle Jake's front porch, weeding an old wooden planter in which several red geraniums were gasping their last breath.

"What's the puss for, Anne?"

"Nothing." My momentary glower betrayed my lie.

"You've been sullen ever since I picked you up."

I looked at my feet.

"Look at me when I talk to you." At my mother's raised voice, Margie looked over from the yard, where she was pushing a wheelbarrow full of grass clippings.

I raised my eyes. My burning cheeks were not from the summer sun.

"You didn't want to leave them, did you?" She spat it like a cougar.

"No," I mumbled. "I liked being with a family where there was a father and other kids."

I felt the hot air on my cheek before her hand hit. I didn't step back. I knew she would follow my retreat. I knew to wait until her hand stopped its swing back and forth like a pendulum eventually losing force. I wanted to touch my stinging cheek to soothe it but didn't dare move in case it set her off again. I could smell the dirt her hand left on my face.

"What's the matter, Mary?" Uncle Jake called through the screen door.

"This ungrateful little brat doesn't want to live with me," she said.

"Now take it easy, Mary. I'm sure the child loves you."

My mother glared at me but didn't argue with Uncle Jake. She didn't speak to me again for three weeks.

This big quiet wasn't a matter of curt responses or communicating the bare minimum required to keep a household going. It wasn't just a withholding of affection. It was total silence. Occasionally, if she really wanted me to know something, she'd say to Margie, in front of me, "Could you tell Anne that . . . ." There was no call to supper. I'd have to slink into the kitchen when I heard the chairs scrape on the linoleum. We ate in silence. There was no other communication, no notes. Just silence. If I tried asking her a question, I was met with stony muteness. If I said "good night," there was no response. This was not the first time she had inflicted the silent treatment, but it was the longest.

Maybe I should have enjoyed the silence. Perhaps it could have given me time to gather my thoughts, get some clarity. I could have pretended to be in a silent movie and created my own dialogue. Maybe it would have gone like this:

Mother: Anne, I'm so sorry I haven't been able to give you a family with a father and brothers and sisters. I really wish I could have.

Daughter: I'm sorry I said I'd rather live with our friends. It's not true—I'd miss you and Margie too much.

Mother: I did feel hurt. I'm very sensitive. I wish I knew how to express my feelings better. But I do love you desperately. And I would be so devastated to lose you.

Daughter: I love you, too, Mommy.

Perhaps I could have filled my days with music. Over the summer I was supposed to be working on the piano pieces Sister Frances had assigned. Or, I could have sung and played tunes from musicals like *My Fair Lady* (my favorite) or *The Sound of Music* (Margie's favorite). Singing and playing piano at the same time required the concentration of my entire body: left brain matching notes to piano keys; right brain bringing emotion to the music; mouth, throat, chest, and diaphragm producing the vocal melodies; hands, arms, shoulders, and back controlling the piano keys; feet teasing the pedals. With my entire body engrossed in this activity, I might not have noticed the silence.

Instead, I ate. I ate double and triple helpings of my mother's meatloaf—determined, it seems, to get some kind of nourishment out of her. I ate four bowls of Alpha-Bits cereal in the morning, not even stopping to spell words out on my spoon. I used my stockpile of cash to buy candy—enough for six or more candy bars a day. I drank milk as if it were the only liquid in a drought. I gained five pounds in the month before school started and continued that upward spiral during eighth grade.

Years later, after I had finally severed all contact with her, my mother retaliated by ridding her home of all memories of her only child—photos of me, my school records, pictures of my two daughters. She couldn't just throw these out—she had to send them to me so I'd know of her purge. Among the materials was a page of my diary from this period.

August 8, 1965
Dear Diary,
I don't think my mother loves me anymore. But I love her so much that I just don't know how to live without her. I'll do anything, anything in this world to get her to love me. I know that sometimes I haven't shown it. And when she won't let me do something I get awfully mad and sometimes I call her names to myself. Sometimes I've lied or disobeyed her, but I'll never stop loving her. Last week I visited some friends. And when I came home I was foolish enough to tell her that I'd rather live there than with her. I said something about I'd have brothers and sisters and a father over there. But I know

now that it wasn't true and that I'd rather have her for a mother than anyone else in the world. And I hurt her terribly. Now, I don't want brothers or sisters or even a father, all I want is her. And if she keeps hating me, I'll just die of a broken heart. Why can't she forgive me? I love her so very much. And I want her to love me too. I'm an ungrateful little brat and I'm going to try and be somebody that my mother can love. Dear God, please help me and please give me back my mother's priceless and undying love.

I picture myself writing the entry, curled up on my twin bed in the converted porch that was my bedroom. Squirrels ran relay races in the ceiling at night, and tiny red mites scurried over my bed. With no radiator, the room was so cold in the winter that the only way I could spend time in there was to crawl under several blankets and use a flashlight to see.

I wonder why my mother chose to keep the particular section of my diary that spelled out my anguish at these events. Was she touched by my emotion? Did she like seeing me grovel on the page like this? Or, less likely, was there a chance that she realized what pain I was in and how she magnified my distress by giving me the silent treatment for three weeks?

When my mother sent me my diary page, I was in my late forties, working as a physician and researcher and married for twenty-five years with two daughters in college. I was as grown-up as you can get, yet reading my diary entry made me feel like a young girl mourning her mother's abandonment. The feeling didn't persist—I knew my mother was trying to strike another blow, to obliterate the person I had become—because I was now the one with the power. She could no longer hurt me.

But as a defenseless girl, her violent silence changed me. My home felt like a vagrant's cardboard box—it gave shelter but not enough to provide warmth, leaving me exposed and vulnerable. I pushed my anxieties and depression along like a homeless person's shopping cart full of dirty rags and plastic, sure that someone could attack me at any time. And I scrounged for affection as if in a soup line, grateful for whatever anyone would dole out.

My feelings for my mother changed soon after I wrote that diary page. Each day of silence made me hate her more and love her less. By the time she spoke again to me, I had vowed to never again allow her to cause me pain. She might hit me, but I'd be like the willow tree that bows with adversity; I'd bend to prevent breakage. She might scream at me, and I'd see the yelling as her problem, not mine. But I still needed to cope, to adapt. So I became an actress. I pretended to love her. I feigned interest in her life. I diligently completed my chores. Secretly, I began to look for ways to hasten my separation from her. I became like the prisoner who makes nice with the guards while digging an escape tunnel, one spoonful at a time.

Chapter 8

The Doughnut Shop

Being female and poor meant living with things that didn't work. My mother and aunt noticed the broken items but announced they couldn't fix them because they were women. A few rudimentary tools languished in a cardboard box: a lady-sized hammer, two screwdrivers, a small pair of pliers, and a few hooks, nails, and screws. To my knowledge, neither my mother nor Margie ever opened that box. I grew up thinking the ability to repair anything was a sex-linked trait: women could fix food or clothes, but only men could fix everything else. My mother had a hi-fi record player that didn't work. The kitchen radio only gave off static. One of Margie's bureau drawers was stuck shut. A lamp with a frayed cord sat in the living room waiting for electricity.

The broken venetian blinds bothered me most. Every window in our apartment had them, with their two-inch metal slats and thick white cords running up each side. When a cord frayed or the mechanisms at the top stopped working, a blind might be stuck in any position, halfway up and crooked, fully down and letting in no light, or perpetually opened like someone caught bug-eyed by a camera flash. Margie once ventured into a hardware store—that male bastion that frightened us all—to purchase a replacement cord, but she wasn't brave enough to use it. She dreaded cutting herself on the sharp slats or metal workings at the top.

I decided to fix the blinds myself. I had seen the ten-year-old boy next door peering into our apartment at night. I didn't tell my mother—she would have kept the lights off in that part of the flat—because every room but the kitchen and Margie's bedroom were on the side facing the boy's house, and we'd be functionally sightless at night. If only my current secret crush lived next door—the delightful Tommy with the dark brown hair and face full of freckles like the generations of Irish before him. I wouldn't mind him seeing me in various states of undress, but this little twerp was a different story. I decided that in order to put a stop to his peeking, I had to fix the blinds.

I knew I had the brains to do it. My IQ was the second highest in my grade in the Archdiocese of Boston. When the nun told me this, I could only think someone had made a mistake in grading my intelligence test. My natural smartness kept me an A student. This helped allay fears of my mother's wrath if I came home with even one B on my report card. It also led to positive attention from the nuns, which my shyness would otherwise prevent. Academic abilities were my only assets. I learned early that when you've got some talent, you need to use it.

So, one Sunday afternoon, I balanced precariously on tiptoes atop a dining room chair next to the window. I reached up to the top of the blind. This particular one had been stuck in the open position for several months, and now the June sun was beating in.

"What in the name of God are you doing?" My mother's voice came from the door leading into the kitchen. I didn't turn my head for fear I'd fall over. I could feel her disapproval of me standing barefoot on the maroon and white striped fabric of her dining room chair.

"I'm going to fix this blind."

"Are you out of your mind? You're only twelve years old. You'll make it even worse than it is."

I didn't say anything. I was reaching up to feel how to get it off the window.

"Margie, can you come help Anne?" my mother called. "She's going to make a mess of this."

Margie's slippered feet padded down the hall from her bedroom. The smoke from her Chesterfield cigarette followed her.

"Jesus Christ," she said when she saw me. By this time, I had one end of the blind out of its socket but couldn't reach the other side to free it.

"Here, I'll hold that," she said.

We took the blind down, gingerly carried it into the living room, and laid it on the salmon-pink area rug. Dust wafted up and mixed with Margie's cigarette smoke. I examined the blind over, up, and down, each side in turn. I studied the top where all the control functions resided, the creature's brains.

"Can you repair it, Anne?" Margie asked.

"Yes, I can," I said. "Where is the extra cording?"

"I'll get it."

By the time she returned, I had a diagnosis and a treatment plan. The cord was broken near the bottom left side. I'd just have to thread the new string through the same path as the current one. I thought at first that I could tape the two cords together and have the new one follow the old one through its various ducts and canals. But looking through the control mechanisms at the top, I could see that the operation would be much trickier there, and I'd have to do that part by hand. I didn't know it then, but these skills would come in handy in my future as a physician—the ability to look at a patient, assess the person's problems, and come up with a reasonable course of action. Plus, threading a cord through a venetian blind is disturbingly similar to easing catheters through patients' blood vessels.

Margie gave me the package of white cording. She had also brought a pair of scissors but didn't hand those over. I figured she imagined blood dripping down my hands.

I mended that blind and the other broken ones over the next few weeks. I'd hoped to gain my mother's tolerance by taking care of the blinds. If she could see me in a more grown-up activity, taking responsibility for something in our household, maybe she wouldn't hit me or threaten to send me away. Unfortunately it didn't work, but it did give me a sense of my own capabilities. I could fix things.

Taking action like this was one way in which I showed my family and myself that I was growing up. I was capable. I could take care of myself and contribute to the household. In doing so, I was fixing myself, little by little.

I needed love and I needed money. While girls of more advanced ages or other circumstances might have fulfilled these two requirements by, say, marrying well or by turning tricks, for a chubby thirteen-year-old Irish-American Catholic there were few possibilities. I decided that an after-school job would provide both a paycheck and a steady stream of potential boyfriends. Now in the first year of high school, my friends began landing after-school jobs—as grocery store baggers, waitresses, and ice cream fountain clerks. I watched the twin toddlers downstairs, but the pay—twenty-five cents an hour—was too low. And while the babies were cute, sitting for them was exhausting even for a teenager. So as soon as I turned thirteen, I applied for working papers and looked for a real job.

My friend Patty also wanted better pay than her regular sitting gig. So together we perused the *Boston Globe*'s want-ad page. We found a listing for afternoon and evening shifts for waitresses at Dunkin' Donuts. How exciting—to work surrounded by the aroma of doughnuts. Chocolate frosted, glazed, jelly, twists, sugar, and grease—couldn't get any better. Patty pointed out that the ad was for the shop on the Boston Common. That was no problem—I'd been taking the streetcar downtown on my own since I was seven years old. Patty called the listed number and learned that they still needed waitresses. I was on my way to fortune and romance. I'd show my mother just how grown up I was.

Patty and I walked into Dunkin' Donuts along with a crush of workers and shoppers. My excitement had me walking on tiptoes. I didn't think it through clearly but I had some vague notion that boys would miraculously appear in Dunkin' Donuts looking for girls. They wouldn't know that I was the class nerd, since none would likely be from Brighton and certainly not from my school. I realized that there was no hiding my weight, but even some fat girls had boyfriends. I could begin again with a clean slate.

A crowd milled around the takeout counter, customers waiting impatiently for their coffee and the little waxed paper bag with their two favorite doughnuts. The lucky ones already clutched their bags and coffee cups and looked smug. In 1966, there were only about 100 Dunkin' Donuts stores in the entire country. People came from all over downtown Boston to get their coffee and doughnut fix at the Boston Common shop.

We skirted the crowd and passed by three bays of counters and stools. The first two bays were populated by women with shopping bags stuffed around their feet and businessmen hunched over the counter. Steam from their coffee cups and smoke from their cigarettes rose to mix with smells of wet coats, cheap perfume, and greasy doughnuts. The women were bright-eyed, perhaps from an afternoon of fighting off competitors in Filene's bargain basement. The men's eyelids drooped from hours of tedious work that wouldn't quite pay the bills. The last bay held an assortment of people: a young olive-skinned woman with a deep cleavage and too much makeup under her teased blond hair; two pale sailors in their whites; a stocky streetcar conductor with the name Vinny sewn on his shirt pocket; and two skinny men with conked hair. All of the men were looking at the woman—the conductor furtively, the others openly. The men called out to the waitresses as they rushed by in their pink and white Dunkin' Donuts uniforms. "Hey, doll, got anything sweet for me today? Why dontcha ditch that no-good boyfriend of yours and go out with me?"

We stopped one of the waitresses to ask where we could find the manager.

"Abe's back there," she said, her long pink fingernail pointing to a smudged glass window through which we could see two men toiling, so covered in flour that I couldn't tell where their white uniforms began and ended. The older one, with stubbly gray hair, gave directions to the younger. Abe wasn't much taller than we were and was surprisingly thin for someone surrounded by doughnuts all day. He looked up as we inched our way in but didn't pause as he repeatedly pressed a stainless steel doughnut cutter into a yard-wide sheet of rolled-out dough.

"Can I help you girls?"

"We've come about the jobs," Patty said.

"Are you the one who called earlier?"

"Yes."

"How old are you?"

"Thirteen," I said.

"Fourteen," said Patty.

"Do you have working papers?"

"Yes," I said.

"What experience do you have?"

Neither of us answered at first. Abe raised a white eyebrow.

"I've got a babysitting job," Patty said.

"I'm an honor student," I said. Somehow I thought this might make up for my complete lack of work experience.

Abe sighed. "Well, you look like nice girls. Ask the waitress out there to get you two application forms to complete. Then we'll talk shifts. I suppose you can only work after school or weekends?"

We nodded.

"Okay, then. And tell the girl your sizes so she can order you some uniforms."

The waitress had teased brown hair and black eyeliner that curved past the corners of her eyes, giving her an exotic look out of character with her pale skin and freckles. Large silver hoop earrings tickled the collar of her pink uniform when she moved her head. She looked old—probably in her early twenties. We asked her the questions we were too scared to ask Abe.

"What is the pay?"

"A dollar twenty-five an hour. We split tips at the end of the shift."

"What are the hours?"

"You're kids so you can't work past 7:00 P.M. and you can't work too many hours a week. Abe will know the rules."

"Do the Combat Zone people give you any trouble?"

"Honey, they're just like everyone else. Some give good tips, some don't. But none of them will ever look down their noses at you. They come in and out by the back door there." She pointed lazily to the dark hallway to the right of the kitchen. "And they always sit in this back bay. If all the seats are taken, they just stand behind them."

"What shoes should we wear?"

"Abe likes us to wear white shoes. He thinks it looks professional. I got these clunky nurses' shoes on sale at Jordan's." We all looked down at her unhappy feet.

It was a relief not to worry about the inhabitants of Boston's Combat Zone. While I had been allowed to take the streetcar downtown starting at age seven, my mother strictly forbade me from going near this red light district. The area centered on Washington Street between Boylston and Kneeland Streets and extended up Stuart Street to Park Square. It got its name from all the soldiers and sailors who frequented it so often that it resembled a war-torn region. They came for the porn shops, peep shows, strip clubs, bars, and, mostly, for the girls who sold the real thing on the street. This was the closest I'd ever been to it. I looked around the residents of the shop's back bay, half expecting one of them to reach out and drag us through the dark hall, out the back door, into the Combat Zone, and that would be the end of us.

As this was my first job, I didn't realize how unusual it was to be hired so quickly. Maybe Abe was impressed by my honor society status after all. Patty and I worked the afternoon shift from three to seven o'clock. I'd do three afternoons a week so I could take piano and guitar lessons on the other two afternoons. I only worked half the weekends because we visited Jake other weekends. Patty worked so many shifts that she soon became one of the insiders. Abe eventually let her into his kitchen to make doughnuts, but he never did trust me with his big machines.

Oh, how I longed to be able to stick those cake doughnuts onto the spoke of the jelly-squirting machine, feel the fullness and weight of the successful fill, see the deep red or purple color, courtesy of cancer-causing food dye, oozing out of the hole, then carefully lay each one on the two-foot silver tray, and carry them to the front of the store like a fine meal in a hoity-toity restaurant on Beacon Hill. If it were up to me, I'd orient each of those doughnuts so that the little hole with the jelly or cream oozing out would face to the front, at about five o'clock for a little artistic value. Only now do I recognize the sexual images in the making of these doughnuts. The round ones with holes in the middle—why were those holes needed? Then there were the twists, long and firm. Finally the filled ones, the making of which was practically orgasmic.

Alas, I was relegated to the lowly role of server—taking orders, making change, bringing coffee and doughnuts. My hands were stained brown from all the coffee spilt on them. Covering the takeout counter offered a little variety and less walking. Sometimes a man would flirt with the counter girl but if there were people waiting behind him, God help her if she so much as smiled in return. An occasional stockbroker would slam a dollar bill on the counter without waiting for change. The fur-clad women grabbed their change with diamond-encrusted fingers and rarely did they add to our tip jar.

At the start of my shift, I'd don the polyester Dunkin' Donuts uniform that made me look like a sausage in bubblegum-pink casing. After tying a neat bow in the white apron with several pockets in front, into which I could stuff customer's tips, I was ready for action.

With over eight years of Catholic school experience, I was accustomed to the anonymity that a uniform gave. But it took some getting used to being called Hey You, Waitress, Honey, Doughnut Girl, Dear, or Coffee Girl. The customers, especially the ones at the takeout counter, did not care that I was an only child living with my mother and aunt, that I played piano well and guitar not so well, that I got mostly As in school, and that I had a crush on the boy who sat in the row next to me two seats up. I was the waitress distinguished from the others only by her snug size fourteen uniform, long baby-fine dirty-blond hair pulled back into a ponytail, and silver necklace with a Saint Christopher medallion pendant to keep her from getting lost on her way home.

After one week on the job, I'd learned all the rules. A coffee regular meant one shot of cream and one teaspoon of sugar. Two shots of cream made it a "coffee light." Coffee "to stay" came in one size only, an off-white mug with the Dunkin' Donuts logo on the side. We gave each customer a spoon placed neatly in the middle of a paper napkin. There were fifty-two varieties of doughnuts, but Abe never had that many at one time. Store policy was for unsold doughnuts to be tossed after five hours, so he and his assistants had to keep up production of the doughnuts in highest demand: plain, dunkin', crullers, glazed, honey dip, chocolate, various filled doughnuts, and a few frosted. The communal tip jar sat under the takeout counter, to be split later. Customers paid, in cash, as soon as they were served.

Dunkin' Donuts was like a church—offering comfort to people from all walks of life. Most of the customers entered the shop through the front door with faces wide-eyed in anticipation of gustatory pleasure. Some scowled, as if thinking of the six-minute walk to get back to their office, where the boss would say, "You're late again." The cops always came in through the front door. A path would clear for them at the takeout counter like the Red Sea parting, with the faces of those in line a mixture of tentative smiles and averted eyes. We didn't charge the cops for their coffees or the dozen assorted doughnuts we arranged carefully in the pink cardboard box.

The back-door people didn't venture up to the front. They sat on their third-bay stools, some for hours, stretching their coffee's lifespan. The men gazed at the women without blinking. A woman might slowly slide her finger around the rim of her coffee cup as she listened to a sailor's story. The hookers got right down to business, responding with luminous smiles if a man offered money, ignoring those who said they were short on cash but really needed loving tonight.

I never mentioned the back-door people to my mother or aunt, but they must have known. Margie's office was a few blocks from the shop—she stopped by occasionally on a long coffee break. She sat in the second bay with the other workers and shoppers. Over her black coffee and chocolate doughnut, she'd watch me work. If she noticed the prostitutes, she didn't let on.

Most of the other waitresses were in their twenties. Some had finished high school; none had higher education. Patty and I were the only high school kids. While I knew I didn't want to become a professional doughnut waitress, I envied their sophistication. They knew how to be nice in just the right way to earn extra tips. They talked with Abe and the other bakers about the Red Sox, Bruins, and Celtics. Their uniforms hung fashionably loose on their bodies made thin from the constant walking on the job and pack-a-day cigarette habits. Their hair and makeup were artfully arranged. Compared with these girls, I felt primitive and ugly.

Some of the girls had boyfriends. There was the beautiful and friendly black waitress whose nylons bunched around her ankles, making me even more jealous of her thinness. Her boyfriend came in often and sat on a stool between bays two and three. He'd drink the free coffee she slipped him, smoking and glaring at everyone and no one. I couldn't understand how she loved this angry boy. Another girl hooked up with a construction worker who came in the back door when he was working on a new high-rise over on Washington Street. The couple would laugh and talk about how hot they felt when they were within two feet of each other. I felt left out of a secret world they inhabited.

Despite some little flirtations, none of the guys who came in the front of the store asked out any of the waitresses. To them, we were back-door people. In Abe's eyes, though, we were all strictly front door, and he frowned upon the waitresses flirting with any of the customers. Or maybe he didn't want the complications that he knew would come as a result. He'd come out from the back in a second if a customer gave any trouble to a waitress.

He often asked us how school was going, making sure we could keep up while we were working. He made us go home early if a nor'easter threatened to close down the streetcar lines. Abe smiled and shook hands with the girls' visiting boyfriends. Abe was our work dad.

One early evening in November 1967, a tall, lanky boy with a dark crew cut, fair skin, and a deep blush ducked his way in through the back door. He stood in the hallway for a minute, as if he wasn't sure he wanted the commitment of taking a seat at the counter. Finally, he sat at the third bay, between two prostitutes. He was too young to be a pimp, wasn't wearing a service uniform, and didn't have construction gear. He stayed for about an hour nursing a black coffee, talking with the other customers. The black coffee suggested he might not be a native Bostonian, or perhaps he had done time in the service. He was back the next night, and the next, and then he started talking with me. One of the other waitresses smiled at me at the end of my shift.

"Our boy Steve is flirting with you," she said, nodding to where he sat at the back bay.

I blushed intensely—no one had ever flirted with me in my fourteen years. "Oh, he's just friendly with everyone."

"Uh-huh," she said.

On the fourth night, he asked me out. I said okay, not having any idea how I'd manage to clear this with my mother. He got up as I passed his bay on my way to the kitchen. He grabbed my hand and gently pulled me into the dark hall. He kissed me so quickly that it felt like only a breeze had swept my lips. I was beside myself with excitement. I had been kissed! Most of the girls in my high school class had been kissed. Some girls told of boys pulling them behind a building or a tree for a smooch as early as age seven or eight. By ninth grade, the cool girls had steady boyfriends. Many of the uncool girls had also been kissed, either on a rare date or after a school dance. Only the awkward ducklings like me still had virgin lips. Even if a boy had wanted to plant one on me, he wouldn't get the chance. If I recognized a boy on a Brighton street, I'd look down and away to avoid seeing what I knew would be a sneer. Often, I'd cross the street in time to avoid a boy altogether. It never occurred to me that the boy might feel slighted by my avoidance, my rudeness. I once was surprised that as I looked away and down, a very cute boy was saying "hi" to the side of my head.

After my first kiss, I floated around the rest of the shift. *Maybe I'm not so gross,* I thought, *if someone wanted to kiss me.* The next evening, the phone rang. I rushed to answer it, grateful that my mother was downstairs doing laundry, and Margie hadn't yet arrived home.

"It's Steve," said a deep voice on the other end after I answered. I struggled to get out a sound.

"Hello? Is Anne there?"

I finally found a voice. "Hi, this is Anne." I sent a few prayers to the ceiling to keep me from fainting, thankful that this boy couldn't see my crimson cheeks.

"I only have a few minutes on my dime. I'm calling from a payphone. I just wanted to tell you how much I'm looking forward to our date Tuesday night."

"Me too."

"You're a really pretty girl."

"Oh." I didn't know what the right response would be. I'd never had a phone conversation with a boy before, nor had a boy ever told me I was pretty.

"I wish we were together right now so I could hold you."

"Me too," seemed like a good reply.

"I thought we could go to a movie."

I was about to say that sounded like fun, when he continued, "It will be nice and dark so we can make out and stuff."

Panicked, I only managed to eke out an "mm." It goes without saying that I'd never made out before, wasn't sure I wanted to do that already, and certainly wasn't ready for "stuff." Still, a date is a date, and I was willing to try anything in my desperate love journey. We talked, or rather he talked, for another minute until the operator came on the line to tell him to add more money.

"Bye, Anne. See you Tuesday at seven o'clock."

After we hung up, I realized he had not told me anything about himself. I wouldn't have known what to ask. Furthermore, his interest in me seemed to be summed up in his one word "pretty," which was fine with me. I didn't care whether he thought I was interesting or clever or nice or that I knew nothing about him. Pretty! A boy thought I was pretty! I could think of little else for days.

The following Monday afternoon Abe called me into his kitchen. Wondering what I'd done wrong, I walked in with pulse racing. Abe didn't look up as he kneaded a one-foot diameter ball of dough. Flour dusted his arms up to his elbows and settled in every crevice of his hands, completely covering his plain gold wedding band. I stood there watching, soothed by the rhythmic movements of the dough.

"You know that boy Steve you've been talking to?"

"Yeah?"

"You know he's completely crazy. You need to stay away from him."

"What do you mean he's crazy?"

"He's just crazy, really loco. You'd better stay away from him or you'll get hurt."

This shook me to my core. Abe would not make something up to scare me away from this boy. He must have known something, some reason why Steve came through the back door even though he didn't have an occupation that would require that entrance. Something kept him from the front door.

I felt devastated but not surprised. Of course, no sane boy would have asked me out. When I saw Steve later that afternoon I told him I couldn't see him. He asked why. I didn't tell him the truth, just said I couldn't, that's all. Steve still came into the shop, but not as often, at least not on my shift. I avoided his gaze until he finally stopped looking at me. Then he stopped coming in altogether. I never asked Abe or any of the other waitresses anything else about him; I was too embarrassed.

After the maniac's kiss, I gave up any idea of finding a boyfriend at Dunkin' Donuts. I still talked with the people who came in the back door and found them to be the most interesting of the customers. But I realized I didn't yet have the ability to tell good from bad, sane from crazy, eligible from taken. My desire for the love of a boyfriend was eclipsed by my desire not to be killed by a crazy guy from the Combat Zone.

Reality hit me hard—I was still a fat, ugly, nerdy girl, and no normal male would ever want me. I started eating doughnuts in earnest—we were allowed to eat all we wanted during our breaks, and I took advantage of this. Plus I could take home some of the unsold doughnuts at the end of my shift. I was in hog-hell as I grew fatter and fatter.

One day, I was the only waitress serving the thirty, seated customers. Patty, feeding a ferociously hungry crowd at the takeout counter, didn't even have time to fix her shiny dark brown hair that kept slipping out of a large silver barrette. A swath of powdered sugar graced one of her cheeks that were otherwise pink from exertion. The shop had been empty when we arrived, but at three o'clock the afternoon coffee break crowd rushed through the doors and filled every seat. I grabbed a bunch of napkins and spoons.

"Hi, can I take your order?" I asked the gentleman in the beige raincoat with a shadow already showing on his chin.

"Coffee regular and a honey dip."

I repeated my question for the lady to his left. She was sweating in her dark fur coat.

"Coffee black, no sugar."

"Do you want a doughnut?"

"Did I ask for one?" She looked like she really wanted her coffee with cream and sugar and a doughnut to dunk, but I humored her.

I repeated the napkin, spoon, and questions to the ten people in the first counter bay then went on to the next bay.

"Hey, aren't you going to get me my doughnut?" It was the man in the raincoat. I ignored him and repeated my question to each person down the row. Pretty soon the customers realized what I was doing. One woman asked, who did I think I was, wasting their time? There was no way I could remember their orders without writing them down. A couple of guys who would come in together started betting on how many orders I'd manage to remember. A few of the other men got in on the action. One customer said he really only wanted coffee but was ordering two different types of doughnuts just to make it more interesting.

I took the orders for all thirty customers and started filling them. First I came around with the doughnuts. I figured it would make them happier, to be able to take a sweet bite while they waited for their drinks. Then I filled the coffee orders and carried them to each bay, ten cups on a tray, three trips. I spilled a few drops on the tray, but I got every single order correct, and no one had to wait more than a few minutes. It helped that most of them, true Bostonians, took their coffee "regular." When I finished serving, the customers gave me a round of applause. Some of the betting men were especially enthusiastic. I smiled widely for my audience. Abe watched, as he always did, from his flour-encrusted window. He wasn't smiling. I realized I hadn't taken the customers' money as I took their orders and had to quickly run around to collect.

Why did I pull this stunt? I must have needed to prove to myself that I had some value. I could memorize and carry out complicated orders. These skills would later be useful in medicine—the ability to listen to people and deliver on a promise. I wasn't beautiful, wasn't the type of girl that boys fell for, but I was smart as a whip. For just a few minutes, these people would value me, might even love me a little, as they took their first sweet bite of doughnut.

During my tenure, I felt at home in all elements of the Boston Common Dunkin' Donuts. I was one of the front-of-store people, a mix of upper, middle, and working classes, seeking a few minutes of pleasure the sweet and greasy confection would bring them. While I'd never be upper-class, I felt solidly working-class, and aspired to be middle-class. Maybe I could be like one of those secretaries who looked so pretty in their bright dresses and high heels, hair perfectly styled into bobs or French twists. At other times, I felt more like the Combat Zone people who came more for the physical warmth and camaraderie of the other customers than for the coffee and doughnuts. I would never enter the life of a prostitute, and I didn't have the physical stamina to be a soldier or sailor, but I understood the back door customers' longing for love. In the end, I used both doors, teetering always between working hard to make a living and searching for love, comfort, and pleasure.

Dunkin' Donuts gave me so much: I earned money, confirming that I'd be able to make my own way in the world; I learned how to please and appease people, a skill I'd find useful as a physician; and I experienced people from different backgrounds other than the Irish-American Catholics who had surrounded me my entire life. This too would help me as a doctor, as I quickly learned you need to provide the same level of care and courtesy to a homeless customer covered in rags and grime as to a wealthy client covered in furs and diamonds. I was playing at grown-up. It was full dress rehearsal, and opening night would come all too soon.

Chapter 9

Easter Treat

On Easter Sunday, 1968, ten days after Martin Luther King Jr.'s assassination, sections of Boston were jumpy. Plymouth was quiet. My mother, Margie, and I went to the 9:00 A.M. Mass at St. Peter's Church, a half-mile up the hill from the diminutive Plymouth Rock that never failed to disappoint a first-time viewer. The scent of lilies weighed heavy in my nose as we walked out of Church. I squinted from the bright sun. My mother and aunt replaced their cat's eye glasses with identically framed sunglasses. Our dresses were pastel: Margie wore lilac, my mother dressed in yellow, and I sported baby blue. We looked like the three fairy godmothers from Disney's *Sleeping Beauty*. Fairy godmother was not a cool look for a fifteen-year-old girl.

Easter was a day of celebration in our family. We'd gorge ourselves as we broke our forty-day Lenten fast. My mother and aunt loved the traditional ham baked with pineapple slices and maraschino cherries stuck to its sides, boiled potatoes, and hot cross buns. I devoured chocolate bunnies, cream-filled eggs, jelly beans, and marshmallow chicks. Sometimes my aunt would bake a cake in the form of a bunny. In my current life as an obesity and weight loss researcher, I wonder if religion-imposed fasting helps with weight control. Even if our post-Lent gorging caused some weight regain, it may not have been enough to counter effects of forty days and nights of significantly restricting calorie intake.

Rather than celebrating that Easter, we were once again in Kingston to visit Uncle Jake, who was living in a nursing home. After visiting him, we would peel off our Easter outfits and put on our cleaning-women rags to do more house and garden work at his place. Uncle Jake had deeded the house to my mother and Margie before he went into the nursing home, so in reality we were taking care of their property.

After Mass, we headed toward a maple tree that shaded the navy blue Chevy Nova my mother had bought with the Rambler trade-in and a three-year loan. We planned to visit Uncle Jake at the nursing home after breakfast. My stomach growled—that little white communion wafer was still stuck to the roof of my mouth, too small to have made a dent in my hunger.

"Where do you want to eat, Mary?" Margie asked.

There was no response. Margie and I turned around at the same time. I half expected a scowl on my mother's face; sometimes her silence hurt my ears. But she wasn't behind us.

My gaze followed Margie's over to a 1960 beige Ford Fairlane. My mother stood with her back to us. Left hand on her hip, right hand clutching her purse and gloves, she was talking with a tall man with thick white hair and glasses who was leaning against the car. The wind straightened her short, jet-black hair. We waited for a good ten minutes. Finally, the man smiled, showing straight white teeth. He opened his car door and said something to my mother. My mother turned around and walked our way. The smile on her face quickly faded as her small brown eyes met Margie's larger ones.

In the car, Margie asked, "Was that Bob Richards?"

"Yes. He said we should get together some time."

"You kept us standing here like a couple of fools. Do you think I have nothing better to do than wait around while you talk with that . . . *man*?"

"Well, if you'd ever get your license and buy a car, I wouldn't have to do all the driving."

"Why did you need to talk so long with him anyway?"

"He says he's divorced now," my mother said. "He has two grown children. He lives on the south side of Plymouth, on Boot Pond."

"Jesus," Margie whispered.

"What do you mean, 'Jesus'?"

"Middle-aged rumbling," Margie muttered.

"What did you say, Margaret?"

Margie didn't respond.

"Who's Bob Richards?" I asked.

My mother didn't answer. I twirled my hair around a finger.

"Ma, who is he?" I surprised myself with my persistence.

"He's someone I dated right after high school, before I met your father."

"You had a boyfriend?" I could not believe this. Mary Helen Smith McTiernan had always been fatter than I was, and decidedly more uncool, and even she had had a boyfriend as a teenager? What was wrong with me that no boys had any interest in me? Maybe God really does want me to enter a religious order, like the nuns told me every year.

The car moved silently except for the tires kissing the pavement. We grabbed coffee and doughnuts for breakfast at a roadside cafe and ate them on the way to the nursing home. The chocolate honey dip helped fill the void of the stillness.

At the nursing home, my mother and aunt pretended all was normal, their voices raised now not in anger but in consideration for Uncle Jake's reduced hearing. The nursing home beat with a cacophony—old people yelling to hear their own voices, nurses and visitors talking loudly and slowly directly into an elder's ear, and intercoms paging orderlies to clean up a ward. Little did I know that in seventeen years I'd spend many hours in noisy clinical settings like this during my medical training. Unfortunately the sounds in Uncle Jake's nursing home didn't distract me from the blasts to my other senses—the mixed scent of urine and Lysol, the heat, and the sight of gnarled and unhappy bodies. Uncle Jake asked about his house. My mother said we'd mow the lawn before we left for Boston.

"You need a man around the house," Uncle Jake said, not for the first time.

After the visit, my mother and aunt spoke to each other but with shorter sentences than normal. Bob's name wasn't mentioned for the rest of the day. We weren't a family given to long dialogues, and anger tightened our lips even more. All the same, we knew each other, our likes, loves, dislikes, and hatreds.

I figured Margie's main problem with my mother seeing Bob was that Bob had made the poor choice of being a man. She also bought into the Catholic Church's teachings on marriage: my mother would be on the road to hell if she took the path of dating Bob. But Margie's main problem was panic about losing her home. She'd had a family, such as we were, for the past fifteen years. If my mother married again, Margie would be kicked out, sent away, discarded like the used Kleenexes she kept stuffed up her sleeve all day before finally throwing them out. While my mother's conversation with Bob had been short, her eyes sparkled with interest.

There may have been no talk about Bob, but my internal drama director had him and my mother married and miraculously producing a family for me with his two children. I wondered when he'd tell me to call him Dad. The thought of a man in my mother's life, and in mine, also frightened me. I knew little about men, other than my father and grandfather surrogates—Uncle Jake, Mr. Johnson, Abe, and Jesus. How should I act around this guy? What should I say to him? Were there other, more sinister, reasons why Margie got so upset about my mother talking with him? Was he an alcoholic like my father and grandfather? Was he a communist spy?

A few weeks later, my mother visited Bob in Plymouth while I attended a mandatory weekend religious retreat. My mother picked me up at Church that Sunday evening. Hit by ammonia fumes when we walked into the apartment, we knew Margie had been cleaning. She stood in the kitchen, back to us, wearing tattered and battered clothes several sizes too big because they were hand-me-overs from my mother. Her Chesterfield cigarette smoldered nearby. She sipped black coffee with one hand while she crossed items off a list she'd penciled on a used envelope.

"Hi Margie," I said. There was no response.

"What's wrong, Margaret?" my mother asked. Still nothing.

"Aren't you going to answer me?" my mother asked.

Margie began to mutter, something about having forgotten to vacuum the living room rug, then she reminded herself to iron her outfit for the next morning. She continued this charade for several minutes. The ammonia fumes made me feel faint in that small airless kitchen, but I didn't dare move for fear it would ignite a blast between the two women. My mother stood watching for a few minutes and then said, "Jesus Christ, what the hell's gotten into you?"

Margie began to cry.

"I have to clean and scrub all weekend with no help because both of you are off gallivanting. You treat me like your servant."

"Christ, Margaret, you're just being a martyr. No one said you had to clean this weekend. And I offered to drop you off in Kingston, if you remember. You said you didn't want to go."

Margie mumbled about middle-aged rumbling and ungrateful people as she shuffled off to her room without looking at either my mother or me.

"Oh, my God, there's something really wrong with her. I shouldn't have to deal with this. Not now, when I finally can find some happiness. I don't deserve her crap."

I silently agreed that something was wrong with Margie, but I did think my mother should deal with it. Something had snapped in Margie when my mother began dating. Shaking, I realized that Margie was upset enough to leave us. I couldn't imagine life without her.

One month later, we were staying at Uncle Jake's house again. On the agenda was visiting Uncle Jake at the nursing home, cleaning the house, and tending the garden. This was not exciting stuff for a teenager, and even my mother and aunt were getting fed up with the grueling schedule.

My mother had a date with Bob on Saturday evening. She emerged from Uncle Jake's spare bedroom looking lovely in a peach shirtdress, white costume pearls with matching clip-on earrings, and white sandals. Looking this fresh presented a challenge in a house where you'd get a black streak on your skirt if you brushed too close to the coal stove, a wood stain on your belly if you pressed into the wainscoting surrounding the kitchen sink, or dust on your shoes on the front walk so narrow in places that you'd have to walk heel to toe like a drunk stopped by a traffic cop.

Rare for her, my mother looked genuinely happy, and she was glowing when she returned home late that night. Margie and I were sitting at the kitchen table, piles of paper, napkins, and ashtrays pushed aside to give us a surface for laying down our rummies on the red-and-white checkered oilcloth.

"Hi, what's everyone doing?" my mother asked.

"Playing gin," I said. Margie frowned at her cards.

"I had a lovely dinner," my mother said. "Bob took me to McGrath's down on the Plymouth waterfront. I had the swordfish."

Margie's scowl deepened. She hadn't yet looked at my mother.

"What's the matter, Margaret?" my mother asked.

"It's not right, what you're doing. You know it's a sin for you to date."

"For Christ's sake, all I want is a little happiness in my life. I've sacrificed all my life for Anne, with no love, no chance for happiness. I deserve this."

"Are you planning to marry Bob?"

"How in the name of God should I know that? I've only been seeing him for two months." The corners of her mouth played with a smile.

I realized with that smile the thought of marriage had occurred to her. But it will be a chaste marriage, I knew. After all, they're too old for sex—she's forty-seven, and he's fifty-four. She has graying hair and fat drooping thighs, and he has white hair. So of course, there will be no sex.

"Well, you and Bob were engaged almost thirty years ago. What's going to stop you now? Where am I supposed to go if you two get married?"

My jaw dropped and my eyes widened: Whoa, what engagement? How come no one ever thought to mention this to me before?

"I don't know. I don't even want to talk about this now." I could feel her unsaid words: *I don't want to jinx it.*

"It's not fair to me, Mary. I've stayed with you to help you raise Anne for the past fifteen years. I've given up my own life for the two of you. I changed Anne's dirty diapers for you. So now you'll just kick me out like I don't matter at all." Her eyes were wet.

"Jesus H. Christ," my mother said and stormed out of the room. I wandered around the kitchen, then stood at the sink, and watched the fireflies blink in the backyard. Margie sat at the edge of her chair, hand covering her mouth, cigarette burning closer to her fingers, coffee long gone cold, eyes wet. We stayed that way for a while.

Margie muttered under her breath, things like "single blessedness" and "middle-aged fools." I didn't bother to ask her what she was saying.

I knew she wouldn't answer. She'd moved into her internal world, trying to make sense of changes that terrified her.

Thinking through the conversation that had just occurred, I realized they used me as a weapon in their messages, leaving me battered and bruised.

My mother continued to see more of Bob, although most of their dates occurred when we came down to Plymouth to see Uncle Jake. This confused me. On television, men drove to women's houses to woo them, not the other way around. My mother told me a little more about Bob Richards. She had met him when she was still living with her father and Margie, while working in a store on Bob's Railway Express delivery route. Bob joined the United States Navy after Pearl Harbor, and he asked my mother to move with him to California where he'd be stationed. Too afraid to leave everything she'd known, she'd declined his offer. He shipped out, married another woman in California, and broke my mother's heart. Easter morning at Church was the first time they'd seen each other in twenty-seven years.

The more my mother saw of Bob, the more Margie withdrew. She'd arrive home at her usual time after work, make a cup of black tea, and take it into her bedroom. While she made the tea, she muttered under her breath. If one of us asked what she was saying, she'd remain silent. Anger swirled around Margie like a fierce magnetic force field, attracting yet repelling me. Attracting because I wanted to ask her what was bothering her, how she was feeling, why she wasn't talking to us. Repelling because I was afraid of a verbal blow or worse, her silence. The sound of rustling paper would drift out of her open door as she made a dinner out of saltine crackers or chocolate-covered peanuts from the five-and-dime. This was the first time the three of us didn't eat supper together every night, not counting my institutionalized years.

One Saturday morning late in May, Margie rustled around her room more than usual. Listening outside her door, I heard drawers opening and shutting, something being dragged on the floor, a thud. Suddenly the door opened. I tried to look like I was just passing by.

"What are you looking at?" she burst out.

"Nothing."

I followed her to the kitchen, not able to hear what she mumbled as she scuffed along. She took a couple of paper grocery bags out from under the sink and rummaged through the cabinets. She took an odd assortment of things: the lime green glass mug she used for her instant coffee, a box of saltines, a jar of Peter Pan peanut butter, and two cans of Campbell's chicken noodle soup. She also took some measuring spoons and cups and two cookie sheets.

"What are you doing, Margie?" I asked.

There was no response. She picked up the bags and went back to her room.

I soon found out what her odd movements were about—she moved into Uncle Jake's house in Kingston for the summer while my mother and I remained in Boston. Margie said she wanted to be closer to Uncle Jake. She did what then was an impossible commute. She walked twenty minutes along a country road to catch the Plymouth and Brockton bus to Boston. Several nights a week, she'd take the bus to its terminal in Plymouth and walk a mile along the coastal route to Uncle Jake's nursing home. Some evenings she'd catch a ride back to Kingston with another visitor or staff member. Other times, she'd take a taxi back to the house. On weekends, she'd take a local bus to the nursing home, which also involved a long walk.

True to her word, she came back to our apartment after Labor Day, looking thin and tired. While she wasn't speaking much, at least she was home. Still, our home life together was forever changed. Margie no longer ate dinner with us. Often, she'd arrive home late, perhaps having eaten at a downtown cafeteria. I pictured her sitting alone with a tray on which were arranged black coffee, a Parker House roll, fried haddock, and a slice of apple pie. She'd read the *Boston Globe* while she ate, keeping it folded lengthwise. She'd skip only the sports and classified sections.

Margie became more like a reclusive boarder and less like a family member. She was no longer either mother or sister to me. It hurt terribly, and I responded by eating less and seeking connections to friends. I couldn't share much about my home problems with my friends, though. Not comfortable expressing feelings, I didn't know how to describe an aunt who'd been more mother than my own mother, a sometimes sister-figure, and a friend. I didn't know how to explain her new strange behaviors, where muttering replaced words, frowns replaced smiles, and cold shoulders replaced hugs. I didn't have the words to say how sad it made me.

My mother and I rarely ate together either. I'd joined as many school activities as I was eligible for: choir, math club, French club, Latin club, Catholic Youth Organization, and the National Honor Society. After my piano teacher was transferred to another school, I began piano and music theory lessons at the Boston Conservatory of Music. There was no admissions process for these classes—you just needed to pay for them—but it impressed the kids at school.

To my chagrin, my new piano teacher informed me I was not playing at the advanced level I'd thought and assigned me to a lower music level. I never told my mother or friends about this setback and even lobbied my mother for a new Baldwin upright piano. I said I couldn't advance with our old clunker, a vain attempt to blame my lack of talent on the instrument. To pay for the piano, my mother took out a bank loan. The new piano was nice but didn't help me advance any quicker. I decided to become a music teacher and didn't listen to my high school choral director who told me my personality wasn't outgoing enough for that career.

My mother took on a second job to pay off her debts. After six months of dating, she and Bob decided to marry. They set a date a year and a half in the future—Memorial Day weekend—immediately after my high school graduation. It felt like my mother couldn't wait to begin her new life without me.

Our household became three bedrooms inhabited by females with separate lives. Home life was dull, lonely, and frightening. There was no one to laugh with, no one to care about me, no one to hug me. That lack of touch was so critical, I can now see through the eyeglasses of time. It resurrected the times I'd been institutionalized with no one to hug or kiss me. Today, I shower hugs and kisses on my husband, daughters, and grandchildren. Back then, longing for connections, I'd do almost anything for love.

Chapter 10

Thanksgiving Famine

A solution to my problem came to me like a miraculous apparition: I decided to contact my father. For fifteen years, I'd fantasized about him turning into a loving and caring parent, a would-be savior. Maybe he could be my family now that my mother and aunt were removing themselves from my life.

My mother and I drove down to Plymouth to spend the Thanksgiving weekend with Bob at his house on Boot Pond. Margie had taken the bus to stay at Uncle Jake's house and would most likely feast on peanut butter, saltines, and cigarettes. The original Pilgrims arrived in Plymouth with hopes of a future filled with community and bountiful riches, things to be grateful for. What I got were Bob and my mother flirting with each other while stuffing the turkey and a day full of Bob's relatives who gorged themselves silly, talked at each other without feeling, and showed little interest in my mother and me. They probably thought my mother was a temporary fling until Bob came to his senses and reunited with his wife of thirty years, who lived across the pond. These people might be my relatives someday, but I realized they would not be my family.

We returned to Boston Saturday night because I needed to play organ for Sunday Mass. On the way home in the car, my mother went on and on about Bob and how good it felt to be accepted by his family. I feigned interest.

It was my first Thanksgiving without Margie. Starved for affection, I came up with the idea of contacting my father. By this time he was forty-seven years old and remarried. He'd never called or sent me a single card, letter, or present. I can see now that the executive part of my brain—the part that controls decision-making—was functioning at half-mast. I don't know what made me think this reluctant parent would have any interest in me.

I wanted him to see me all grown up. He'd immediately realize what he had missed by not being in my life. He would apologize for abandoning me and say that he'd want to be a good father to me. He'd pay the child support he'd stopped sending years earlier. Maybe he'd even give me a present now and then. I no longer had the fantasy of my parents getting back together, but I could still dream about him coming back to me.

The problem was that I had to involve my mother. She was the keeper of his secret information: his address, where he worked, and his phone number. I only knew that he lived somewhere in or around Boston. I had searched in my mother's desk for any information about my father's whereabouts but to no avail. Even if I had found his address, I still would not have dared to contact him without my mother's permission.

I fretted all Thanksgiving weekend. In my head I practiced how I would ask my mother, how she would react—she'd be furious, of course—and how I'd handle it. I finally settled on a simpler goal. I'd ask if I could send him a Christmas card. After all, a good Catholic girl sends Christmas cards to her relatives and friends, so how bad could it be for me to ask to send one to my father? This simpler goal still had me worried. What if she hit me? Well, I'd survived her previous blows. What if she sent me away? Maybe I could stay with a friend. What if my mother refused to give me my father's address? I'd be no worse off than I was now.

I approached my mother at home after Sunday Mass. I figured she'd be in a pretty good mood because she'd gotten Church out of the way for the week, didn't have to work until the next day, and had her two toasted coconut doughnuts. I followed her into the dining room, waiting until she was on the other side of the table. I stared down at my clenched hands.

"I thought I'd like to send my father a Christmas card," I mumbled.

My mother didn't say anything. I felt myself shrinking back toward the wall. Finally, I raised my eyes. Her face was stark white against her dark hair; her small brown eyes were mere slits; her mouth with its remnants of orange lipstick was pulled back tight.

Finally, she said, "Why? Why do you want to send a card to that son of a bitch? He's never sent you a card; he's never been interested in you at all."

"I don't know. I just want to do it."

"Well, go ahead. It's clear that you're not grateful for everything I've done for you, you little shit. So go ahead and send your card to the bastard. I'll send you to live with him so he can take care of you for a change." She turned to leave the room.

"I don't have his address," I said in a small voice. "I'll need his address to send him a card."

Well, that's that, I thought. Now she's mad at me, and I'm no better off because she's not going to help me find him. I just hoped that she wouldn't stay angry for too long and wouldn't follow through with her threat to send me away.

About an hour after she'd left the room, I was sitting at the dining room table doing my homework and playing with a strand of my hair when my mother came into the room. Without saying a word, she walked over to the table, placed an index card down in front of me, and left the room. I picked up the card. James McTiernan, she had written at the top. An address in Auburndale, Massachusetts, was listed under that. It looked like all the other index cards she kept for people with whom she exchanged Christmas cards, except this one didn't have any years listed on it and no mark to indicate a sent or received card.

While my mother had done as I asked, her action shocked and confused me. Did she feel guilty that she had not helped me to know him? Maybe she, too, harbored a longing for him to take a role in my care, to relieve her of some of the burden. In those days, a father's rejection of his children was seen as the mother's failure. Was she ashamed? Or, perhaps she thought that allowing me to see him would speed my growing-up trajectory. A girl who is mature enough to ask to contact her father surely will not need care much longer. She might have felt giddy with relief.

Excited and terrified, I decided to write the Christmas card right there and then, before I lost my nerve. I went over to the hutch and took out the boxes of holiday cards my mother bought last January at half price. I needed to see all the possibilities to choose the perfect card.

I carried the boxes over to the table and sat down. I hopped up to search for a pen in the kitchen drawer stuffed with envelopes, pieces of paper, rubber bands, and broken pencils. I stood up to turn on the overhead light. A trip to the bathroom followed, after which I felt very thirsty. It had been several hours since my cup of cocoa with the chocolate glazed Dunkin' Donuts. I drank a couple of big glasses of water. Cool and soothing, the water made me feel in control. More importantly, it helped me to procrastinate working on the most important Christmas card I'd ever sent.

I opened the first box. The picture on the top told me that this contained the religious cards, the ones my mother sent to good Catholics. *Hmmm,* I thought, *how does Hallmark say, To my father whom I've never met, whom I've dreamed of meeting all my life, when he'd sweep me into his strong arms and say how sorry he was for abandoning me, and he'd stay with me now, forever, and love me always, wishing him a Merry Christmas?*

I opened the first card. "May the Christ Child bring you blessings and joy this Christmas season." No, the reference to the Christ Child might be too much of a reminder of how he had deserted his own child. And I didn't really want him to have blessings or joy. The next one started with "Hark the herald angels sing." I recognized this as the beginning to a Christmas hymn, but I didn't know what herald meant. I wanted to understand every word on the card for this momentous occasion. The next one said, "God loves all His children, especially this time of year." No, this one wouldn't do either. I wasn't sure God loved me, and He'd better not love this bad father if He didn't love me.

Okay, I decided, religious isn't working. I opened the next box, which contained the ones we sent to little kids. "If you're very good this year, Santa will bring you lots of wonderful presents." Would he think I was trying to coerce him into being a good father? Or would he think I was angling for gifts for myself? I set this one aside. The next children's card had a picture of Rudolph with a huge shiny red nose. I rejected that one right away. My mother told me that my father was a drunk, and I knew that drunks often had red noses. I didn't want him to think that I was pointing out one of his failings.

It was time for the secular box. These were the cards my mother sent to her non-Catholic friends and acquaintances, especially the Jewish people she worked with and complained about so much that I wondered why she sent them Christmas cards. The top one was silver with "Seasons Greetings" embossed in white italic lettering on the front. Inside, the sentiment continued, "and Happy New Year." Perfect. No hidden meanings. Now all I had to decide was what to write on it.

I realized that this was going to take some thought and practice, so I stood up to find some scrap paper. I didn't want to send my first card to my father with scratch-outs and erasures; it had to look nice. Settled back at the table, I began my task. "Dearest Father," I wrote, "how are you? I am fine. Well, I'm not fine actually. It's driving me nuts, making this contact with you. I'm also mad that you're not making the first move to get in touch with me." *Hmmm, maybe this isn't the best first approach.* I crumpled the paper and started again.

"Dear Daddy." No, I'm fifteen years old, after all. "Daddy" sounds like I'm five. I crumpled this paper, too.

"Dear Dad." This didn't feel right either. I'd never met the man, so how could I call him Dad? I'd heard my friends call their fathers "Dad," and it was always with the familiarity of knowing this person their entire life.

"Pops? Papa? Daddyo?" This wasn't working.

"Dear Jim." Perfect. It was his name after all. It felt strange to call him by his first name but less strange than the alternatives.

"Dear Jim," I wrote inside the card just about above Hallmark's "and Happy New Year." Underneath I was about to write "Love, Anne," but this felt really wrong because I didn't love him at all. So I just signed it, "Your daughter, Anne McTiernan," in case he'd forgotten that he had a daughter or what my name was. I decided not to write a note on the blank side of the card. I just didn't know what to say. I inserted the card, addressed the envelope, wrote my return address on the back, and stamped it. I put it into my book bag to mail the next day because I didn't trust my mother to send it.

After I'd posted it, I felt elated at the thought that my father would receive the card and immediately realize his mistake in never being in my life. He'd phone me right after he opened it, of course. He'd call me honey and sweetheart and ask me if I could ever forgive him. We'd talk for hours. He'd ask me all about my life, and I'd tell him about school, my friends, and my musical talents. I'd tell him about my mother and how she treated me. He'd say that all of that would change now; he'd make sure of it. Or, maybe he would come to our house without calling. Maybe he'd want to see me right away.

I knew little about this man, only the snippets my mother told me over the years. His parents emigrated from Ireland at the turn of the century. His father was a gardener, his mother a stay-at-home alcoholic. Jim McTiernan was the eldest of two sons. Speed and agility characterized his youth: he fast-talked women and was an avid ice-skater and ballroom dancer. My father also had a remarkable memory for numbers, helpful when your job in an auto parts department requires memorizing long strings of numbers in pre-computer days. He didn't qualify for the army in World War II—something about flat feet. Interesting that he could dance and skate but could not march. A few years after the war, he did give some number of months to the United States government when he served time in a federal prison for tax fraud. Seems he thought it was a good idea to claim his dead parents as dependents on his tax return. I have no direct proof of his having spent time behind bars, only my mother's say-so. But hearing about a possible prison time confirmed my certainty that he was a bad man. Still, I desperately longed for him to be in my life. He may be a bad man, but I wanted him to be *my* bad man.

The days and weeks passed with no calls, no father showing up at our door, not even a Christmas card from him in return. Maybe the card never arrived. Maybe my mother gave me the wrong address. But I realized that the post office would have returned it if the address was wrong. Maybe he called when my mother was here, and she didn't tell me. Christmas came and went with no word from my father. I knew then that I would never see him.

I carried an inner secret that made me so horrible that no one wanted to come near me. It made my mother hate me enough to abandon me, threaten to send me away, and beat me. It caused my father to stay as far away as possible. I knew in my heart that this thing was part of me. My great dilemma was that I didn't know what *it* was; therefore, I didn't know how to fix *it*. I couldn't figure out how to make the inner me loveable.

Then one evening in late January, my mother said, "Your father called me today." Her brown eyes were snapping as hard as shot pellets.

I looked up at her, surprised. "What did he say?"

"He wants to meet you."

My heart did jumping jacks inside my chest. I hoped she couldn't see it through my sweater. I didn't want to seem too excited.

"Can I?" I asked.

CHAPTER 11

Icing on the Cake

The room spun. I couldn't breathe. Or maybe I was hyperventilating. My lips and hands had gone numb. I dug my nails into my palms to get some feeling back, while managing to pull in some air. My mother stood at the sink with her back toward me, taking forever to say yes or no. I felt part of my biology melting as I sat at the maple wood table in our little kitchen with its mint green painted walls. If only I could see my father, touch him, and smell him, then I would know where I came from. Maybe then I could find my hidden evil and clean it out like an exorcism.

Finally, my mother turned around and looked straight at me, as if she too was peering inside the wicked Anne.

"I guess so, if you're sure you know what you're doing."

"Yes, I want to," I eagerly replied.

Cool, calm, and collected on the outside, the inner Anne did midair splits like the elite high school cheerleader I could never be. My mother and father. My parents. Oh, how wonderful to think of those words together, related to me—I'd never done that before. It sounded so normal. *Maybe now I'll be normal*, I thought.

My parents arranged for the three of us to meet at two o'clock on Saturday afternoon, February 22, four days after my sixteenth birthday. My father chose the venue—a bar in Allston, northeast of Brighton. Kids were allowed into taverns then—how else would the Irish-American mother of thirteen children send the older kids to fetch their father from his barstool? I'd never been in a bar, however, not having had a dad to rescue and my mother and aunt being near-teetotalers. Not that I missed the experience—the establishments I passed in Brighton Center reeked of stale beer, urine, and vomit. Worst of all was the sadness in the men stooped over on their stools, clutching glasses.

For this occasion, however, I'd walk into hell itself in order to meet the man I'd dreamed about for almost sixteen years; the man who would rescue me from my life of drudgery and fear; the man who would turn me into a stunning princess from the ugly toad I was, just by saying I was beautiful and that he loved me.

During the next three weeks, my inner Drama Queen was in full mettle. She created a new Anne for this momentous meeting. She had me miraculously lose twenty pounds. (In actuality I could hardly eat, so I probably did lose a few pounds.) While she did this, she also made me beautiful—thickening my hair, lifting the little droop in my eyelids, decreasing the length of my ski-slope nose, and slimming my Irish-peasant hips. She created brilliant discussions in which I'd be a fascinating and humorous conversationalist. My father would hang on my every word, and my mother would smile and look on proudly. None of these imaginary conversations had a single word of anger in them: not from my mother railing at the man who'd left her for women and booze; not from my father protesting that she was the one who arranged the legal separation; not from me complaining to them both that they'd failed as parents; and not from me raging at the man who'd had so little interest in me that he hadn't even bothered to sign a child support check for years, let alone call, write, or visit me in all of my conscious life. No, the meeting in my imagination would be as perfect as humanly possible, given that it was in a bar in a working-class slum of Boston, involving three estranged working-class Irish-Americans.

My anxiety had me shaking like an aftershock. I was on my best behavior with my mother. That meant I couldn't be my usual sullen teenager self. I pretended to be happy, in control, serene—nothing bothered me. Ma, no problems for you. Yes, of course I'll clean the house. I'll do it after I get home from my Dunkin' Donuts shift and finish my homework. No, I'll be fine if you go down to Plymouth to see Bob and leave me alone again for the weekend. No, I don't need money for anything; don't worry about me at all. You need the bathroom right now? Of course I'll wait until you're done. I'll deal with the nuns' wrath at being late for school.

About a week before the big meet, the Drama Queen took an insidious turn. She twisted my inner dialogues into something from an Alfred Hitchcock movie with dark undertones to each line and the grave potential for danger lurking behind every doorway. In her new play, my father spoke at length about what an ugly baby and child I had been, so spoiled and obnoxious that he couldn't bear to be with me. When his own father passed away, the man who'd nagged him continuously to see me, he finally had his freedom. My mother talked about how miserable her life had been raising me, how she'd gotten no thanks from me for the many sacrifices she'd made over the years, how I was a failure at so many things that she couldn't keep her head up as she went to Sunday Mass. Oh, wait—that was how my mother always talked—the Drama Queen didn't have to make up any dialogue for her. My lines were now blank—I had nothing notable to say—and I sat there blushing and sweating. Typical Anne. The Drama Queen was running out of creativity here.

For the meeting, I'd have my usual peachy-pale skin with crimson cheeks, dirty-blonde hair, and blue eyes, while my mother would be sallow-pale against her brown hair, brown eyes, and brilliant red lips. I pictured my father looking exactly as he had in the photos in my mother's desk, in various shades of gray. Just for completeness, I imagined the bar and its other inhabitants also in gray. My mother and I would be etched in Technicolor against a black-and-white film.

I couldn't hear his voice in my head, though. I hoped it was deep and melodious. I liked a deep voice in a man, like Father McNulty who could mesmerize the entire Church with his booming words and arms spread wide like he was folding the congregation into his embrace, protecting us from the evils of the world.

I imagined my father would shower presents on me. After all, he owed me sixteen years of Christmas and birthday gifts. He'd lead us to the sidewalk outside the bar, where he'd have parked a large station wagon borrowed for the occasion. The back would be piled high with presents of every shape and size, wrapped in various shades of pink paper. He'd load them into my mother's navy blue Chevy Nova, taking up the entire trunk and back seat, and even then I'd have to hold a couple on my lap.

Back home, it would take a couple of hours to unwrap all the presents. Ooh, there was a baby blue cashmere cardigan in my size. I didn't know anyone who owned cashmere. A matching white cashmere scarf, gloves, and hat—very smart. A small bottle of perfume with a French name. Two tickets to the Boston Pops and another pair to the ballet. Oh, how sweet, he knew I liked classical music and aspired to sophistication. A real leather purse—that must have set him back a good penny. Piles and piles of clothes, all fitting me perfectly. Gift certificates to Jordan Marsh and Filene's so I could get even more clothes. Books, including leather-bound classics, works of art, and classical music scores. A gift certificate for my favorite restaurant—Marliave's—Italian food to die for. Then would come The Beatles records: *Help, Rubber Soul, Sgt. Pepper's Lonely Hearts Club Band, Magical Mystery Tour.* I would make sure to stack them carefully in a corner so I didn't step on them as I jumped around in glee. And what's this big box? A GE portable record player of my very own! Ah, here was a Brownie camera with ten extra rolls of film. I would record my friends' smiles for posterity, but first I'd snap photos of the presents in a pile, in case someone didn't believe my story.

I turned sixteen in the midst of this angst. Sweet Sixteen. My mother took me to dinner at a nice steak house, a special treat—I could count on one hand the number of times I'd eaten steak. It was my first birthday without Margie, not counting the ones I'd spent in institutions. I couldn't help feeling some sadness that she wasn't celebrating with me. She hadn't even wished me a happy birthday or given me a gift. She wasn't home that evening; I envisioned her alone in a downtown cafeteria. I couldn't understand what I'd done to make her so angry with me. In part, I knew, it was because she was so estranged from my mother. But it was more than that. Like Peter Pan lamenting Wendy becoming a mother, Margie couldn't forgive my growing up. But her actions couldn't completely douse my excitement at turning sixteen. This was the year I could drive. Theoretically I could marry without parental permission—as if there was any chance for romance for me. And I was just over a year away from graduation and total freedom from my mother.

After we returned home, my mother asked me to put in a load of wash. It didn't occur to me that the birthday girl shouldn't have to do laundry. I was trying really hard to keep in my mother's good graces. Only four days more to behave. After that, everything would be different. Light crept out from under Margie's door, but she didn't come out. I grabbed the laundry and headed down to the dark basement, making sure to flip switches on as I went. I was always on guard for bogeymen, especially in the part of the house most resembling a crypt.

I opened the cellar door and nearly dropped the basket when the lights suddenly splashed on and eight teenage girls yelled at the top of their lungs, "Surprise!" They topped this shout with giggling.

"Happy birthday, dear," I heard my mother say from behind me. Shaking, I continued into the basement room, its concrete bleakness hidden with multi-colored balloons and streamers. Dumbstruck, a fairly common state for me, I looked around at my grinning girlfriends: Gina, Kathleen, Patty, Barb, Susan, Katie, Lucy, and Maureen. I couldn't believe my mother had arranged this for me. I'd only had one birthday party before, when I was eleven years old. Exhausted then from the effort of hosting a handful of boisterous girls, she swore she'd never do it again.

Before they sat me down for presents, cake, and silly games, I looked around again at my friends. I had the fleeting audacity to be disappointed there were no boys. What did I expect? Even if my mother had been willing to allow a boy-girl party, as it was called then, I knew no boys for her to invite. It's not like I had a Rolodex full of male acquaintances. This all-female party underscored my failure as a girl in 1969 Brighton, where being able to attract a boyfriend was the single most important achievement to which a girl might aspire. The cool kids had been having boy-girl parties since sixth grade. Here in eleventh grade, I was having an infantile all-girl party. I hope I kept this selfish disappointment off my face and instead showed gratitude for this lovely group of females who'd come together to celebrate my milestone.

I had told my best friend Patty about the plans to meet my father that weekend, which meant by now they all knew. They asked me a little about it after my mother went upstairs, and everyone wished me luck. Mostly they wanted to know what I was going to wear.

February 21, 1969. I lay in bed staring into the dark, fretting about the following day. Maybe it wasn't real, only a dream. Sleep wouldn't come and wouldn't come some more. I didn't bother putting a light on to read. I wouldn't have been able to concentrate on a single word. Plus, I couldn't risk waking my mother for fear she'd cancel the meeting out of spite.

What if he hates me on sight? What if he shudders at the ugliness of me? What if I start crying and it drives him away again? So many difficult scenarios to imagine with such a long stretch of night to feel their terror.

As soon as I saw my mother the next morning, I knew it wasn't a dream. Her hair stood at wild angles to her head, her nostrils flared, and her hand shook as she took her first swallow of coffee. We didn't reveal our thoughts, not being the sharing types, but the air sizzled with our anxiety. This must have been terrifying for her. She hadn't seen her former husband for thirteen years, and most of their communications had been through the City of Boston courts in my mother's vain attempts to re-establish regular child support payments.

Over the past three weeks, I'd agonized over what to wear. I'd flipped through *Mademoiselle*, *Glamour*, and other fashion magazines at the drugstore. Not one gave advice on what to wear the first time you meet your father. Back home I perused my bare closet. Finally, I chose my best dress, a white wool A-line I had sewn from a Vogue pattern and remnant material. That morning I snagged runs in the first two nylon stockings I tried to put on. Washing, setting, drying, and styling my hair took up most of an hour. In the end I wasn't happy with what glared back at me from the bathroom mirror, but I had to live with what I had.

I waited impatiently in the kitchen by the back door for my mother. At 1:30 P.M., she emerged from her room in a navy wool skirt, topped with a kelly green sweater set and a three-stranded pearl costume necklace. She wore her ever-present pancake makeup with red lipstick and eyeglasses with one little rhinestone sparkling in each upturned corner. Her back swayed unnaturally from her high heels.

She took a deep breath. "Okay, let's go."

The day spat a mix of rain and sleet. Snow banks stood tall along the streets from a storm two weeks prior. On the car ride to Allston,

I cracked every knuckle I owned. I worked my worries through my head but didn't let them venture out of my mouth.

"Of all places, of course he had to pick a bar," my mother said. "A bar is no place for a young girl."

I kept quiet, wishing her to just keep driving. It would not be out of character for her to turn the car around at the last minute and announce we weren't going through with this. The venue was the least of my concerns right now, although I did wonder why she didn't insist on someplace else to meet. This was not typical for her. Perhaps she was not as strong-willed with men as with Margie and me.

I walked into the bar behind my mother. My cheeks burned like the top of Uncle Jake's coal stove. I weaved to avoid brushing the grimy tables with my white dress. The bar was so dark that I could barely see the forms of men hunched over their glasses and so quiet that I could hear the ice clinking as they lifted their drinks. A mixture of cigarette smoke, musty wood, and the sweet and sour odors of whiskey and beer attacked my nose.

"Hello, Jim," my mother said to one of the men. My heart pounded in my ears. Surely this slightly stocky man could not be my father with his slicked-back, thinning, light brown hair, tiny blue eyes darting behind bifocals, and little red veins running all over a turned-up Irish nose. I had thought I might look like him since I didn't inherit my mother's dark hair and eyes. But while I had his coloring, this man appeared so worn by time that I couldn't see myself in him. He stood quickly, and I could see that he was average height, maybe five-foot-ten, a half foot taller than I was. Under an unwrinkled beige raincoat, he wore a yellow wool cardigan over a white polo shirt. I wondered if his clothes and gold pinky ring were expensive.

The big grin on his face surprised me. I wasn't expecting a friendly man. His manner suggested someone meeting old friends. I wanted to see tears of joy and contrition at seeing his grown daughter for the first time. I would have liked him to fall to his knees, begging my forgiveness.

"Hello, Mary," he said in a raspy, deep voice. "You look wonderful."

My mother responded with a lift of her chin.

"And this is Anne Marie," he said, barely glancing at me.

The use of my middle name surprised me. No one called me Anne Marie any more. Then I remembered my mother telling me that my father had chosen my middle name. I'd always hated that name but couldn't say why.

"Hi," I said, at a loss for any other words.

My mother and aunt hadn't taught me much in the way of social graces, and the nuns didn't cover this particular situation in class, so I didn't know what to say or not say, sitting in a bar with my stranger-father. I just knew that I felt overwhelmed. I was finally meeting him, this man who had appeared as a shadow in my dreams and daydreams. This figure I couldn't quite see, couldn't hear, couldn't feel but I knew must exist. He had been both my imagined savior and the dreaded bogeyman to whom my mother threatened to send me when she said I'd been bad.

Here he was, finally in front of me. I could see him, and he wasn't handsome as I had imagined. I could hear him, and his voice didn't sound gentle and loving as I had heard in my dreams. I could smell him, and he sort of smelled like I had thought men might smell—like strong aftershave, cigarettes, and whiskey. I couldn't touch him. He didn't reach out his hand to shake mine, nor did he try to give me a hug, which was fine with me. My soaking wet palm would have been a dead giveaway of my anxiety, not the cool and sophisticated demeanor I wanted to portray. But things didn't look good for my fantasy coming true of Daddy sweeping me into his arms and saving me.

He pulled out a chair across from him for my mother. I sat next to her.

"Would you like a drink, Mary?" he asked.

"No, thanks."

"Anne Marie, would you like anything?" he asked.

"I'd like a ginger ale, please."

He drained his drink and went over to the bar. He came back with my ginger ale and a new scotch-on-the-rocks for himself. Frank Sinatra began singing "Strangers in the Night." My father must have asked the bartender to play a record, I realized. It made me feel a little special.

"Mary, do you remember Joe McNally?"

"Uh-huh."

"He died last November."

"Oh?"

"He was a customer of mine. I manage the parts department in the Newton Ford dealership. Joe drove a 1969 Ford LTD, like mine." He puffed out his chest.

I waited for my mother to ask why, if he was a manager and could afford a top-of-the-line Ford, he couldn't come up with child support payments. I wanted her to ask.

"Oh," she said.

"How is Margaret doing?"

"Fine. She spends a lot of time in Kingston now."

"She was always so good to you and Anne Marie."

"Yes, she was." Hanging in the air were the unspoken words of how Margie had filled in for my father's absence.

"Boy, that Mr. Nixon is going to do a great job," he said. "The country will be going in the right direction with a Republican in charge."

Now this shocked me. In my predominantly Irish Catholic working-class school, there were no Republicans. How could I have descended from a Republican? Republicans were pro-business, pro-war, and decidedly against unions, peace, and rock-and-roll. I couldn't tell my friends about this part of the conversation. They'd shun me.

Good God, how this man could talk. We learned he had season tickets to the Boston Celtics. Once again, my mother said nothing about him being able to live high on the hog while she struggled to pay rent and put food on the table for their daughter. By this time my mother was doing a great imitation of a *Valley of the Dolls* character. While I had no reason to suspect she'd downed a Valium, I couldn't understand her calm.

My father moved a lot as he talked: shoulders shifted, hands gestured, drink moved to his mouth and down. His eyes roamed the room, focused on my mother, checked on his drink, but he barely glanced at me. He wasn't a calm man. He didn't talk to me, didn't ask me about my life, my interests, or about school or my friends.

My disappointment lay heavy on my shoulders like a soaking wet wool coat. I started to feel angry at being ignored. While watching my mother and father have their little conversation was interesting, albeit mostly one-sided, it wasn't what I had hoped for.

What about me, me, me? I thought. *I'm the one who got this whole thing started here. Why isn't he talking to me?*

After about a half of an hour, which felt like five minutes, my mother stood up.

"We have to go now," she said.

I didn't want to leave him, still hoping that he'd pay attention to me. I sat for a beat without moving, staring at the man who clearly wasn't going to be my salvation. He had barely even looked at me, for God's sake.

"She's lovely, Mary," he said then, in his deep voice. "You've done a wonderful job raising her."

My head could have burst with pride. Finally he'd noticed me and had complimented me. My mother lifted her chin at his compliment to her. I waited to hear her say something like, "No thanks to you," but she merely murmured, "Thank you."

He smiled at me then and reached down under the table. As he straightened up, his hand held a box, about six inches long and four inches wide and high. It was wrapped in pink paper with a white bow.

"Happy Birthday, Anne Marie." Still smiling, he handed me the gift.

"Thanks," I squeaked. It was the first present he'd ever given me. I wanted to kiss it and rub it across my cheek. I held it tight, as if afraid someone would try to wrestle it away from me.

"Goodbye, Mary," he said, smiling.

"Goodbye, Jim," she replied. She reached for her purse.

"Goodbye, Anne Marie," he said.

"Bye," I said, looking at the floor.

I followed my mother outside, eyes squinting after the darkness of the bar. We got into my mother's car. I was shaking as I ripped the paper off his present. Inside was a bottle of Heaven Scent cologne and matching bath powder. It must have set him back all of seven or eight dollars.

Disappointment smothered me in so many ways. My father, who I'd thought would come to his senses on meeting me and beg me to come back into his life, clearly had little interest in me. The cheapness of his first gift showed that he didn't think I was worth wasting his money on. My hopes that he'd save me from my current life were dashed. I had to face the facts. I was ugly, boring, and unworthy of my father's love or attention. I caused my mother grief and anger by my very existence. Even Margie was pulling away from me as she distanced herself from my mother and her new beau. I might as well not even exist. Maybe if I died they'd at least shed a tear over my casket. But the thought of my death was not something I could linger on for too long. It was a mortal sin to commit suicide, and I was terrified of eternal damnation, which sounded even worse than my current life. So I had no physical escape.

The next morning I came upon my mother sitting in her usual chair on the far side of our kitchen table. Her salmon pink chenille bathrobe flowed onto the linoleum. With hair spiking, she sported the punk look long before it was cool. Her gaze remained on the *Boston Globe*, which lay open on the table.

"Well, are you satisfied now?" my mother asked.

"Huh?"

"That was the hardest thing I've ever had to do in my life. I hope you're happy."

I didn't know what to say.

"Why don't you just go live with him? Then I can be free of you. And good riddance it would be."

"I don't want to go live with him." My voice caught on the tears that began to drip down my throat.

"You should get down on your knees and beg God's forgiveness for what you've put me through." She finally looked up at me, small black eyes narrowed to slits.

I turned away and headed toward the back door.

"Don't you dare turn your back on me! Where the hell are you going?"

"To Church. I have to play the organ at nine o'clock Mass today."

I left without waiting to hear what she had to say. Later, I walked home slowly, afraid of what was waiting for me. I'd been surprised by her outburst this morning. Not because it was out of character for her, but rather because she had seemed so placid the previous day at the momentous meeting with my father. I hadn't realized how difficult this must have been for my mother. She was the "all powerful one" in our family, the one to be feared, not the one quaking with anxiety. Yet she'd been so meek and mild-mannered in the bar yesterday. It was as if she still wanted his approval.

Thinking back, I realized my mother had dressed nicely, answered his questions politely, and thanked him for his compliments. She'd had no harsh words for him; certainly no physical punches were thrown. So where was all that anger toward him that she'd shared with Margie and me over the years? Had she held onto a fantasy of him, just like I did? Did she want him to be the rescuing kind of man, come in on a white horse, and save her from her life of misery? I would never learn the answers to these questions.

When I next saw my mother that evening, I realized that she no longer towered over me. Both of us in slippers—me in the purple ones Margie crocheted for me the previous winter, my mother in her peach-colored scuffs with the instep puffball—we stood eye-to-eye. My mother had always been the tallest of our female family. Margie never topped five feet one inch. In her twenties, my mother had been six inches taller than Margie, but she developed a premature dowager's hump and now matched my five feet four inches. Yes, she outweighed me by thirty pounds, but her excess was all fat. Plus, I had youth on my side. I was no athlete but could move quickly if need be. This realization of her vulnerability made me feel a little bit stronger. I began to see my mother as a weak, middle-aged woman. I was losing my fear of her.

"What do you want for dinner?" she asked.

"I already ate."

"What did you have?"

"A bran muffin and a Tab."

"That's not enough food."

"It's all I wanted."

She sighed but said no more.

"I have to do homework." I went to my room.

I leaned uncomfortably against the wooden headboard of my twin bed, knees to my chest. I tried to concentrate on a history essay, but my blue pen would only doodle on the blank page. I drew circles within circles, circles overlapping other circles, big and little circles. I thought about my real parents—mother, father. I thought about my substitute parent/sibling—Margie. I could see that none of these people were going to be the type of parent I needed, none would love me unconditionally, and none would commit to be there for me as I went through the rest of my developmental years.

My mother didn't seem interested in what I needed; she just gave me what she thought I deserved. She considered herself a good mother. She hadn't retreated like my father. Yes, she'd institutionalized me during my infancy and preschool years and repeatedly threatened to send me away again, but as long as there was a roof over my head and access to food, she thought she was doing a pretty good job. But I needed a mom to love me for who I was, unreservedly. Unfortunately, she couldn't, or wouldn't, do this.

Margie needed a mom more than she needed to mother me. After her own mother died when she was twelve years old, Margie had elected her reluctant older sister to be a mother substitute. Now that my mother was heading toward a second marriage, and I would leave for college in less than two years, Margie knew that her family would soon disintegrate. Margie's subsequent anger pulled her away from me.

Then there was my father. How odd to call someone "my father." I don't know why I expected to morph in the space of one day from a half-orphan, fatherless child to a golden girl with a loving mommy and daddy like on a television show—that wasn't going to happen. It was my fault, of course. Shy mouse that I was, I was not interesting enough to hold any male's attention. I was disappointed that he paid me so little attention, but why didn't I open my mouth and talk? Why couldn't I be like the popular girls at school, the ones who knew how to have a conversation, how to smile sweetly at a boy, how to make a boy fall for them? One of those pretty, pert, talkative girls would have engaged my father, made him laugh. He'd have listened to their stories and asked them questions about school, friends, hobbies, and boyfriends.

As I ruminated on my shortcomings, I drew circles. Looking back, I see these rings as representing family, love, and connections. Circle of love. Circle of friends. Today I loop my arms around my daughters and my grandchildren. I wear a gold band on my finger to show my lifetime commitment to my husband. On birthday cards, I write circles and Xs below "Love, Mom" and "Love, Grandma." I drew those circles that day, perhaps unconsciously graphing my desire to be surrounded with love.

I didn't realize then, and wouldn't learn until my husband and I first saw our daughters after their births, how parents suddenly and absolutely fall in love with their babies. The child doesn't have to perform—her existence is enough to trigger and sustain deep, unbreakable, unconditional, unending love. The circle contains, it holds, it protects.

I can see the changes that occurred in the young me as a result of meeting my father. While the actual event was less than spectacular on the surface, underneath it represented a major accomplishment. I felt some amount of pride at setting things in motion for the big meet. Clearly, my parents would not have initiated it. It required them facing their broken marriage and their failures at parenting. I learned that I could accomplish a difficult thing from start to finish. I was a closer; I got the job done. If I could bring together two people who hated each other to the point of complete avoidance, then I could tackle other seemingly insurmountable obstacles. I would soon need these skills to handle several challenges during my remaining years of high school.

CHAPTER 12

Purging

Something was wrong. I could smell it. I stood in the cramped hallway outside our second story Boston apartment. At five o'clock, darkness had already fallen on this early March afternoon. My mother would be home in thirty minutes.

Fresh, pungent cigarette smoke clung to the air. This was odd—no one was home. Another smell hit me—maybe sweat. My green school bag slid off my shoulder and thudded to the floor. *Oh, great,* I thought. *If a murderer is waiting for me behind the door, now he'll know to expect me momentarily.*

The silence felt stifling as I let myself into the flat. I quickly closed the door. Flipping on the kitchen light switch, I began my rounds, looking in closets and under beds to make sure there were no bogeymen hiding. I knew I was too old to be doing this, but I couldn't break an eight-year habit. Then I saw Margie's partly opened bedroom door, the one she always kept closed to hide the piles of old newspapers, magazines, clothes, and other junk she couldn't bring herself to discard. Her room always contrasted starkly with the neatness of the rest of the apartment.

I gently pushed her door open and turned on the light. The emptiness rushed out and pulled the breath out of me. I leaned against the doorjamb, hand still clutching the glass knob so hard I could feel the edges dig into my palm.

All Margie's furniture was gone, as if a giant Hoover sucked it up in one swoop. Gone were her matching mahogany bed, chest of drawers, and low bureau with its attached mirror. I once scraped a key along the footboard of her bed, for which she'd quickly forgiven the four-year-old me. The white lace doilies covering her bureaus were taken, as well as the pink music box with the twirling ballerina on top. *She kept that in here for me. How come she didn't leave that?* Gone were the stacks of coupons that she'd spent hours cutting out from the Sunday *Boston Globe*. The piles of clothes she'd thrown on a rocking chair had disappeared, as had the chair. The room echoed with the sound of my loafer striking bare wood as I stepped into it.

I opened her closet. Her work skirts, dresses, blouses, and cardigans—gone. Her collection of black pumps—fifteen pairs in various states of disrepair—all gone. The clothes she'd kept for the past twenty years in case they ever came back into fashion had disappeared. The shoeboxes and Filene's bags she'd stuffed into every corner of the closet were missing. Even the hangers had been removed, including the pair of pink satin-covered ones I gave her as a Christmas present one year. The closet looked cavernous now.

She planned this for some time, I thought. *She must have had movers here today*. A strip of wallpaper, lilac with clusters of purple and pink flowers, peeled away from a corner. We'd hung that paper together four years ago. I could still picture her on that first wallpapering day dressed in a yellow cotton, ruffled sleeveless blouse that stretched across her wide chest and left gaps between the tiny white buttons. Her madras plaid capris were ones I'd outgrown in my steady march to obesity, but they were a little loose on her. One of her navy Keds, my mother's castoffs, had a hole in the right shoe where the little toe hit. Her thick, graying brown hair, wrapped up into a blue-flowered kerchief, kept slipping out in spite of numerous bobby pins.

Now my world was falling apart. My Margie, my sweet, sweet Margie had gone. Margie, who read me stories when I was little and rubbed my back until I fell asleep. Margie, who had comforted me when I skinned the same knee over and over again from roller skating. Margie, who played cards with me when we were both bored. Margie, who tempered my mother's anger toward me. Gone, without a word to me, no goodbyes, no hugs, no "sorry, Anne, I'll miss you," no note. I sunk to the hard floor; the room's emptiness now closed in. The scent of her Chesterfield cigarettes lingered like a dog marking its territory. Mixed with this was the odor of her Jean Naté toilet water, cloyingly sweet. Then I realized I couldn't smell anything, my nose filled with snot and tears, and I sat and cried for my Margie to come back to me.

The sound of the kitchen door unlocking unnerved me. My Timex wristwatch said that only thirty minutes had elapsed since I made my discovery.

"Hello, I'm home," my mother announced, her nightly greeting. I jumped up, ignored a head rush, and ran out to the kitchen. My mother's work clothes sagged—white blouse askew under a navy cardigan whose sleeves were wrinkled from being pushed up to the elbows repeatedly, navy skirt wrinkled from sitting. A coffee stain flared from the front of her blouse; it would have annoyed her all day. Scuffed navy pumps wanted to be kicked off. Her perm was growing out, the roots straight and ends frizzy.

"Margie's stuff is all gone," I said.

"Jesus, Mary, and Joseph," my mother said. "How can she do this to me?"

She followed me into Margie's room and pulled her breath in sharply at the door.

"Holy Mother of God."

"Where did she go, Ma? How will we find her? Why didn't she say goodbye?"

My mother stood still without speaking. "Well, there's one good thing," she said, finally.

"What?"

"She took the damn cat. I noticed the litter box and food dishes were gone from the hallway."

"Oh, no."

Lucky was *my* cat. And now Margie had kidnapped him and left no ransom note, no hope of reprieve.

"I'll have to come up with her half of the rent now," my mother said, talking to herself as if I wasn't there. She looked around the room. Then she looked at me.

"Oh, stop crying like a baby, Anne. This won't affect you. You're not the one who has to worry about paying Margie's half of the rent and all the other bills."

"I can work more hours at Dunkin' Donuts."

"Yes, you'll have to. Thank God I won't have to pay for your upkeep much longer. After high school, you're on your own."

Margie couldn't have moved to Kingston. That house had no central heat, so it would still be cold with only two coal stoves for warmth. Uncle Jake had lived in those primitive conditions for seventy years, but he was a man and used to a rudimentary life. Margie had become a city girl, soft and accustomed to comforts. Moreover, the walk to the Boston-bound bus had no sidewalks and would be treacherous if March turned snowy. So she must have rented another apartment in Boston. But where? Would I ever see her again?

I suddenly realized I'd be alone with my mother now. I'd lost the cushion between us. If she decided to send me away, she could move in with Bob, which would solve her money troubles. Where would I go? I had no relatives who'd take me in. The nuns would be of no use—they'd cite the commandment to "honor thy father and thy mother" and tell me it was my fault that my mother treated me as she did. My friends' parents could ill afford to add another kid to their households, and I couldn't think of a single one who would accept me without money for room and board. I couldn't survive on the streets—nighttime temperatures were dipping below freezing. I shivered violently at these thoughts.

That evening, my mother and I ate a dinner of minute steaks and salad with Ken's dressing. My mother read the paper. I stared at an open page of a library book while picking at my food. Whatever bites landed in my mouth tasted of salt from my tears. I kept my head down for fear that my mother would see my crying, knowing it would enrage her.

After I cleaned the dishes, I went to my room and lay under the covers, still crying. I couldn't help but remember that when my mother and Margie left me at Rosary, Margie had turned around at the last minute to say they'd be back soon and she loved me. This time, Margie left silently with no words of love, no words at all. It felt like she'd died. Later that night, when I heard my mother's snores, I crept out of bed and walked silently to Margie's room. I stood inside the doorway, breathing in what remained of her.

Looking back, I see that two incidents changed my life forever—Margie's leaving and meeting my father for the first time. These two people, one whom I knew so well, the other whom I fantasized about so perfectly, had disappointed me greatly. Critically, I had hoped they would protect me from my mother—Margie as she had done when I was younger, my father as he had done in my daydreams. But it became crystal clear that neither would shelter me. I understand now that both of these parent-figures were tragically flawed. They couldn't love a child unconditionally and wouldn't take responsibility for their own failings. I couldn't depend on them.

These events set several things in motion. First, I could no longer hope for someone to swoop in to save me from my fears and answer my longings. I'd have to fend for myself. Second, I resolved that if I ever were to marry, it would have to be to a man who was reliable, stable, and likely to be an excellent parent. Finally, I had to become a breadwinner. Margie would no longer be a source of funds. My father, with his history of paying little child support and no evidence of current generosity, would not be showering me with cash. My mother had made it clear that she'd soon be cutting the apron strings. I needed a trade.

I wasn't helpless. Indeed I'd been training for this all my life. I'd cried myself to sleep as a little girl with no parent figure to hold me and protect me from my fears. I nursed myself through illnesses. My hard work at school had rewarded me with top grades. After-school jobs provided steady, albeit modest, paychecks. I had skills and experience but I needed a plan.

From books, newspapers, and television, I'd learned that further education equaled higher job prospects, which would bring financial stability. I might not be able to control my emotional demons but I could pay my bills. My first major goal was to go to college. It would be the tunnel through which I'd break out of the prison formed by my mother's control over me. Eighteen months—that's how long until I could leave home.

My most immediate threat was the danger of physical harm from my mother now that we'd be living together alone. So my second major goal was to keep her from killing me. While I was beginning to see her as less than powerful, my insights did nothing to lessen her outbursts when angered. I was now as tall as she was and more agile and theoretically could make an immediate escape. But when she started swinging, years of training made me stand there and let her make contact; I was still the stationary punching bag.

So I developed several tactics to limit my risks. I was careful never to answer her back and keep my eyes downcast so she couldn't see the hate in them. I practiced avoidance. I attended every meeting and event at my school. Together with my job at Dunkin' Donuts and piano and guitar lessons, these activities kept me out of the house every evening and much of the weekend days. I still had chores to do, housework and laundry mostly, but I could do them late at night after my mother was in bed or on the weekends when she went to Plymouth. I was in full retreat, but it was safer than putting myself in harm's way by hanging around the apartment when she was home.

I also honed my acting skills. I understood by now that my mother desperately wanted to be loved. I continued to pretend to love, care, and worry about her—this helped stroke her fragile ego. It paid off. One day, my mother said she and I were more like best friends than mother and daughter. I smiled and nodded but mentally stuck my finger to the back of my throat.

Years later, during my medical training, I would learn these containment principles when working with psychiatric patients. First rule—never let yourself be alone in a room with a volatile patient. Second rule—sedate or restrain the threatening ones. Third—know how to rally immediate help if a patient endangers you. And finally—develop a discharge plan as soon as you admit the patient. Get him out of your hospital for his own good as well as yours.

My discharge plan for my mother was to get her the hell out of my life.

By protecting myself in these ways, my fear of my mother slowly began to abate. By no means was it a sudden cure—I would struggle for years with guilt and anger from her accusations that I was a bad daughter, an "ungrateful brat." I finally cut off contact with her when I was in my forties. But for the teenage me, who couldn't break ties with my mother without suffering consequences of homelessness, avoidance and appeasement worked to improve my margin of safety.

If I could go back in time, I'd like to take this poor lost teenager in my arms. I'd hold her warmly even though she'd stiffen in my embrace—she wasn't used to physical affection. I'd mother her and grandmother her, holding her until I felt her soften, until she felt safe. In holding her, I'd feel the strength in her spine, and I'd be able to tell her that she'll build a good life, create a family, and make a contribution to the world. I'd even tell her she'd one day be a doctor and a researcher, write a book on how women can use exercise to fight breast cancer, publish over 400 scientific manuscripts on how to prevent disease and improve health. But I know she wouldn't believe me.

Chapter 13

Hungry for Love

I needed love, and I needed it badly. So in addition to my first two goals—college and safety—I had one more major goal: put some effort into my appearance. It might lead me to the high school Holy Grail, a boyfriend, which would provide immediate affection and give me experience for later landing a husband.

I was on shaky ground here. I had a few glimpses of interest from boys, but I interpreted them as inconsequential. *That boy wasn't really looking at me—he was interested in the pretty girl beside me. That other boy wasn't flirting with me—he was just naturally friendly.* I believed I had limited material to work with in the looks department. But, desperate times call for desperate actions, so I swung into full gear, which involved a starvation diet, adding makeup as an essential step in my daily routine, and improving my hair situation.

I strategized with all the cunning of a four-star general. To get a boyfriend, I had to be pretty. To be pretty, I had to be thin. Twiggy and all the other fashion magazine models were slender, and they were obviously beautiful. Plus, the cool girls at my high school, the ones with boyfriends, were skinny. You'd think that, having been a fatty most of my life after escaping Rosary Academy, becoming thin would seem daunting. But while I knew it would take some time, I figured the actual doing would be easy. I had cut back considerably on eating after the momentous meeting with my father and loved the feeling of control it gave me. So I thought eating less would feel even better.

The cool girls also had beautiful hair, shaped eyebrows, wore makeup, and showed several inches of their thighs below their school uniforms. Daily hair washing would be critical for my new Mod Squad style of long straight hair, which looked effortless but actually took some attention. The part had to be exactly centered and the hair had to have just a little body with no frizz. Washing my hair every day turned out to be a challenge. We didn't have a shower—only a claw-foot tub with a little pink rubber hose that sprayed water everywhere in the bathroom no matter where you aimed it. My new ritual would be traumatic for my mother because I had to do it in the morning while she got ready for work. But I had no choice—I had to rid my scalp of oil buildup from the previous night, so that my baby-fine hair wouldn't separate into greasy strands like wet duck feathers.

The first morning, I happily relaxed in the tub when the door opened. Cigarette smoke wafted in, followed closely by my mother in her short peach and white negligee, clutching the *Boston Globe*.

"Sorry, I have to go," she said. The prospect of what was about to happen made me shoot out of the tub like a sperm whale jumping for a tourist boat. I grabbed my towel and fled. After this, sleep seemed less important than looking good, so I got up an hour early to secure my bathroom slot before my mother awoke.

Plucking my eyebrows came next on my agenda. I had been blessed with thick Irish brows that looked like slabs of brown peat growing above my eyes. The hairs grew perilously close to the middle, giving the impression of one swath of hair stretching from left to right. I perused the fashion magazines at the local pharmacy until I found an article on brow tweezing. I bought a copy of that month's *Mademoiselle* with its clear instructions: "Beautiful Brows in 7 Steps! Look Just Like Twiggy!" *I can do this,* I thought.

According to the article, the only equipment I needed were a pair of tweezers and a mirror. With two hours until my mother would arrive, I set myself up with the *Mademoiselle* article open and lying across the sink, tweezers in hand. I grabbed a hair under my right brow, yanked, and felt a knife stab me right over my eye. *Jesus, Mary, and Joseph*, I screamed inside my head. My eyes immediately watered up, tears flowed, and I couldn't see anything, including my reflection in the mirror. I was paralyzed with pain and then realized with horror that I had about 500 more hairs left to pull before I'd have beautiful brows in seven steps!

When my eyes started to clear, I reread the article: "If you feel any discomfort, applying an ice cube to the skin can help." I guessed that this qualified as discomfort. Reeling into the kitchen, I faced my aversion to taking ice out of the freezer because it involved holding the metal ice tray in one hand, while yanking up on a handle to release the cubes. The resulting screeching sound wounded my ears as much as my mother's angry voice.

Holding ice to brow, I returned to the bathroom. After a minute, I peeked under the ice to look at the damage. A puffy, beet red eye glared back at me. *That looks pretty good. Time for the next one.* To my surprise, the second pluck didn't go any easier than the first. The ice hadn't numbed the skin, contrary to what *Mademoiselle* said. But I was sixteen years old, and pain could not stop me. I tweezed for an hour, most of which time passed waiting for my tears to clear. I ended up with two, one-eighth-inch thick eyebrows. Underneath them were eyes swollen like water-filled balloons, a red and runny nose, and lips chafed from biting through the pain. But I had beautiful brows!

The next order of business was to wear makeup. *Mademoiselle* said I needed eyeliner, eye shadow in blue or green, an eyebrow pencil, and mascara in order to make my tiny eyes into big, sexy, eyes. Rouge would help give me a healthy glow. It didn't occur to me that my constantly blushing cheeks might not need more color. If *Mademoiselle* said I needed it, I needed it. And lipstick was a requirement, preferably in several colors so I could choose the right hue for each of my outfits. I looked down at my skirt and vest and wondered which shade coordinated with Catholic school uniform forest green.

Now I knew what I needed, and I knew where I could find it. My mother "put on her face" every morning. I could raid her stash. Rummaging through the supplies artfully strewn over her bureau top, I found Max Factor pancake makeup, plus several Revlon lipsticks. Her shades didn't look anything like the pale pinks and peaches from my *Mademoiselle*, and the magazine specifically said to use liquid makeup for the most natural-looking skin. Pancake makeup would not do.

A quick trip to the Woolworth's in Brighton Center netted goodies, including mascara in brown, bright blue eye shadow powder, navy eyeliner, a brown eyebrow pencil, a bottle of liquid makeup in ivory bisque, pale pink blush powder, and several Revlon Natural Wonder lipsticks: Ivory Blizzard, Frozen Peaches, Sheer Shaver Pink, and Nothing Frosted. Back home, I crowded them into the little ledge around the porcelain sink and commenced my artwork. By the time I heard my mother's key in the lock, I was at the dining room table pretending to do homework.

"Hi," I said as my mother came in. I didn't look up, afraid she would yell at me about the makeup.

"Have you been crying?" she asked.

"No," I said, "why?"

"Your eyes look swollen."

"Well, I wasn't crying."

She looked more carefully at me. Sweat beads formed on my upper lip. I worried that my makeup would start dripping.

"You look nice," she said.

"Thanks."

"Where did you get the makeup?"

"At Woolworth's."

"How did you figure out how to put it on?"

"I read how in a magazine."

"Will the nuns allow you to wear it at school?"

"All the girls wear makeup."

"Oh, okay then." She paused for a few seconds, then said, "Katie McGuire called me today."

"Who's that?"

"My second cousin. She lives up the street from Uncle Jake's house. She says she's seen Margie coming and going from the house."

"Oh," I said, drawing out the word. So she did move into Uncle Jake's house after all.

"That house is half mine, and I pay half the utilities on it, but she acts as if it's all hers."

I nodded.

"Maybe I should just deed her my half of the house. That way I'm not stuck with those bills. And Bob couldn't get his hands on it in case anything happened to me."

I smiled, at a loss for words. She didn't want my opinion, just an ear. I was surprised she was trying to protect an asset from her future husband. I thought when a man and woman wed, they'd want to share all their worldly goods.

I had mixed feelings on learning Margie's whereabouts. I was annoyed that she hadn't told us where she was but felt sorry for her having to take on such harsh conditions: the long and cold walks to the bus, the coal stoves, and the lack of central heat.

The next day, I arrived at school in full makeup like the little actress I was becoming. My friends all noticed and said I looked really pretty. Most of them wore makeup, so we spent our lunch period comparing products. If any boys noticed my new look, I wouldn't have known because I still couldn't make my eyes meet theirs.

Next on my boyfriend-getting list was to wear my skirts short. The nuns had strict rules about skirt lengths—the knee had to be covered. The cool girls got around this rule by hiking their uniforms up on the way to school, at lunchtime, and after school. As they were leaving school, their books carried by their boyfriends, they'd reach under their jackets and pull up on their skirts, rolling the waistband over, until the hem stopped several inches above their knees. The academic and nerdy girls didn't do this. We were afraid of the nuns catching us outside of school and didn't want to look "fast." No matter, I decided, I would be one of these cool girls. I practiced shortening my skirt at home in front of my mother's full-length mirror. When I'd gotten the hang of it and the hem looked straight all around, I became one of the skirt-rolling girls.

My starvation weight loss plan turned out to be more difficult than I had thought. I'd forgotten about the hunger issue. Some things helped. My mother was also dieting so that she could look better for her new beau. As a result, there were no desserts in the house. Margie was no longer there to bring home chocolate-covered peanuts or bridge mix from the five-and-dime store. Actually, without Margie's salary to help with expenses, food was scarce. Tab lent a helping hand when we could afford it. Coffee and tea provided both a buzz and a foil for my mouth that was screaming to have things put into it. Having a realistic, reachable goal helped too—mine was to look like Twiggy.

I learned how to measure out food and look up calories in the little diet guide my mother kept in the kitchen drawer. This was one of the few books we owned. Our collection included a musty-smelling nineteenth-century family Bible with paper-thin pages and a dictionary. Margie had taken her Reader's Digest condensed books, and I kept a revolving set of schoolbooks that I had to return each June.

With guidance from our diet-bible, I learned how to write down everything I ate and drank with calorie counts beside each item, which helped me realize that the Jordan Marsh blueberry muffin I craved would provide enough calories for an entire day. I'd tally the numbers several times during the day to make sure that I kept well under 1,000 calories. The "best" days were ones in which I could keep under 500 calories. I knew if I wanted to lose weight I had to give up the good stuff: candy, cookies, cakes, pies, pudding, and—horrors—the doughnuts, all the things that made life bearable.

As a weight-loss physician and researcher, I now know that the very low calorie diet I kept for days running was dangerous without medical and nutritional supervision to ensure adequate intake of critical electrolytes and nutrients. Continued long enough, this kind of dieting in a young person is similar to anorexia nervosa, and it can be deadly. In my clinical trials, my nutritionists watch our patients carefully to make sure that none are over-restricting their calorie intake. I was starving myself on my diet, repeating what I'd done at Rosary.

After Margie moved out and left a gaping hole in our apartment like a missing front tooth, my mother announced she'd always sacrificed the better room and moved into Margie's old space. I was okay with not having the better room—I didn't want the nightly reminder that I was there because Margie wasn't. I moved from the porch into my mother's room. I loved my upgrade. But it needed to look more like me and less like a forty-nine-year old woman.

My newly lenient mother—I wanted to ask who she was and what she had done with my real mother—said I could decorate my room and pick out the paint colors, linoleum design, and curtain fabric. Deciding to go whole-hog into mod style, I chose white for the walls, cerulean blue for the trim, blue-patterned linoleum, and flower-powered blue fabric for curtains. I used three weeks' salary from my Dunkin' Donuts waitressing job to pay for the supplies. The landlord didn't care about anything since his wife had left him, so we didn't even bother to ask him if I could redecorate.

I did the painting and linoleum-laying myself. While this was definitely not women's work, no one else would do it—we didn't have money to pay workmen, and my mother had other things to do. Luckily I'd interned under an expert—Margie—who'd uncharacteristically taken on the men's work of painting and wallpapering. So I knew how to remove old wallpaper, sand down rough edges, spackle plaster cracks, mix paint, and apply it with rollers and brushes. After two weeks, I had a perfect nest for the newly transformed Anne.

Over the next few months I lost thirty pounds. At 125 pounds and five-foot-four, I was a little chubbier than my skinny Irish peers. I still saw myself as obese. If a few boys looked at me, I still couldn't talk with them or even look them in the eye. Somehow in creating Anne's list of "How to Get a Boyfriend in 5 Easy Steps," I'd left out some of the most critical items. I forgot to work on my interpersonal skills, self-esteem, and ability to relax and smile at a boy. Because I knew so little about boys and men, I didn't realize that they were people, too. I didn't know that boys craved love, attention, and companionship, just like I did.

With no boyfriend prospects, I became desperate. My girlfriends were all going steady. It came to a head one afternoon in May. My friends and I stood in a tight circle at lunch like little girls playing Duck Duck Goose. Gina, red-haired and freckled, had told the group how she and her boyfriend spent entire evenings talking when he could get to a pay phone. Gina and I were the smartest girls in the group, and we often had a little rivalry about who would get the best grade on a math test. The other girls chatted about their boyfriends. I remained silent while this went on for what felt like hours. I knew I was such an ugly monster that I'd never have a boyfriend. Mortified about my shortcomings, I felt like I would explode.

"I'm seeing a boy, too," I blurted out. Blushing furiously, I'd shocked even myself with my revelation.

"Really!" several of the girls said at once. Their faces mirrored my surprise.

"What's his name?" asked Kathleen. Annoyingly tall and thin, Kathleen was the prettiest of the group. Her steady apprenticed at the local undertaker's.

"Kevin," I said.

I surprised myself when this name popped out of my mouth. It was a good Irish name. I must not have imagined dating anyone other than an Irish-American Catholic boy, even a make-believe one.

"How did you meet him?" asked Patty. For the past year, she had shared with me the troubled peaks and troughs of her relationship with her beau.

"At the Boston Conservatory," I replied. "He takes piano lessons right before me."

As they asked more questions, my new boyfriend took shape with ease. He was tall and slender but with wide, powerful shoulders. Straight brown hair fell into his eyes when he lowered his head. He was cute but not the most handsome boy (otherwise there's no way he'd be interested in me—I was trying for realism here). A dedicated musician, he'd won several competitions. With his two parents and older brother, he lived in a large white house in Weston, a wealthy suburb of Boston. A year older than me, he would start college at Harvard the following year. My friends didn't question the veracity of my statements. Either they were very gullible, or they humored me so that I wouldn't be embarrassed. I suspect it was the latter.

I soon discovered that a make-believe boyfriend was limited in what he could do for and with me. He couldn't take me to a movie or put his arm around me as we walked around town. He couldn't slow dance with me. He didn't talk (actually this could be an asset or a limitation, depending on the situation). He couldn't make me feel loved and special and couldn't meet my friends. I soon tired of having to report my Kevin-lie every week to the priest at Saturday confession.

By the time school began in September, I'd broken things off with Kevin. I told my friends it was because it was too hard for him to get away from his college classes to see me. It was a lame excuse, but I was running out of creativity.

I felt so ashamed of having to create a pretend boyfriend. It forced me to admit that I was too deformed to have the real thing. I was a failure of a girl, a creep, an untouchable. Added to my humiliation was my immaturity in creating a make-believe love. I was no better than the little Anne who had invented an imaginary friend to keep her company as she moved from one institution to another. That friend, whom I named Charlene, was a mother with nine children. At the time, I'd desperately needed mothering, so I invented my own mother. Now, I thought having a boy to love me would solve all my problems and fill the emptiness in my life. I craved love like an addict, as if I'd tasted the real thing and needed more.

Chapter 14

Sugar and Spice

In October of 1969, my high school was fairly insulated from the turmoil happening around the country. I wouldn't hear about Woodstock until after graduation. We knew about Vietnam, but no one protested—we didn't realize we could do that. No one skipped school on October fifteenth to join The Moratorium to End the War in Vietnam. The St. Columbkille's kids worried about more immediate things: Would there be food in the house when we got home? Could we find and keep a part-time job? Could we maintain our grades?

He's looking at me again. I know it. No one is sitting behind me, and only boys are sitting in the three seats ahead of me. So his swiveled head looking toward the back of my row has to be aimed at me. But it can't be—boys never look at me. Well, not since sixth grade when the entire class turned around to look at me and giggle after Sister said it was sinful to be fat with so many starving children in the world.

The head swiveling happened all through history class. I was so sure that he could not be looking at me that I turned around several times to make sure none of the cute girls had dragged a chair over behind me. My thought process made no sense because the schoolroom's 100-year-old wooden desks and chairs were securely bolted to the floor.

This boy's attention confused and scared me. I'd follow anyone around like a sick puppy if they noticed me. And this boy was popular and an athlete. Six feet tall and muscular, he had brown hair and dark brown eyes you could get lost in. What was he doing looking at me, the Queen of Nerds? What on Earth would this boy want with me instead of the pretty and popular girl who everyone knew had a major crush on him? I wondered if the boys were playing a mean trick on me. What fun it would be to make big, fat, smart Anne think the most popular boy in the class liked her, and then they all would have a great laugh when the joke was revealed.

In the middle of my confusion I remembered that I wasn't so fat anymore. By now, my no-eating plan had brought me down to 110 pounds. My body was thin, although my brain thought I was fat. But this boy didn't seem the type to pull a mean stunt on a girl, even big, fat, smart Anne. Yet I still couldn't believe that he might like me until a girl in my homeroom gave me a hint.

"Anne, Dan told Jimmy that he likes you and wants to invite you to the Snowball Dance," said the girl who dated Dan's best friend.

"Are you sure?"

"Jimmy said so."

I stared at her, dumbfounded. She didn't look quite as surprised as I felt. Instead she smiled.

"It's so cool," she said.

I nodded. My heart had stopped beating. I hoped it would start up again soon.

"Well, what should I tell Jimmy to tell Dan?" she asked.

"Tell him I'd like to go with him." She had to bend her head close to hear me.

I floated through the rest of the day. A boy wanted to take me to the winter formal! That meant he wanted to buy me a ticket to the dance and a corsage for my dress, pick me up at my apartment, drive me to the dance, dance with me—which meant he wasn't disgusted by the idea of touching me—and then maybe take me to an after-dance party. What's more, we would walk arm in arm as we joined the procession of couples into the decorated gym at the beginning of the dance. I was immediately smitten. I didn't know much about this boy, other than that he was a nice guy. We didn't travel in the same circles. He was not the academic type. The only boys I dared talk to were fellow Math Club members and my friends' boyfriends.

Dan called to ask if I'd like to go out the following Friday, a month before the Snowball Dance. I mentally checked my empty calendar and said, "Sure, I'd love to." I was as surprised by this date as by his Snowball invitation. Not only did this boy think me worthy as a formal dance partner, but he also wanted to spend time alone with me—as if I was normal!

I couldn't concentrate on anything in the week leading up to my first real date. I expected Dan to call at any minute to say he'd come to his senses and of course there's no way he'd take me out, wanting nothing to do with me. Waves of panic roiled me like a series of small earthquakes as I faced the dire fact that I didn't know how to talk to boys. What would I say to him? My *Glamour* magazine said asking a lot of questions would keep a conversation going because boys liked to talk about themselves. *Okay, I can do that,* I thought. I ran through several conversations in my head, just for the practice.

Anne: So what do you like to do for fun?
Dan: Well, I play football.
Anne: Oh, yeah.
[Brief pause.]
Anne: You have lots of brothers and sisters, right?
Dan: Yeah.

[Anne's underarms start to get squishy, so she decides to take a different line of questioning.]

Anne: What kind of music do you like?

Dan: Rock.

Anne: What's your favorite group?

Dan: The Stones.

Anne: What's your favorite Stones' song?

Dan: Dunno.

[More sweat from Anne.]

Anne: Oh, do you like . . .

Anne [to herself]: *I hate the Stones so much that I can't think of a single song of theirs. Wait, there's "I Can't Get No Satisfaction." Oh, God, I can't mention that song. It's all about sex. He'll think I'm fast.*

Clearly this wasn't working. All the little conversations I could come up with lasted about thirty seconds, followed by uncomfortable silence. Even in my head it was uncomfortable. I hoped he didn't ask me questions about myself. What would my answers be?

Dan: What do you do for fun?

Anne: I read, play piano and guitar, watch television, and hang out with my girlfriends.

[Dan yawns.]

Dan: Do you have any brothers and sisters?

Anne: Nope, no brothers or sisters. *Just wait until he hears that I lived most of my life with two women and met my father for the first time last winter. And I was mostly institutionalized until I was five. He'll think I'm insane or deformed.*

Dan: What's your favorite group?

Anne: The Beatles, absolutely. *Mustn't mention the mad crush I still have on Paul, and I'd give anything for a chance to be Paul's girlfriend.*

Dan: What's your favorite Beatles' song?

Anne: All of them; every single one.

But I realized I didn't have to practice this type of conversation. *Glamour* said I should get him to talk about himself, not the other way around.

At school I tried to play it cool. My friends showed more excitement than I did.

"What are you going to wear?" asked Gina.

"I don't know," I said. "I don't have that many clothes."

"Wear a dress," said Patty. "You have to look pretty."

"No, wear slacks," said Kathleen. "You have to look casual, like you're not trying too hard."

"No, no, no," said Mary. "You should wear a tight sweater and a short skirt. Boys like foxy-looking girls."

"You should wear your hair up," said Patty.

"No way," said Kathleen. "You look really pretty with your hair down, like it is now. Plus if an up-do gets messed up your mother will know what you were doing."

The other girls nodded. I nodded too, pretending to know what she was talking about, although I couldn't see how my hair was going to get messed up. I did like the suggestion to wear it down, though, because I couldn't afford a trip to the hairdresser's in addition to the one required for the formal dance.

My new lenient mother said yes, I could go on the date. Given what I now understand about her, I think this development would have made her happy because it signaled my further maturation. Little girls don't date. Big girls do. My mother wanted the little girl out of her life. She said it was a big sacrifice for her to wait for half a year before marrying Bob. Looking back, I can appreciate her arranging her life around mine, but it really was the simplest solution. She was legally responsible for me while I was in high school and had no options for where she could stick me for half a year if she moved to Plymouth with Bob.

"I should have said yes the first time Bob asked me to marry him," she told me one day. "I've regretted it all my life."

I mentally mouthed the words *then I wouldn't have been born.*

My mother insisted that Dan come up to the apartment to meet her. I could hear them chatting while I finished getting ready. Mostly my mother was asking questions, and Dan was giving polite answers. *Hmm, she must have read my* Glamour *magazine.* I had a sparse closet, especially with my new weight loss, so my choice of clothing didn't take long. I emerged in the same white wool dress I'd worn to meet my father. It was a lot looser now. Over it I wore a yellow hand-knit Aran cardigan that a friend of Margie's had brought back from Ireland. It was too small for Margie so she had sadly given me one of her few possessions from the "old sod." Dan said I looked nice.

We got in his car, and he took me to Howard Johnson's. I was a little disappointed. In my fantasy first date, a waiter with a towel over his left arm bent over the candlelit table and asked how the young lady would like her lobster prepared. Instead I got a bored waitress asking, "Do you want fries with that burger, honey?" I wasn't thinking about how even buying hamburgers was a stretch for a poor Irish boy from Brighton. Back in the car afterward, Dan turned toward me.

"Do you want to go park somewhere?"

I thought he meant we could talk some more and get to know each other.

"Sure," I said. He smiled at the enthusiasm in my voice.

The winter night was so dark I couldn't see where we were headed. Dan pulled into what looked like an abandoned lot. As we bounced over the rutted pavement, I saw several other cars parked in random formation at some distance from each other, steamed windows hiding the occupants. Dan stopped, away from the others, and turned off the engine. We sat for a minute. I looked straight ahead, biting my lip. Dan said something.

"What?" I asked.

"I said come here."

He pulled me over toward the driver's seat. I soon learned what "go park somewhere" meant. At least I learned the first-date version, which involved a lot of kissing. Ugh, what was that tongue doing? My knowledge of kissing was from television and books. Neither prepared me for this. I'd never been this close to a boy. His cheap herringbone tweed sports jacket scratched my cheek. He smelled of Irish Spring soap.

I smelled of panic mixed with Heaven Scent cologne. *Glamour* said fragrance was essential for a date, and it was the only bottle of cologne I owned—the one my father had given me for my birthday the previous winter. I didn't get the irony of my fragrance's name in view of the present sinning, but I did wonder whether the whole night of kissing constituted one sin or each kiss would tally up to hundreds of sins.

After some time, a car pulled up close to ours on the driver's side. Dan rolled down the window.

"Hey, way to go, O'Rourke!" said the redheaded boy behind the wheel. A slender girl with beautiful big hair sat close beside him. Her broad smile matched her boyfriend's. I recognized them from school. Neither would have given me the time of day before now. (Or maybe I wouldn't have dared look at them. It's kind of hard to say "hi" to someone who is staring at her feet.) This scene replayed itself several times as other cars pulled up. Some flashed their lights, others quietly tooted horns. I wondered how the other boys knew Dan had planned to come here this night. I also couldn't help admitting to myself that the kids were congratulating him on being there with me, not pitying him.

The Snowball Dance went off without a hitch. My feverish preparations included designing and sewing a green velvet ball gown with gold trim and a white brocade evening coat. I used my Dunkin' Donuts wages to pay for the materials as well as for the hairdresser's appointment for my upswept, lacquered hairdo.

I swallowed a momentary disappointment when I saw that the corsage Dan gave me had a silver ribbon, which I knew would clash terribly with the gold braid of my dress. In the 1960s, it was a crime to mix gold and silver in the same outfit. Thankfully I was smart enough not to say anything to Dan about this, and I wore the corsage as if there was not a single thing wrong with my perfect outfit. My "boy muteness" helped me here. I didn't know how to say much of anything to this boy, much less complain about his nice gift. My mother saw us off to the dance. She snapped pictures that showed Dan smiling comfortably and me grimacing as if a gun was pointed at my face instead of the Brownie camera.

The Snowball Dance was a night of firsts. It was my first upswept hairdo. This required a visit to a salon solely for the style, no haircut involved. So much hairspray was applied that I could have done a headstand and still had a glorious crown of stiff curls. It was my first formal gown. The only long dress I'd ever worn was a flannel nightgown, several sizes too big because that's how Margie said we should wear them.

And it was my first slow dance with a boy. For years, I'd watched them from my place pressed against the wall, my heart pounding, as I hoped a boy would ask me to dance, yet terrified one might. Now I knew that joyous feeling of a boy's arms around my waist: pulling me in close, my arms around his neck, the strength of his wonderful broad shoulders. Dan quietly sang along to Stevie Wonder's "My Cherie Amour." I willed the music never to stop. This was my Cinderella moment.

If I had spread my arms I would have floated up to the ceiling, past the round silver-mirrored strobe-light ball that shot colored lights across the entire room. I would have glided over a room full of girls with stiff updos, overstated eye makeup, understated pink lips, and pastel formal dresses and their skinny dates looking like kids dressed in their fathers' too-large tuxedos and shoes. The girls looked at least ten years older than the boys. On closer inspection, the girls' dresses were mostly borrowed or hand-me-downs, and the boys' tuxes rented. Probably most had worked extra hours at their part-time jobs to pay for hairstyles, shoes, tux rentals, and flowers. As I floated, I would have seen a boy-band with its freshman and sophomore class members even smaller than the dancers. Finally, I would have observed the black-and-white-clad nuns surrounding the dancers like penguins encircling peacocks.

That night was also the first time my breast was fondled. This followed the after-dance party, in the darkened car outside our flat. No one, with the exception of one aggressive bra saleslady at Jordan Marsh department store, had ever touched my breast. I kind of liked it (from the boy, not the saleslady), but the guilt put a serious damper on the pleasure.

After the dance, Dan and I dated steadily. We spent our lunchtimes together, walking hand in hand up to Brighton Center to Brigham's Ice Cream Shop. With my hand in his, I felt secure. He led me through a journey to a new life as a lovable person. This was as unreal to me as I imagined a psychedelic trip to be. But unlike the acid trip, this was a voyage I'd been longing for all my life. The reality was so much better than I'd imagined.

I attended Dan's sporting events, proud to sit beside him on the team bus. My ignorance was a real handicap as I watched his games.

What I saw were boys dressed in costumes with padding to make them look like they were actual men rather than skinny kids, bumping rudely into each other, and sometimes running back and forth on the field. That a ball was thrown and points scored was lost on me. When the crowd on our side of the stands got up and cheered, I did the same and with such gusto that my voice would be hoarse the next day. But I had no idea at all what I was cheering for.

Dan and I went out on dates every Friday and Saturday night—actually we just parked. I had not expected this when I'd worked on my beautiful brows in order to get a beau. And my pretend Kevin and I never went parking. Admittedly, this was because I didn't know anything about this activity until my first date.

Desperate to keep my boyfriend, I never complained, never asked to do anything else. I would have appreciated an occasional movie, or bowling, or ice-skating. This is what dating teenagers did on television sitcoms, my only real source of dating information other than my fashion magazines. I thought some more conversation would have been nice, although it would have been one-sided because I still didn't know how to talk to boys. So it would have involved a lot of me smiling and nodding, but at least I would have learned more about this boy than what I learned in the car. I knew only that he came from a large family, loved his parents, and had leadership aspirations.

I shared little with him about my family. He knew my mother was controlling from the strict curfews she imposed, and the absence of a father was obvious when Dan came to pick me up for dates. But I didn't tell him about my past institutionalizations or my mother's continued liberal contact of her hand with my face. I didn't tell him that my father had no interest in me. I also neglected to mention fantasy Kevin and maniac Steve, letting Dan think he was my first love. As might be expected, the car activities progressed over the next several months, although my virginity remained intact.

Before becoming exclusive with someone, it might have been healthier for me to have started going out with groups of girls and boys then ease into casual dating. But external forces shaped my romantic life. The cool girls had steady boyfriends, and I wanted to be a cool girl. Dan seemed smitten with me and wanted to date exclusively. To know that someone liked me and wanted to spend time with me gave me a glorious dopamine-fueled high. I needed to be loved and feel special after a lifetime of neglect. So I became a steady, a girlfriend. Dan gave me his class ring, the Irish working-class high school equivalent of a two-carat diamond engagement ring.

CHAPTER 15

Power Hungry

"Oh dear God," my mother said. Her hand squeezed the black telephone receiver so tightly I could see the outlines of tendons against white knuckles. "When did he go?" she asked. She nodded, saying nothing. "Well, at least he didn't suffer at the end." She listened, nodded some more. "Ok, Margaret, I'll drive down tomorrow. I'll pick you up at the house." She put down the receiver. "Oh sweet Jesus, I don't need this now."

"Don't need what?" I asked.

My mother looked up, seemed surprised to see me there. "Uncle Jake died tonight."

"Oh, no." I hadn't seen Uncle Jake in a month because I didn't want to see him as his spirit faded in parallel with his failing heart.

"Oh, Christ, I hope I don't get fired for taking time off from work for this. You'll need to come with me to help with the arrangements," she said.

"What arrangements?"

"The wake and the funeral. There will be a hundred things to do. Okay, we need to start packing. Bring a dark dress. Jesus, they're forecasting more snow for tomorrow."

Overwhelmed with a numb feeling, I went to my room. It was a cold December night. I had dates with Dan that weekend. I'd have to call him to cancel. I was also supposed to accompany the choir at the Sunday Morning Masses. I wasn't sure how to reach the music teacher who arranged the Church organ music, but I'd somehow have to get word to her. Then I remembered the big exam I had the next day.

"Ma," I called.

"What?"

"I just remembered I've got a big math test tomorrow. I can't miss it."

"Jesus Christ, can't they let you take it later?"

"I can't. I need it for my college applications."

"Okay, then, you'll have to go to school tomorrow and take the bus down to Kingston. But pack your suitcase tonight and put it in the trunk of the car so you don't have to lug that thing on the bus."

Surprised that my mother was thinking about what I had to carry, I returned to my room. I felt relieved that I'd see Dan and the music teacher at school to explain in person. As I started packing, I realized my mother and Margie had just had a conversation over the phone. Maybe taking care of the arrangements together would heal some of their differences. But the stress could deepen their rift. Hopefully they'd at least be civil at the wake and funeral.

I'd not seen or talked with Margie in nine months. I wished for a new beginning to our relationship like a new life that is created in that period of time with a pure, new soul—no bitterness or sin or craziness, only the unconditional love a good mother gives instinctively. Mostly I just wished she'd speak to me.

Before class the following morning, I delivered a note to my homeroom nun that my mother had written in her beautiful penmanship, asking to excuse me from school for at least a week for the wake and funeral. As opening prayers came over the loudspeaker, I was surprised to hear Mother Superior pray for Anne McTiernan's uncle's soul. I kept my eyes down, feeling important to have this recognition but realizing I should be putting on a show of piety and sorrow. I was still numb and didn't feel anything about Uncle Jake's passing. He was the first relative to die whom I actually knew and loved. Looking back, I see that I repressed feelings about Uncle Jake's death because that was easier than facing the permanence of his leaving.

The wake was the traditional three days and nights of body viewing and praying. As a result, there was plenty of time for my mother and aunt to talk, smile, and laugh with old friends and relatives. Margie's eyes were red from crying, but my mother and I had matching bone-dry eyes. It was an open casket similar to all the other wakes I'd ever been to. Uncle Jake looked like he always did—a little old man with round wire-rimmed glasses, bald head covered with age spots, and a little beard stubble. Fingers gnarled by arthritis clutched a rosary as if he was fervently doing last-minute praying before the judgment. Kneeling by his casket, I still felt nothing. My heart was hardened, as Margie would say.

It seemed as if the entire town of Kingston stopped by the funeral home over those three days. All the Catholics came because Uncle Jake had been the Church and cemetery gardener for the previous twenty years. The neighbors up and down Elm Street arrived, some to pay respect, others to find out if Uncle Jake's house would be sold. A line-up of storekeepers arrived, reversing the rounds Uncle Jake used to make on his shopping trips to downtown Kingston—the pharmacist, baker, newspaper hawker, grocer, and butcher. The relatives were the friendliest to me.

"Jake used to talk about you all the time, Anne," one said.

"He thought the sun rose and set on you," commented another.

"He was so excited when his Little Miss Boston was coming to visit," another added.

I loved hearing that Uncle Jake told people about me, although I was a little surprised since he hadn't expressed much love directly to me, never gave me a big bear hug. All the kisses between us had been instigated by instruction, as in, "Anne, give Uncle Jake a kiss goodbye now," and I'd obediently endure a little pain on my lips from the ever-present cheek stubble and his old-man smells of tobacco, mackerel, and unwashed clothes.

Finally, my mother and I headed home to Brighton. I drove—my mother had discovered the benefit of paying for my driving lessons was that I could chauffeur her. I didn't mind and felt grown-up behind the wheel. The upside of the week was that Margie was talking with us again. She even let us take her grocery shopping, where she piled her cart so high the clerk said she must have a big family.

"I'm spending the Christmas holidays with Bob," my mother said to me after we'd merged onto Route 3. "Bob said you can come, too." Her voice wavered a little with this last part. It was a relief to keep my eyes on the road. I didn't want to see the annoyed look on her face. Then I started thinking. *She doesn't want me in the way. Or Bob doesn't want a kid hanging around. Or both.*

"Thanks, but I thought I'd spend Christmas with Margie." I felt proud to be thinking on my feet.

"Oh, so you think she'll want you?"

"Well, she seemed friendly enough this week."

"You never know with her. I hope you're right."

My shoulders sank. My mother didn't want me around, and now she suggested that Margie wouldn't either. I could easily be alone for this holiday, I realized, the one when my greatest longing for family surfaced. Christmas was the embodiment of love and warm cozy feelings if you had people in your life who wanted to be with you. If you didn't, it would be a miserable goddamn day.

I exhaled a big sigh of relief over the phone after Margie said yes of course I could spend Christmas week with her. When I told my mother, she said, "I hope she doesn't change her mind. If you're coming with me, I need to tell Bob ahead of time. It's only fair."

Christmas with Margie was surreal. She acted as though the months of separation hadn't occurred. But her pretense of normal served to get us through the week. My mother reluctantly let me borrow her car, so I was able to take Margie shopping and on errands. Margie went whole hog at the grocery store. For just the two of us, she bought a fifteen-pound turkey, a five-pound bag of potatoes, a dozen rolls, parsnips, carrots, and two kinds of cranberry sauce. It took two large shopping carts to haul her purchases to the car. Back at her house, we made Toll House cookies, a real feat in that old coal stove with its irregular heat.

We set up Margie's crèche. Before she moved out, it had always been my job to unwrap the worn tissue from around the figurines and place them in and around the stable. After I finished the set-up, Margie would move each figure a few millimeters.

Next we assembled Margie's six-foot artificial tree. It took her two hours to string the tree lights because she had to rearrange them several times. In the remaining twenty-five years of her life, she never took that tree down. Sitting year after year in her living room, waiting for Christmas to come around again, it collected enough dust to look like a snow-covered pine.

A couple of days before Christmas, a snowstorm dumped a foot of snow. It was a beautiful setting for Christmas in the country. We were happy that we'd done such a big shopping trip already. We had provisions.

Christmas dinner was a stretch. We'd played sous chef to my mother for holiday meals, but neither of us had ever planned or executed a formal dinner. Margie's worn *Fannie Farmer Cookbook* got us through the preparation, and afterward I felt as stuffed as the turkey. After dinner, I tried telling Margie about my current problems with my mother. She replied only, "You should thank God every day that you have a mother." My hopes for a new, open relationship with Margie were dashed.

I missed Dan terribly during my stay at Margie's. This was the longest we had been apart in our two-month relationship. Margie wouldn't allow me to talk with a boy from her phone, so Dan and I were out of communication for the entire week. The situation became bleak when a nor'easter blew in late Christmas night, leaving another two feet of snow. I was stranded even longer than planned and didn't see Dan until after New Year's Day.

I delayed the college application process as long as possible. I kept my grades up and continued my school activities, but the thought of leaving my new love, even to move across the city, was unthinkable. Plus, Dan was not a scholar, and I was afraid that he'd lose interest in me if I were better educated than he was. Finally, with deadlines looming, I broached the topic with Dan during a stop for air in one of our Friday night make-out sessions.

"I'm thinking of applying to college," I said.

"Yeah, you should go. You're smart."

"You wouldn't mind?"

"No, of course not. You should go."

"What are you planning to do after high school?"

He paused for a few seconds. "I've thought about the priesthood."

"What?"

"I dunno. I kind of feel like I have a calling."

The room tilted. He'd seemed so intent on intimacy. I suddenly realized that he meant more to me than I did to him. Tears formed, but I willed my eyes dry. Embarrassed by my neediness, I couldn't let him see how this news upset me. It was no surprise, though. I'd been a fool to think a boy could commit to me.

After Dan dropped me off at home, I fed my sorrow with a peanut butter and marshmallow creme sandwich. Convinced that I was destined to be an old maid, I recognized that I couldn't rely on a male taking care of me. I'd start on the applications in the morning.

The descendant of a long line of Irish peasants, I would be the first person in my family to attend college. I'd met few graduates in my life, other than the lay teachers who occasionally popped up at St. Columbkille, such as the Adonis-like English teacher who every girl developed a crush on, the slender young French teacher who reportedly hid hickeys under her turtleneck sweaters, and the football coach who used field plays to demonstrate geometry problems in sophomore math class. I don't know if any of the nuns had higher education credentials—we never thought to question the adequacy of their teacher training. I suspect that many were under-educated and ill-prepared to teach.

The nuns prepped us strenuously for the PSAT and SAT exams, but there was no college guidance counselor, no person I could ask, "I want a good education so I can get a job afterward to support myself because my family will have no place for me after I've finished high school, and I have no money, so I'll need a full scholarship, where should I go?" When I told my homeroom teacher of my aspirations, she replied, "You should become a sister." With difficulty, I refrained from blurting out that there was no way in hell I'd become a nun. I'd had enough living in a religious, female-only household to last a lifetime.

Out of my depth, I didn't know how to find out about colleges, how to determine which ones might accept me, and how to apply. I knew about the famous Boston-area universities, such as Harvard and its annex for women—Radcliffe. But Harvard-Radcliffe was for the Brahmins who lived on Beacon Hill and for the daughters of wealthy families who lived in the towns stretching along Route 30 west of Boston. Our high school library provided some brochures on Massachusetts Catholic schools and universities—Boston College, Holy Cross, Merrimack, Regis, Stonehill, and Emmanuel—which would admit an Irish Catholic working-class girl. But there were no brochures on secular schools. I needed more information and I knew where to get it.

"Where are you going?" my mother asked as I headed for the back door the next morning, purse slung over my shoulder.

"To the downtown library."

"Do you have to do it today? I need you to do laundry."

"I have to look up colleges. The applications are due soon."

"You're quite above yourself, aren't you? I wish I could have gone to college. I was smart enough, you know. I would have made an excellent teacher. My life would have been so much easier."

I don't know why my mother wanted so badly to be a teacher, except that it was one of the few intellectually challenging careers available to women in the 1930s. She didn't particularly like children and would have been as much of a terror as the worst of the nuns. But she had great organizational skills, so perhaps she could have risen into an administrative position. That is, if she didn't marry or have children, both of which were career-enders in those days.

"You'll need to get a scholarship," she said. "With all the money I've spent on you over the years, there's nothing left for me and certainly not for a highfalutin education for you."

"Yes, I know I have to apply for scholarships," I replied as I walked out the door.

A bus and train took me to Copley Square. There, opposite the old Trinity Church, stood the grand dame, the Boston Public Library's main campus. For an avid reader, it was like coming to the mother ship. I'd devoured practically every book in the local Brighton library branch, so for new fixes I had to come downtown. I'd done all of my research for school projects at this library. There was no Internet then to surf for instant answers. Our family was too poor to own an encyclopedia, so I didn't have the luxury of a quick search in a dad's wood-paneled den.

I loved the Boston Library's main reading room with its elaborately carved arch ceilings, the old wooden tables with their green glass-shaded lamps, and the smell of well-worn books. Unfortunately, the higher education reference books were kept down in the stacks, the musty and dingy low-ceilinged floors that lay beneath the main rooms' grandeur. I climbed down several flights of rickety stairs. I hoped I wouldn't be alone, or even worse, with one of the creepy guys that seemed to populate the stack floors. Often, I'd come upon one hiding in a back carrel. I never saw any illicit activities—just a guilty look or a leer.

The stacks held *Barron's Profile of American Colleges* and catalogues for virtually every college and university within a 100-mile radius of Boston. I spent several hours poring over them, learning which schools had scholarships and which had music programs. Pictures of smiling, confident, young women looked up at me from the catalog pages. They were uniformly beautiful and well-dressed with straight teeth. Clearly, I didn't belong. My mother was right. Still, I persisted.

I didn't think about the rarity of someone from my background obtaining a higher education. I didn't realize that only about a third of high school graduates at the time went on to college, or only about three-quarters of kids graduated from high school. In my insular Catholic high school, we had lost a few kids who were slacking; the nuns would not invite them to return if they failed a year. But these were rare cases—even if a student had cognitive deficits, if he or she was willing to try, the nuns would work steadily to get a basic education into the student. No kid left St. Columbkille High School without being able to read and write.

Despite my mother's claim, I didn't think of my college plans as highfalutin but rather as a necessity. At the time, it didn't strike me as ironic that I planned a teaching career, as my mother had fruitlessly hoped for. I thought of music teachers as being fundamentally different from classroom teachers, so of course I wasn't trying to achieve something my mother had not been able to do. I chose music because I felt no passion for the basic high school subjects. If I'd had a crystal ball, I'd have been shocked to see my academic career later move from music to medicine and research.

The catalogs confirmed my suspicions about Harvard-Radcliffe: They awarded few scholarships, which rarely covered the entire tuition cost. They accepted a minuscule proportion of applicants. And, given the list of notable graduates, it was clear that a poor girl whose name began with "Mc" would not be wanted. Of all the Catholic schools, Emmanuel College appeared to have the best music program. It was far from Plymouth where my mother would live after her wedding, and it provided a few full scholarships each year.

By the end of my search, I had a list of four schools with music majors. Boston University, with its elite music department, would be a long shot for me. Brandeis University, also with a notable music program, primarily admitted Jewish students, but I thought it didn't hurt to try. I was pretty confident that Framingham State would accept me; Massachusetts state schools were developed for poor and working-class families who could not afford private institutions, and my grades exceeded the typical state school applicant. Emmanuel would be my one Catholic school application.

Over the ensuing weeks, I struggled to complete the applications. I was a terrible typist. I'd taken to heart my mother's admonition against becoming a secretary and avoided the expected female proficiency in typing. As a result, the forms had quarter-inch thick blobs of correcting fluid. But my greatest challenge was with writing a personal essay. I didn't know what to say about myself. After multiple drafts on onion-skin paper my mother had brought home from her office, I had an essay that pretty much said I wanted to help people.

Years later, after I'd married and had two children, I would write a personal essay for my medical school applications. That time, I wrote about my early life, including meeting my father for the first time at sixteen years of age. This disclosure would get me admitted to one school where my interviewer, a pediatrician, said he was amazed that I could thrive in spite of my meager family beginnings. I wanted to hug him.

I submitted my college applications and waited.

Chapter 16

Extra Virgin

My period was late. I checked my Hallmark pocket calendar for the twentieth time that day and counted back. Yes, it was now mid-February, and it was still forty days since my last period. My mind sped so fast I couldn't finish a thought other than *Oh God, Oh God, Oh God*. A very reassuring thought would have been that pregnancy was unlikely because I was a virgin, but the memory of our one sex-ed class in junior year maimed my usual linear thinking. A scowling nurse in white uniform, shoes, and cap had sat alone on the auditorium stage facing 150 squirming girls. She told us of pregnancies occurring in virgins when the male ejaculate came near the female's vagina.

That class was forty pounds ago, when I had no hope of having a boyfriend, but I'd listened with rapt attention like the good Catholic girl I was. I'd vowed never to get myself into that predicament. Now, three days after turning seventeen, I was in that predicament. I tried praying to the Blessed Mary for redemption in the form of my period showing up. But then I remembered that she got pregnant and gave birth as a virgin, so she might not have too much sympathy for my plight. Just buck up and deal with it, she might say.

At school that day I could barely look at Dan. I didn't want him to see how ugly I was with tear-swollen eyes. He cornered me between classes.

"Anne, what's wrong?"

I couldn't look at him.

"Anne, what is it?" He put his hand on my arm.

"My period's late," I whispered.

"Oh my God. Are you sure?"

I nodded.

"Maybe you're just a little irregular."

"I'm never late."

We stood there without talking for what felt like an hour. It was probably ten seconds.

"We'll get married."

"What?"

"If you're pregnant, we'll get married."

"Are you sure?"

"Of course. I love you. I'll take care of you and the baby."

Shocked that he loved me and wanted to take care of me, relief flooded through me. I wouldn't have to have an illegitimate child, a bastard. Still, I worried that my mother might not agree to the wedding and send me to an insane asylum or home for unwed mothers. Over the next few days, I realized I was terrified of having to marry so young, losing the chance of going to college. I'd remain poor forever. Dan's life would be ruined—he'd have to take a menial job to support us. And all through this, shame engulfed me. This was how God was punishing me for my sexual sins.

To make matters worse, the following weekend my mother and I were going to Bob's house. An hour alone together in the car. She'd smell my fear.

Sure enough, as we pulled off the highway in Plymouth that Saturday morning, my mother's voice sharply cut the tense silence that had occupied the bench seat between us since we'd left Boston an hour earlier. We were the only car in sight; scrub pines stretched endlessly on both sides of the road.

"What's wrong, Anne?"

"Nothing."

Silence again. I pulled my royal blue wool coat tighter and curled my fingers within my gloves. The car's heater wasn't touching the cold.

"Are you late?"

I burst out crying.

"Jesus H. Christ. What the hell have you been doing, Anne?"

We turned onto Boot Pond Road. Blinding light reflected off the pond's surface as we bumped along the dirt road. I looked down at my lap.

"How late are you?"

"Three weeks," I whispered.

"Goddamn it. How can you be so selfish? I told Bob about it. He was very concerned."

At least Bob cares about me, I thought. I wasn't surprised that my mother had suspected I was late. There was no hiding the fact of menstruation in that apartment with one bathroom. My mother might even have recorded my periods along with her own on her day calendar.

My mother went on, "He said he couldn't marry me if I had a pregnant daughter. Now you've ruined my chance for happiness. You should get down on your knees and beg God's forgiveness for what you've done to me."

So much for Bob caring for me. Earlier that morning I couldn't imagine anything worse than being seventeen, single, poor, and pregnant. But that was just a practice run for my desperation now. As we entered Bob's house, the sweet smell of pine wood smoldering in the fireplace brought on a wave of nausea. *Oh, great, I'll improve things by getting sick all over Bob's olive-green shag rug.*

I left soon afterward to pick up Margie in Kingston. My mother had invited her over for the day to help celebrate my birthday. Despite living over a mile from the nearest stop for buses that ran as rarely as in a third-world country, Margie still didn't drive, although she pretended to be self-sufficient.

Some birthday celebration this weekend was turning out to be. As I bounced and swerved my mother's blue Chevy Nova down Bob's rutted dirt road, radio blasting The Beatles' "All You Need Is Love," I had the urge to cut the wheel hard and spin myself into one of the ponds I was driving past. With my luck I'd get stuck in a snow bank and then have to answer to my mother for ruining her car as well as her chances for happiness. Nope, not worth it. I was not much of a suicide risk.

Over a lunch of lasagna and salad, only Bob and Margie spoke. My mother sat like stone. I picked at my food, staring at the red-streaked noodles with their brown lumps of meat and mushrooms and green specks of oregano. Margie looked nervously back and forth between my mother and me. She tried to break the tension by complimenting my mother on the lunch. My mother grunted.

Finally I could stand the pressure no longer, stood up, and walked the few steps into the house's one bathroom, where I almost fainted when I saw blood on my underpants. For once I didn't despair over the stain that had seeped through to my wool slacks and would require the expense of dry cleaning. Oh, God, that beautiful, beautiful red. It was always my favorite color. And now it signaled reprieve like a last-minute Supreme Court stay of execution. I wouldn't have to have the shotgun wedding Dan had suggested. I could still become a music teacher. And my mother would not be so angry.

I emerged from the bathroom smiling. My mother stared at my face for a full minute then let out a big breath. She looked meaningfully at Bob, whose sole focus was on his third helping of lasagna.

"You're a great cook, Mary Helen," he said. They clearly weren't having a Vulcan mind meld.

The three adults sang a wobbly Happy Birthday to me over the chocolate layer cake Margie made, which smelled of her cigarettes. I had a strange moment of genuine joy. Life had so many possibilities now and so much to be thankful for. My mother, aunt, and Bob were together in the same room and no one was fighting. My mother even smiled—there was no sign of her earlier rage. I wasn't even disappointed by the small number of presents they gave me—a white cotton turtleneck from Margie and a navy blue cardigan from my mother and Bob.

Later, when no one was within earshot, I told my mother I'd gotten my period.

"I figured," she said. Relieved, I thought the event was really over. It wasn't. The next evening, as we drove home to Boston, my mother said, "You should be ashamed of yourself for what you've been doing."

I said nothing. I was ashamed.

"You must really hate me to do this to me," she said.

"Do what to you?"

"Acting like a pig with that boy."

Again I said nothing. The pig comment was kind of a conversation stopper.

"As I told you earlier, Bob is very concerned about keeping up his reputation here on the pond. If you get pregnant, he won't marry me.

"You're not going to see Dan anymore," she continued.

She finally found a weapon that hurt me more than her hand and her threats to send me away. I wanted to clutch my belly to stem the blood her blade had drawn.

"But I love him."

"That's just too bad. You've proven that you can't control yourself."

"But I'm still a virgin," I said.

This time she was quiet.

"And he says he loves me, too."

"When a boy loves you, it's even harder for him to control himself."

I had no idea what she meant by this. It didn't seem like the right time for a conversation about men in love. I felt like I'd been handed a jail sentence for the next six months until I left home for good. It was my mother's Irish-Catholic version of birth control.

We didn't speak again that evening. My mother broke the quiet the next morning before I left for school.

"Tell Dan I want to talk to him."

"What about?"

"Just tell him to call me."

Later that day when I told Dan my mother forbade me from dating him, he said he had to see me, and we'd have to find a way.

"Why can't we still go to your place after school?" he asked. With his big brown eyes, he looked like a puppy asking for a belly rub. "Your mother's never come home when we've done it before."

"She says she wants to talk with you."

"With me?"

"Yes, with you. Without me."

"What about?"

"I don't know. She wouldn't tell me. She says you should call her."

Dan did call her, and they arranged a meeting at our flat on a night I was at choir practice. I arrived home at 8:30 P.M. He was already gone.

"Did Dan come over?" I asked my mother. She was sitting at our Colonial-style maple wood kitchen table, newspaper in front of her like a shield.

"Yes."

"What did you talk about?"

"None of your business."

I fumed inwardly at her refusal to tell me but was not at all surprised. No problem, I figured. Dan would tell me. Anyway, I wanted to hear his version of the encounter.

I cornered him at school between classes. Green uniforms and woolen sports jackets swarmed around us as students rushed between classes. The hallway smelled of teenagers: cheap cologne, hairspray, dried sweat, and hormones. The wooden railing I leaned against was worn smooth from 100 years of students' clutches.

"What did you and my mother talk about last night?" I asked, wanting and not wanting to know the answer.

"She made me promise not to tell you."

"So what? You can't keep secrets from me."

He shook his head. "I can't tell you."

I struggled to control the fury that threatened to explode out of me. These two people, so critical in my life, colluded against me, treating me like the child that I had never fully been. Even the President's national security team had more leaks than these two were giving me. Did they make a pact to keep this conversation secret to their graves? Still, I subdued my rage because what man would ever stay with an angry woman? My mother's anger had driven my father away, so the same thing could happen to me.

Two forces pressed on me now. On one side, my mother was firm. I couldn't date Dan at all, period. She wouldn't discuss it with me. If she noticed my red-rimmed eyes, she didn't let on. On the other front, Dan pleaded with me to sneak around. I faced a choice of dangers. There was the threat of my mother sending me away (parents could commit teens to asylums in those days, and she hadn't balked at institutionalizing me before). The other danger was that Dan would leave me. He didn't say that he would do this, but I knew that men leave women. I skated on thin ice in keeping this boyfriend. If I couldn't keep him satisfied, what incentive would he have to stay with me instead of going with one of the pretty, popular girls?

I chose Dan. He professed to love me, and hearing those words was like a drug I couldn't get enough of. So I entered into a clandestine life, feeling like a Cold War spy. I quit my Dunkin' Donuts job and took a lower-paying grocery cashier job. The grocery job had later shifts and was just a few blocks from my house, so I could be available for after-school trysts.

Dan and I developed an afternoon schedule. We walked to my house together. He waited outside while I went in to make sure the coast was clear. Inside the apartment, I made my usual rounds, looking in all the rooms, but this time the bogeyman was my mother. I didn't have to check the closets and under the beds because I knew Dan would protect me from whatever lurked there. By now it was three o'clock. I let Dan in, and he pulled me into my bedroom. There, he undressed me and went as far as I let him. I stayed firm about remaining a virgin, not because of religion, but because pregnancy scared the bejesus out of me. Boston in 1970 was no place for a seventeen-year-old girl to obtain birth control. And even if I'd been willing to use condoms (that same scowling nurse had told us condoms occasionally break, which I interpreted to mean they always break), very few pharmacists would sell them to teenage boys.

At 3:30 P.M., my mother would call. The irony of talking half naked on the hallway phone that sat next to the Infant of Prague statue of Jesus was lost on me. I'd play with the lace around the Infant's cape while we talked. I provided one-word answers to her series of questions about homework and work, in an attempt to get off the line quickly while not arousing her suspicions. I'd return to my mod blue and white room with Dan stretched out on the twin bed that was too small for him.

Soon, the shame of what I was doing consumed me. I was evil through and through. We Irish-Catholic kids were clear on sex—anything beyond kissing was a mortal sin in our eyes, even if not in official Church dogma. I was a brazen sinner. I should have rubbed ashes all over my body, beat myself with the string of my book bag, and lain prostrate in front of St. Columbkille's door.

I didn't need the Church to make me feel shame. There had been so much during my life to feed my own disgrace: fat, no father, no sisters or brothers, shy, awkward, institutionalized, and frequently beaten. Now I had done shameful things of my own volition. On top of the immoral acts I was committing with my boyfriend was the terrible offense of disobeying my mother. The Church may not have classified disobeying a direct parental order as a mortal sin, but my mother did. And so I did.

I was headed straight to hell. To make matters worse, I couldn't bring myself to come clean to the priest at my regular Saturday confession. I could barely think about the unspeakable, dirty things I was doing with Dan. I certainly couldn't tell anyone about it, especially not a priest, the representative of God on Earth. What if the Father wanted details? Would I have to admit what I did for Dan at his urging, and what I let him do to me? I didn't even know the terminology for these terrible acts.

I was sure that if I did confess my sins, the priest would give me a penance so severe my knees would bleed from the hours of prayers at the altar. Then everyone would know what a horrible person I was. So I never confessed. I stopped going to communion because that was only allowed if you were in a state of grace, attained by never sinning at all or by going to confession. To take communion otherwise would add even more sins. With all my transgressions piling up on me like a homeless person's wardrobe, I was in a constant state of disgrace.

I still attended Mass each week to avoid adding the extra crime of missing Mass. I'd sit in the back of the Church with the other sinners who avoided communion. A few times I went to Mass with Dan, who surprised me by trotting up to the altar to take communion. He must have been comfortable in the confessional. Luckily, my mother was usually in Plymouth on the weekends, so she didn't see my communion avoidance.

One afternoon, after Dan had been satisfied, we lay on my twin bed staring up at the blue painted trim around my ceiling. I broached the subject.

"Don't you feel guilty about what we're doing?"

He thought for a minute, then said, "In God's eyes we're already married. So we're not sinning."

"You want to marry me?"

"Of course. I love you. You love me. We belong together."

I fell in love again every time he said he loved me, and now here was the blue ribbon prize. It wasn't a traditional proposal, more like a statement of fact. There was no bending of the knee, no little diamond he'd saved up for, no "Anne, will you do me the honor of marrying me?" But I didn't care. Like Maria in *West Side Story*, I was loved by a wonderful boy. This made all the sins, guilt, and threat of mother's ire worthwhile. I'd walk over coals for this boy.

We made vague plans. He agreed with my going to college but didn't want me to move away. He would also attend a local school. In four years, we'd marry and start a family. We'd have at least eight kids. He'd be head of the household, of course. I'd be a housewife.

While I wanted a large family, these plans irritated the back of my brain like a gnat I couldn't swat away. I pictured myself fat and soft from a dozen pregnancies, living with Dan and our brood of skinny, freckled kids in one of the Boston Projects built for poor, oversized Catholic families. I'd have a vacuous smile on my face for Dan when he arrived home. Kids would be hanging from the ceiling and hiding in closets and under beds. I'd sit with a baby on my lap and a toddler at my swollen feet, slowly moving laundry from one pile to another. I'd feed the kids oatmeal for dinner, same as breakfast and lunch. But I'd have my man, I'd be happy, and when he wanted loving, I'd oblige without birth control because we were good Catholics.

I didn't dare disagree openly with Dan's plans. I didn't want to lose this one person who loved me enough to say it. I couldn't believe it most of the time, but even if it was a charade, it was something to be thankful for. I'd finally obtained what I'd been searching for all my life. That meant I must be lovable. I was so grateful that Dan took a chance on me, this Nerd Queen. He could have listened to the other kids' opinion of the girl who had so recently been fat, who was so awkward, especially with boys. But instead, he reached out and in doing so pulled me out of a self-pitying, miserable abyss.

At the same time, I was sure that I'd do something wrong or stupid to make him lose interest in me. I acquiesced to all sexual moves (except the virginity thing), even though I was very uncomfortable with moving so fast. In addition, none of the enjoyment was for me, but Dan solemnly informed me that the pleasure for the girl was in pleasing the boy. I never disagreed with him, no arguments. I paid careful attention to my appearance, including daily makeup and hair washing, and I starved myself even thinner after he mentioned that his previous girlfriend had a better figure. I didn't flirt with other boys even if I had known how to flirt. My new status as Dan's girlfriend elevated me to someone worth looking at, and a few boys approached me, but I never accepted any date offers.

The romance caused periods of anxiety to outright panic. They say that inside every fat woman is a thin woman. I was just the opposite—inside the new Thin Anne was the old Big Fat Anne screaming for food. I worried that the old Anne would burst loose from her cage and eat everything in sight; she'd not only gain weight back but she'd rocket straight into morbid obesity.

Through all this, I worried relentlessly that my mother would find out about my sneaking around with Dan and do something drastic. She could kick me out of the house, and I had no other place to live.

"Why won't you go all the way with me?" Dan asked. He was walking me to the supermarket, where my cashier shift started in fifteen minutes. I worried I'd be late. It was sunny and cold, early March, a week before St. Patrick's Day.

"It's too dangerous," I said. "I don't want to get pregnant. I told you this already."

"If you really loved me, you'd show me," he said. My stomach clenched. *Glamour* said this is what boys say to girls to pressure them into sex, and you should stand firm in your resolve. But the magazine didn't tell me how to keep a boy interested in *me* without giving in to his demands.

We'd reached the end of Brooks Street. Close to the store, we passed the cute Boston Latin boy who always flirted with me on our shifts.

"Hi," said the boy.

"Hi," I said.

"Who's that?" asked Dan after we were barely out of earshot.

"That's one of the baggers," I said.

"Why did you say 'hi' to him?"

"Because he said 'hi' to me."

"I don't want you talking to him."

"Why?"

"Because you're my girl."

"I've gotta go in. See you tomorrow."

Dan grabbed me. "Promise me you won't talk to him."

"Okay, I won't talk to him." I agreed with this silly request so I could begin my shift on time. If I was late, the manager could easily find other teenagers eager to work. I couldn't afford to lose this job.

After work I called Margie to ask if she'd like me to visit. Her neighbors had reported to my mother that Margie had grown very thin, and I worried that she was starving herself. I planned to take her food shopping and stock up her larder. My concern about Margie's weight loss was ironic, given that I was always on a diet, always hoping to see just one less pound on the dial of my mother's bathroom scale. My mother said Margie was playing martyr with her claim of having no way to buy groceries. I wasn't so sure. I thought Margie couldn't take care of herself. So I wanted to help her, even if it only meant driving her to the store.

"Hello, my Anna Banana," she said when she heard my voice. I loved it when she called me this.

"Hi, Margie," I said. "How are you doing?"

"Oh, I'm so sick of work," she said. "The walk to and from the Boston bus is exhausting. And it's pitch-black when I go in the morning and when I come home. I fell the other night, caught my heel in a hole."

I wanted to ask her why didn't she move back to Boston, or learn to drive a car, or just quit her job. But any time I asked these things, she listed off reasons why she had to keep doing things the same, difficult way.

"I thought I might come down to Plymouth next weekend," I said. "Could I stop over and visit you? I could take you grocery shopping. And we could have lunch."

"Oh that would be wonderful, Anne. Thank you so much. I could really stock up. I'll have to make some Irish bread for us."

My heart sped up; I loved her soda bread, chock full of raisins and currents, but worried about the calories. Still, I didn't want to discourage her from eating. I made a mental note to buy a St. Patrick's Day card for her.

"Okay, I'll call you when we get to Plymouth."

"Who's the boy who visits you after school?" she asked.

My heart stopped and started a few times.

"There's no boy visiting me," I lied. *Dear God help me,* I thought.

"Oh, a friend of mine said she'd seen a boy going into the apartment with you."

"No, there's no boy."

"Oh, okay."

"See you Saturday," I said.

"Bye," she said. "I love you."

"Love you, too."

I'm finished. Some nosy neighbor must have told Margie about the trysts with Dan. It was especially annoying since I didn't know any of the neighbors. Some biddy was prying into my life by watching what I did and reporting it back to Margie. But whoever it was didn't have the decency to be a real neighbor to us. No "hello how are you," no coming to the door with a pie, no invitations to coffee. I was petrified that Margie would tell my mother, or the snooping neighbor would tell my mother. Either way, I was screwed. My mother would first scream, then hit, then kick me out of the house.

The next day, I told Dan what Margie had said.

"Don't worry about it," he said.

"What do you mean, don't worry? My mother will kill me if she finds out."

"I thought you said your mother and Margie weren't speaking?"

"They're starting to talk to each other."

"Don't worry, you can just deny it like you did with Margie."

"I don't think you should come to my house anymore."

"So your mother's more important to you than I am? I thought you loved me."

"I do love you."

We started making out.

"Let's just do it," Dan said.

"No, not until we're married."

"Please, I just can't wait."

"No, I might get pregnant."

"Then we'd get married."

"We can't afford a baby now."

"I need you to prove that you love me."

Lately, Dan turned on this pressure every time we were together. Today, however, something was different. Today, I really worried that he'd leave me. Still, my fear of getting pregnant far outweighed worry of his abandonment.

Chapter 17

Meatloaf

"I have to tell you something," Dan said. He took a big breath. We lay entwined on my narrow bed. I'd been enjoying the smell of his sweat and the broad expanse of his chest, which was as hairless as mine.

"What?"

His long pause allowed my mind to race through several scenarios. Had he decided to become a priest? If so, I'd lose my chance to marry and I would no longer have a boyfriend. Then, there'd be the huge "ick" factor of having been intimate with a priest. *Oh, great, my first kiss was with a raging maniac, and now I've been sinning with a boy destined for the clergy.* Or, maybe it's not that at all. Oh no—could he have been drafted for Vietnam? Or, had he joined the crazies and decided to enlist?

"I went out with Kris Heidelberg." His large brown eyes were already pleading.

The sweat on his upper lip was new.

The room swayed as this news hit me. Dan and I had an exclusive relationship, or so I thought. I also thought his insistence that I not date anyone else, not even talk to other boys, was proof of his commitment. Not that there was much chance of my cheating—I was still a shy little thing and would never initiate a flirtation.

The exotic Kris Heidelberg had joined our high school in our junior year. She dealt with difficult shunning from the girls by dating, and reportedly sleeping with, many of the boys. I had no idea if the latter was true—it could well have been a vicious rumor started by girls who were jealous of this girl's obvious appeal to their boyfriends. Still, I thought if he went out with her, it wouldn't have been just for burgers and fries.

"What do you mean you went out with her?"

"I took her out."

"Like on a date?"

He nodded.

"What did you do with her?"

He shook his head and looked away. If his first admission was like a dagger piercing my heart, his unwillingness to be specific was the knife slicing up all four of its chambers. I imagined the worst.

"How many times did you go out with her?" My voice was stronger now.

"A few times."

"How could you do this to me? I thought we were getting married."

"We are getting married." He had the audacity to scowl at me.

"I'm not marrying you if you're going to cheat on me."

"We are getting married." He paused, then continued, "My dates with her were just friendship. They didn't mean anything. You're the one I love."

"Did you go all the way with her?"

He wouldn't look at me. This put me into a state of shock. While popular culture didn't put much emphasis on a boy being a virgin at marriage, I still hoped the complete lovemaking experience would be something he and I could share when the time was right. That wouldn't happen now.

We went back and forth like this for several minutes. He never apologized and didn't seem to understand why I said we couldn't get married now. Finally I said it was time for me to go to work. I got dressed and told him he had to leave. I turned my head away when he tried to kiss me. He grabbed my shoulders. I stiffened in his embrace.

"Tell me we are getting married."

"Okay," I said, but only to end the conversation. I knew our relationship was over.

Over the ensuing hours, I wavered about my decision to end it with Dan. I had hit the jackpot, undeservedly in my mind, in landing this very nice, popular boy. But he'd shown that he could not, or would not, stay true to me. He must have gone from our lovemaking right to a date with her, I realized. It was too reminiscent of my parents' marriage. My father's cheating played a large part in my parents' break-up and my subsequent life without a father. And with Dan's actions, I'd been abandoned again.

I couldn't tell my mother about my change of heart—I wasn't supposed to even be seeing Dan. I couldn't tell Margie—she couldn't understand why I wanted anything to do with a boy, let alone marry early. And if she learned about the things I'd done with Dan, her head would spin around like a possessed soul in need of an exorcist.

I decided to keep mum about my decision to break up with Dan. I'd ride out the rest of the school year with my elevated status of girl with a steady boyfriend. I'd act proud to be his date at the Senior Prom in two weeks. (Besides, I'd already spent hours making my pink tulle prom dress with the empire waist, and I wouldn't be able to get another date this late.) But there would be no more afternoon trysts at my flat. It was time to protect myself.

I finally realized I'd allowed this relationship to progress too quickly. In the space of six months, I'd bypassed all the incremental steps in learning how to date and plunged right into an everlasting love commitment. My early desires to do something on dates other than make out resurfaced. I'd never gone to a movie with a boy and never had a real dinner date. I didn't know how to talk with a boy, how to get to know him, or how to share my own thoughts and feelings. I'd been flattered by other boys' attention—like the grocery store bagger who went to the competitive Boston Latin high school and was headed for the Ivy League. He flirted with me nonstop and made it plain that if I broke up with Dan he'd be there for me. Then there were the boys at my high school who had taken a second look at the old fatso Anne, now that she was thin and dated a popular boy. I realized that I was no longer desperate to hold onto Dan. I'd evolved.

There was no denying that the change was big. Seemingly in one day I went from doing whatever I could to please this boy, trying to keep his love, to realizing that he wasn't the one for me. He was a very nice boy, but I deserved someone who would not cheat on me. He was not my future.

The one-hour drive to Plymouth that night seemed interminable. My mother ranted on about the sad state of her finances.

"I'm afraid Bob won't want to marry me," she said.

"Why not?" I asked.

"Because I owe so much money. The biggest problem is the loan I took out for your new piano last year. That on top of the other bills each month, I can't cover them."

An immediate pang of guilt hit me—once again I was the cause of my mother's troubles. But then I remembered the money she'd spent having her two diamond rings combined into one cocktail ring, the new car she bought every three years, and the cost of gas driving to and from Plymouth to see Bob. I was just one piece of her misery.

"Can't you ask Margie for help?" My mother and she had reconciled slowly over the past few months. They would never live together again, but they were at least speaking.

"I don't dare ask Margie. That might put her into a snit again. She'll just say that I have a man now to take care of me—as if that were possible. Bob doesn't have a pot to piss in other than that shack he calls a house, that and his old car. At least he doesn't have debts, or I don't think he does. I'll have to see if I can extend my credit at the bank. After you graduate next month, and I move in with Bob, I'll be able to pay off the loans pretty quickly."

I didn't know the magnitude of her income versus expenses. She'd never shared the specifics with me, but I knew that she worried constantly about money. I couldn't help her. I paid for my own clothes, music lessons, sundries, and such, out of my part-time wages. I ate very little at home. But I didn't make enough money to contribute to the rent or utilities. I thought she must be terrified of being evicted from our apartment or having the lights or phone turned off, but her fear focused on Bob.

"Anne, you can't say anything to Bob about these bills or the loans. I can't risk losing him. I'd have no one then."

I didn't tell her she'd always have me because it wouldn't be true. I didn't want to be the one she could depend on. I just wanted to take care of myself.

While my mother was desperate to keep her man, there were many strings attached to his affection. One of the conditions was that my mother had to keep me in line. After they married and lived in his house, I would be a temporary, and apparently annoying, visitor. Even my use of water created an issue.

"Bob says you need to wash in the pond," my mother said Saturday morning.

"What?"

"He said you use too much water in the shower. It's backing up his septic system."

I stared at her, my breath gone. To not be able to wash, especially my hair, was unimaginable. I wouldn't be able to face the world with oily, stringy hair. What was next? Would they tell me I was breathing too much air? Finally, some words fell out of my mouth.

"Washing in the pond is disgusting."

"No it's not, Anne. Bob does it all the time."

"Do you do it?"

"No, my feet hurt me too much to walk barefoot on the sand. You know that."

"So you get to take showers."

"I can't help it. Plus I don't wash my hair in the shower." This was true. My mother had her hair styled each week at a beauty salon. She didn't need to wash her hair every day.

"But it's freezing out there."

"It's supposed to warm up to the sixties today. Once the sun is out on the pond you'll be fine."

The concept of bathing in a pond the size of a lake, in full view of other people and surrounded by frogs, fish, and vegetation, was utterly foreign to me. I'd never been camping, and anyway, the good nuns had spent twelve years carefully indoctrinating me not to bare all in public. I was sure this would be one of those occasions of sin.

Swimming was banned in Great South, the reservoir pond behind Bob's house. Therefore our baths had to be taken in Boot Pond, which unfortunately had more houses on it and a larger audience. Later that morning, I watched Bob as he headed out the door clad in a faded green plaid swim suit with a towel slung over his shoulder and a bar of Ivory soap clutched in his hand. Thin from a three-year stint as a bachelor, he nonetheless had pale flab hanging over the top of his trunks.

With a spring in his step, he walked the twenty paces to Boot Pond, placed his dingy, frayed towel on a stone wall, and strode into the pond. I expected him to drop his trunks at any minute and tensed to avert my eyes if I saw his hands go anywhere near his waist. Bob quickly soaped his head, trunk, and extremities. Oh, so that's how you deal with the private parts, I realized—you don't. Then he dunked completely underwater and came up shaking his head like a dog. As he emerged, he called hello to a neighbor sitting on her dock. She looked up only to smile and nod, then went back to her paperback novel.

I was greatly relieved for two reasons: First, the pond baths did not involve getting naked in public. Second, the neighbors treated this as a normal occurrence.

My mother and Bob gave me big smiles when they saw me heading off to my pond baptism. Since I hadn't packed beachwear, I had to use an old bathing suit left from when Bob's daughter was a teenager. It was snug enough to make breathing a challenge. Feeling very poor white trash—oh wait, I was poor white trash—I walked to the water's edge, clutching my bar of soap and shampoo. Although I'd swum in Boot Pond the previous summer, I'd never thought of it as a bathtub.

As I waded into the cold water through pond lilies and swarms of little black fish, I silently cursed Bob and his shitty septic system. Gradually I became used to the temperature, or maybe I was just numb. I noticed how soft and silky the water felt, almost like a lotion. The short walk back to the house was painful; the air hitting my wet skin was not as warm as my mother had promised.

Bob's septic tank also didn't take kindly to any kind of grease, so we had to wipe all oil residues from the dishes and toss the dirty dishwater out the kitchen door instead of letting it go down the sink. In my opinion, if God wanted dirty water to be tossed out a door, He wouldn't have invented drains. I wondered if we'd have to throw the toilet contents out the back door.

Later that afternoon, I sat at Bob's kitchen table, savoring the spectacular view of Great South. Several delicate pine trees complemented the view. Beyond a large sandy beach, Great South sat low and wide, stretching farther than I could see to the left or right.

Across the pond were small hills, part of Plymouth's Miles Standish Reservation. A bald eagle soared overhead, looking for field mice to sustain him on his migration north.

As I sat there, I was feeling very proud of my diet control that day, having had only cucumber and lettuce for lunch. Bent over the sink, Bob peeled potatoes. The earthy smell of the potatoes was cut with the stink of sulfur whenever he ran more tap water. My mother opened the olive-green refrigerator and started talking to me from behind its door.

"What are you doing?" she asked. The irritation in her voice was palpable. I wondered what had set her off this time.

"Nothing," I replied.

"Supper will be at six. I need you to make a salad and set the table."

"What's for supper?" I asked.

"Meatloaf."

I loved my mother's meatloaf. It was the ultimate comfort food. Tender and soft, almost as easy to chew as a baby's first cereal. Savory and a little sweet at the same time. Just the right amount of spice and salt to tickle the tongue. Grease with its sensual massage to the palate. But then, my internal calorie counter went into hyperdrive. I knew the ingredients to my mother's meatloaf by heart: full-fat hamburger, Quaker oats, Campbell's cream of mushroom soup, onions, and several spices. Each one-inch slice would hold about 300 calories. I'd probably sneak several more tiny pieces that would easily add up to another 300 calories. It was too dangerous to my diet.

"I don't want any," I said as I stood up, ready to leave the room. I may have put my ski-slope nose in the air.

With one step, my mother crossed the few feet between the refrigerator and me, holding the one-pound package of raw hamburger, uncovered, in her right hand. As if in slow motion, I saw it coming toward my face in a perfect arc before it made contact with the left side of my head. The raw meat exploded into hundreds of smaller globs. It dropped from my face and my hair and fell onto the floor.

I stood frozen, horrified, as questions formed. If I moved would she hit me again? Was I supposed to clean it up? My head hurt—was it injured? Had the package cut me? Was I supposed to say, "Oh my mistake, I really do want meatloaf after all?"

At the far side of the kitchen, Bob's open mouth told me he'd seen the hamburger attack. This made it even worse—the shame of having a witness.

We three froze in place. I was the first to thaw.

"Fuck you," I screamed.

I walked to the bathroom where I took a very long and hot shower. I washed the hamburger and grease off my face, neck, and hair. I scrubbed until my skin was as red and raw as the hamburger. I watched as the chunks of meat fell down the drain. The hot water cleared my vision as well as my thinking. I washed away the victim Anne, the one who allowed this woman to treat me like I was something evil in need of punishment, and the inner, strong Anne emerged. I would no longer tolerate this woman's treatment or hope for her love or support. She was incapable of loving me.

I wanted to hurt her, badly. I wanted to run out to the kitchen and start punching her. I imagined my fist hitting her flab like beating bread dough into submission. I wanted to grab a sharp knife and slash her, beginning with her ugly face and progress to her hands and arms that had hurt me so much over my lifetime. Then I'd plunge the knife into her heart, over and over, to be sure I'd hit the mark in her organ that had never given me the warmth that a mother's heart is supposed to give. But as quickly as these thoughts arose, I squelched them. I was not a violent person and would not allow myself to become like my mother, who solved her problems by lashing out, physically and verbally. Now, on the cusp of adulthood, I would take care of myself but not with my mother's weapons.

I drained the hot water heater completely. Hoping I'd overflowed their goddamn septic tank, I went upstairs and got dressed. I packed my things, dragged my suitcase down the narrow stairs, and walked outside. I didn't bother to look into the kitchen to see if my mother or Bob realized I was leaving. I caught a ride to town with a neighbor and took the bus back to Boston.

CHAPTER 18

Bearing Fruit

That night I entered a dark apartment, which had the closed-in feeling of a hot day with no air circulating. I walked through the apartment, opening windows and turning on lights in every room. Good—no bogeymen hiding. Ordinarily I would have been freaked out about coming home late to an unlit, empty flat. The landlord, in perpetual beer-induced anesthesia, would not hear if someone broke in or attacked me. Tonight, however, I was still so pumped up with anger that if someone came after me they'd be the victim instead of me.

I then attended to the mail I'd stepped on inside the front door. There were three large envelopes, several bills, and a couple of circulars. It was unusual for us to receive large envelopes. All three were manila and addressed to me. I tore them open. The first two—from Framingham State College and Boston University—were acceptances. Their cover letters said I could qualify for student loans. I breathed a sigh of relief. I could go to college! But mixed with the relief was the realization that I could never afford the Boston University tuition, and even the state school's costs would be a stretch. Then I opened the third envelope, which was from Emmanuel College. My pulse sped up; my mouth gaped open. Emmanuel offered me a full scholarship—all tuition, fees, room, and board paid. I sat down, shaking. Someone, some people, wanted me enough to pay me to come. I'd have a home.

The Bible says that Emmanuel means "God is with us." I remembered the Christmas hymn that began, "Oh, come, oh, come, Emmanuel, and ransom captive Israel." As in the hymn, Emmanuel would be my salvation. It would free me from captivity. Emmanuel College promised to provide shelter and sustenance. It would give me the skills and credentials to become an independent, self-sufficient, professional woman. It would help me save myself.

With still-shaking hands, I spread out the contents of the envelope. I started on the acceptance form right away. When I checked the box beside "I accept your offer," the words on the page began to swim. That's when I realized I was crying. I stood up, walked into the bathroom, and returned with a box of tissues.

Relief flooded through me when I saw that no parental signature was required since I would not have to pay any costs upfront. Given the chance, my mother would derail my plans just for spite. Where the questionnaire asked for emergency contact, I listed Margie's name and number.

A piece of yellow paper asked questions about housing. *Do I need to live in the student dormitory?* Oh, if only they knew. I checked "yes," since there was no box to indicate I'd be homeless without college housing. *Diet restrictions?* None, unless you count my near-starvation diet to stay thin for my boyfriend or future boyfriends. *Did I have any physical infirmities?* None. My infirmities were all psychological. The medical history questionnaire was robin-egg-blue. I checked "yes" for all of the childhood infectious diseases. It didn't ask about whether I'd ever had failure to thrive brought on by lack of loving. And there were no questions on anorexia nervosa, binge eating, or queries about domestic violence.

Emmanuel College's similarity to Rosary Academy was lost on my seventeen-year-old brain that didn't appreciate irony. Both were Catholic educational institutions. Both had female-only, communal bathrooms, and cafeteria food. Each was run by nuns in black habits and had ubiquitous icons of Jesus and Mary and the Crucifix. I'd not considered the parallels as I made my college applications, and I didn't think about them that night. I could only see the sanctuary in Emmanuel—this institution would be my salvation.

I filled out the forms, making sure I'd answered every question. I lined up all the completed pages, folded and creased them with just the right amount of pressure, and inserted them into the return envelope. "No postage needed," the envelope said, which provided some relief because I wasn't sure how to determine the mailing costs. I licked the flap slowly and pressed the edges together. Grabbing only my house keys, I dashed out of the house to the corner mailbox. With a big intake of breath, I lifted the heavy metal hinge and inserted the envelope. The sound of metal slapping metal reverberated through the quiet street like a clap of thunder. I'd slammed the door to my old life and opened the door to my new life.

CHAPTER 19

Full

While I took monumental steps as a teenager that helped me recover from my addictive relationship with food, the path to my life's work was circuitous and long. I didn't have a plan to focus on diet or obesity. I wasn't a fitness freak. I didn't even study nutrition in college, and there was no specialty in obesity medicine when I did my medical residency. But I was in training for this career my entire life, and it led me to where I am today—a medical doctor who leads studies on nutrition, physical activity, and health.

I was seventeen years old when I left home, became responsible for my own finances, and freed myself from the control of my birth family. I would still interact with my mother and aunt, but I kept them at arm's length—literally and figuratively.

My mother never hit me again. I think that was in part because of the distance I kept and in part because she realized she could lose me forever. Maybe she felt some shame. Bob, now her husband, had witnessed an especially egregious strike; maybe he said something to her about it.

I wish I could say that college was a breeze for me and once out on my own, away from my mother, everything was miraculously okay. But my road was bumpy in the 1970s, and the social upheavals of the time caught me as they rolled along. While Emmanuel College was an insular all-girls Catholic institution, revolutionary ideas drifted onto our campus like fog rolling in off the Atlantic coast. Boston, with over fifty colleges and universities, was a hotbed of student protests. We were anti-war, anti-establishment, and we didn't trust anyone over thirty years of age.

I majored in music—piano was my instrument—but hated practicing four floors up in a turret of the music department while the social revolution was happening at ground level. I hung out with other radicals, discussed Vietnam as if I knew what was really going on, went to demonstrations, and shouted, "Fuck you, Agnew," outside a Boston hotel. My piano teacher would sadly shake his head at my weekly lessons. My music theory teacher couldn't understand why I had trouble discerning notes in his 8:00 A.M. Monday class. Didn't he understand that ears needed some recovery time after being blasted with rock-and-roll at 100 decibels in a bar until 2:00 A.M. the previous night? I suspect the music department arranged this class at that unfortunate time to weed out those who were not serious about a career in music.

I passed my classes that year but switched to major in sociology. I was interested in people, groups, family, and culture. A lost young woman, I was trying to understand my own tribe. I was a big hit with a sociology professor after he read my essay on growing up with a single mother and spinster aunt in an Irish-American Catholic home. He rubbed his hands together with glee as he told me how typical that was in Irish families—the father leaves the home, the children are raised by the poor, downtrodden mother, and often an unmarried relative moves in to help. I didn't tell him about the institutions my mother had sent me to, thinking that might make him too deliriously happy.

I didn't blend well with most of my classmates, girls from middle- and upper-class, intact, Catholic families, who had goals to be engaged by junior year to a stockbroker, doctor, or lawyer, married immediately after graduation, and settled in a house with a couple of children by the five-year reunion. My goals were to find the money to pay for incidentals such as books, food, Ripple wine, and upkeep of my 1963 navy blue Ford Galaxie. I went back to waitressing at Dunkin' Donuts in order to make a salary and made liberal use of the free doughnut policy to supplement the inedible cafeteria meals in the dining hall. After about six months, one of the husband-seeking girls told me I looked like I'd gained weight. I couldn't think of a quick retort, so I stupidly agreed with her. I quit the doughnut job, admitting that I couldn't surround myself with what we in obesity research call *trigger foods*—foods that a person with eating issues can't avoid binging on.

I don't recall a single mixer or party held at Emmanuel; we lived our social lives off campus. On one freezing, soggy night in March 1972, two friends and I wandered over to Cambridge to hear an Irish folk singing group. One of us—the least Irish—said he knew the place, which turned out to be an old brick Harvard dormitory that fronted the Charles River. Realizing we were not in a concert venue, we sat in the foyer to rethink our evening's entertainment.

As we pondered our dilemma, students stumbled down from an upper floor. "Man, what a party," one said. We sent the least Irish guy up to check it out. A half-hour later, when he had failed to return, the two of us crept upstairs. On the fifth floor, we found an open door that led to a small apartment with a smattering of students, mostly male. Each clutched a can of beer with "Maximus Super" printed in a circle around a lion holding a sheaf of malt. Several people wore T-shirts with the same logo. Rock music played, not very loudly. So we wandered in, surprised that no one took notice of us.

Finally, a tall, skinny guy with long, bushy brown hair and John Lennon glasses came over to talk to me; his name was Martin. He was wearing one of the Maximus Super T-shirts and turned out to be host of the party. I liked that Martin was smart, funny, and not a jock. I liked that he wasn't Irish Catholic and drank a little but not very much. Later, I would get a lot of vicarious pleasure watching him pack away eight hamburgers at one sitting without feeling full and without gaining weight. Mostly I liked that he liked me.

Emmanuel College turned out to be less salvation and more damnation. The Catholic tradition with nuns patrolling the dormitory, required religion classes, and ban against men on campus didn't fit in with the hippie-revolutionary-peace-and-love lifestyle I came to desire. Music at the time urged my generation in a different direction: Marvin Gaye challenged us to examine what was going on in our lives, Joni Mitchell pointed to the environmental disasters, and Helen Reddy wanted us to be strong women. I felt that an isolated Catholic all-girls college kept me too hemmed in. In my third year, I transferred to the very secular Boston University, even though it meant losing my full scholarship and having to take out student loans.

I rented an apartment with roommates who provided a feeling of family. One of these girls was a friend from high school. We roomed together for two years but fell out over a green blanket we both claimed to own. The falling out also had something to do with her reluctance to pay for rent or utilities on time, which was in contrast to my compulsively early payments. I was jealous of her beauty and the steady number of boys who fell in love with her. Had she been plainer, I might have let her take the blanket without a fight.

After the Harvard party, Martin and I saw each other regularly. He provided entertainment, always playing it cool, and we never spoke of love. Perhaps I was less than loveable then.

I saw my mother and aunt occasionally during college. They had an annoying penchant for calling me in the morning to announce they'd be staying overnight at my apartment, as if my home was their own pied-à-terre. My roommates and I would scurry to hide alcohol and evidence of live-in boyfriends. I'd breathe a sigh of relief the next morning after they left. I never dared tell them to stay away—I was afraid they would take me at my word. Despite my teenage longing to be free from my mother, she and Margie were my only real family, and I wasn't confident of my ability to face life entirely on my own.

College graduation loomed with no job possibility, so in 1974 I enrolled in a master's program in medical sociology at the State University of New York at Buffalo. Like many people in my generation, I was putting off entering the job market by staying in school, plus sociology majors weren't in great demand. Studying medical sociology sparked my interest in becoming a doctor, but it would be several years before I'd realize this possibility. Also during this time, Martin began his graduate program in computer science at the University of Toronto in Canada.

The two-hour drive between Buffalo and Toronto strengthened our bond. In 1976, we married in St. Peter's Catholic Church in Plymouth with some associated drama. Margie didn't speak for a day after I told her Martin and I were engaged. My father, who drifted in and out of my life after our first meeting, reluctantly gave me $2,000 to pay for the wedding. My mother raged about my father's involvement. She demanded that I carry flowers—I refused. She insisted that we use her friend's printing service for the invitations—I agreed. My father threatened not to come if he couldn't walk me down the aisle—I relented. Martin's mother trembled as she escorted him down the aisle, and the ushers complained that their tuxes were not identical. Several relatives told me I couldn't love Martin because I didn't plan to change my name, and another insisted that the marriage would not last. Another relative said it was unseemly that I spoke at the ceremony., and there were complaints that Martin and I drove to the Church in my car rather than a limousine. I was delighted to have the wedding behind me and start on the path of creating our own family.

I joined Martin in Toronto, and our oldest daughter was born two years later. For the first twenty-four hours after her birth, the nurses took her to the nursery between feedings. Each time they rolled her bassinette away from me, I felt like part of me was ripped away. Recovering from epidural anesthesia, I couldn't get up to run after them and snatch her back into my arms. So I fretted in my four-bed labor and delivery ward and didn't sleep until Martin brought us home. I finally understood the fierce love of mother for child and vowed that nothing would separate me from this precious baby again.

My mother and aunt sent numerous baby gifts and visited a couple of weeks after the baby's birth. They were both smitten with her and squabbled about who got to hold her the most. My mother called her "my baby." I wondered about this, given that she hadn't seemed to want her own baby. After they left, I relaxed. For the next three months, my daughter and I explored Toronto, little wisps of red hair appearing over the edge of the Snugli that held her to my chest wherever we walked.

Motherhood was filled with many surprises. The first was the ferocious bear who lived within me and would destroy anyone and anything who threatened my baby. While I never let the bear loose, she growled as a nurse took blood from my little one's heel soon after birth. She glared at the doctor who prodded and poked and made my baby scream right before he made her smile. When my daughter was older, I struggled to keep the bear from demolishing a child who'd bitten my daughter's cheek.

Another surprise was that my daughter connected me with food, from the very first time she latched onto my breast. When I came within view, she immediately went from placid to ravenously hungry. Later, she could be playing happily with Dad or a sitter but demanded milk or juice or a snack as soon as she spied Mom. Still later, she wanted Mom's own food, including the best bites I'd saved for last, which I gave up without a fight. It was as if this little person knew intuitively that Mom's primary job was to nourish her. It began *in utero* and continued throughout childhood and beyond, even as the nourishment changed from primarily physical to primarily emotional.

As much as I loved being a mother, I wanted a career. I couldn't imagine making Martin support me long term. In my experience, women brought home a paycheck. I was not much more employable with a master's degree in sociology than with a bachelor's degree. So when Martin applied for computer science faculty jobs after completing his doctorate, I applied for PhD programs in epidemiology—a close cousin to medical sociology—and luckily the University of Washington in Seattle accepted both of us.

In 1978, we drove across the country to the Pacific Northwest with our three-month-old baby. We settled into the first house I'd ever lived in and furnished it with cast-off furniture from relatives that we had trucked out from the east coast. I was now 3,000 physical miles away from my roots, and even farther away emotionally.

Seattle in the late 1970s was a sleepy frontier town. Everyone knew someone who worked at Boeing; Microsoft was a start-up working out of a garage; and Starbucks didn't exist. For a computer science faculty wife, social life consisted of a series of potlucks where the moms stood around and compared their babies' progress. Sooner or later, the babies all reached the milestones, but the moms didn't talk about how slow their little ones were to turn over, crawl, or walk.

There were also mom trends I tried to follow. We read Dr. Spock cover to cover. We breastfed but didn't pump. We brought our babies to swimming classes and our toddlers to ballet. We pushed our infants in unwieldy perambulators and later in rickety umbrella strollers. We used cloth diapers because they were cheaper and worked better than disposables. We brought our babies to our bed at night if our husbands tolerated it, or if our babies refused to sleep otherwise. Those moms with bigger budgets dressed their toddlers in OshKosh; I dressed my daughter in whatever clothes our relatives sent and sewed outfits from remnant material.

I benefited greatly from the other faculty moms. I knew little about parenting and had vowed to do everything differently from my own childhood experience; that told me what not to do but didn't teach me how to be a good mother. I had no siblings, never took a child development course, and had little babysitting experience. From the other moms, I'd learn about play dates, educational toys, and grinding my own baby food. I felt like I was stumbling along, but our little girl was happy, healthy, and delightful. I assumed she was somehow resourceful and was developing beautifully in spite of my ineptitude.

Our second daughter, preciously redheaded and delightful, was born in 1982. I fell in love with her just as hard as I had with her sister. She and our older daughter quickly became inseparable. She refused to nap—I think she didn't want to miss any time with her big sister. This time, I knew more about mothering, so I had more confidence. She brought laughter to our household and taught us all that family life is fun.

In my PhD program, I studied the causes of cancer with the goal of finding ways to prevent the disease. Diet as a possible cause of cancer was dismissed as frivolous, and obesity was thought to be related only to diabetes and heart disease. I learned the nuts and bolts of designing and conducting studies as well as statistical and programming techniques for analyzing data. I was sure I'd make a career as a PhD epidemiologist, if only I could get someone to hire me after I graduated.

In June of 1982, I completed my PhD. I was now highly trained but still not very employable. During my PhD training, I discovered that there were two classes of epidemiologists: the physicians and everyone else. The diseases we studied in classes were just words on paper to me. To the physicians, they were real causes of suffering. These doctors had treated actual people, knew what their diseases looked and felt like on a physical exam, and had seen patients suffer through diagnoses and treatments. The physician-epidemiologists also had their pick of jobs, were paid more, and were always called "doctor"—I wanted into their elite circle. To my great surprise and gratitude, Martin agreed to support my application to medical school and move, if it came to that, which it did.

In 1985, we moved to Westchester County, New York, where I would attend medical school at New York Medical College in Valhalla. In Norse mythology, Valhalla is the home of dead heroes, but I had learned that medical school is all about living heroes: those who keep patients alive, those who care for dying patients, and the patients themselves.

IBM Research made Martin a very nice offer, so we had enough money for the move and living expenses. Martin's mother loaned us the money for my school tuition. We paid her back within a few years after I graduated, but I felt a combination of guilt and pressure not to fail. Mostly I felt gratitude and learned that this is what family does for family—something I never experienced growing up.

For four years, I'd leave the warmth of our split rambler in Yorktown Heights to drive fifteen miles down the Taconic Parkway to New York Medical College or one of its affiliated hospitals farther south in New York City. At thirty-two years of age, I was older than most of the students, and only a handful had children. The medical school curriculum was developed with a young, single man in mind, not a suburban mom who drove a Volvo station wagon. The classes required long hours of study, which luckily I could do at home when our daughters finally fell asleep. But I had to show up for lab sessions, 6:00 A.M. rounds, and hospital rotations. Plus there were mom things to do like making grilled cheese sandwiches, driving to ballet lessons, and pushing cherry flavored liquids to get us through feverish nights.

I tried to blend with the twenty-two-year-old medical students, but it didn't work. A perm gave me big 80s hair, but nothing could give me slim New York hips, and I couldn't afford the skinny designer jeans even if I did have slim hips. I had no time in the morning to put on make-up. While Martin made breakfast on school days, I was the official finder, as in, "Mom, where is my blue sweatshirt?" or "Mom, I can't find Sealie. I can't go to school without Sealie."

So here I was, big hair, slightly pudgy by New York standards, in mom jeans, sitting in a sloped auditorium every day with 100 glamorous female medical students who got the attention of the 100 male medical students. Many would pair off during our training and were on their way to being future power couples bringing in enough money to easily pay off student loans and buy his and her BMWs.

When Martin had agreed to my attending medical school and all the family disruption that would entail, I'd said it would just be for four years. I wasn't being misleading—at the time I thought all I needed was the diploma saying I was an MD. I'd be one of the top-tier physician-epidemiologists and would land a prestigious, high-paying job. What I hadn't planned on was falling in love with patient care.

The first two years of medical education consisted of memorizing facts about human biology and what goes wrong when people get sick. The last two years consisted of practical rotations, where I was assigned to a team to take care of surgical, medical, or pediatric patients. I loved these clinical years. I finally learned the medical facts that eluded me in the first two years of book-learning, liked seeing first-hand how diseases manifested, and loved helping patients through the difficult processes of diagnoses and treatments. I was grateful to the patients for sharing their experiences with me, for helping me learn to be a doctor. So toward the end of medical school, I realized I wanted to be fully trained in internal medicine so I could practice as a real doctor. Four years would turn into seven.

Martin, the lovely man that he is, agreed to this change of plan. I applied to internal medicine residency training programs in cities where Martin received faculty position offers. On a nerve-wracking Residency Match Day in 1989, we learned with glee that we'd be coming back to Seattle. Our daughters, now aged eleven and seven years, took some convincing to be excited about the move back. This involved promises to return to New York to visit friends, assurances that their old friends from Seattle would still remember them, and several Dairy Queen Blizzards.

My mother and Margie drove from Massachusetts for my medical school graduation, the first graduation ceremony I'd attended since high school. I ate white cake and drank champagne and basked in the glow of my achievement. After the ceremony, my whole family walked en masse to the parking lot. My mother and aunt hugged me goodbye; neither had said they were proud of me. As Margie walked away, she turned to say, "Bye-bye, Anna Banana," and I burst out crying. It had reminded me of her walking away at Rosary.

My residency training took place at the University of Washington and its affiliated hospitals. There were similarities to *Grey's Anatomy*: there was life-and-death drama. We doctors in training were exhausted. But real-life residents don't have perfect make-up and scandalous affairs. They wear dirty scrubs and lab coats and rotate among hospitals and clinics so often that forming relationships is difficult if not impossible.

I was accepted into the primary care internal medicine program, the main benefit of which was that I was clinic-based for six months out of each year. I only had to do overnight call—every fourth night—during the six hospital months. This was a lifesaver. I don't know if my family or I could have survived any more call nights than I had.

My challenges centered on the demands of medicine versus the needs of my family. All too often medicine won, and Martin and the girls took the brunt. On one on-call day in my first year, I was scheduled to be working for thirty-six hours straight. Martin called in the morning to tell me that one of the girls was sick and had to be picked up at school. He had to teach, so I'd have to get her. I told the second-year resident, my boss for the month, that I had to leave for a few hours.

"I'll have to cover for you. Get back here as soon as you can," he said.

His scowling face said it all. He was a single young man with no responsibilities other than learning to be a doctor. He was not happy covering for an intern. Not one of my senior residents had children, so none understood my competing responsibilities. After a night on call, I'd rush to finish up with my patients and sign out early to the covering team. I couldn't compete with the other interns who stayed late even on non-call nights, checking and rechecking on their patients. They were the favored ones, the ones who won prestigious fellowships or were named as chief residents, not me.

I measured myself against any mothering yardstick in sight. There were so many ways in which I quantified my bad mom-ness. I didn't volunteer at my kids' schools. I opted instead to spend my precious non-work time with our daughters. This sounded good in my mind and to whomever would listen to me, but inside I fumed with guilt. On my rare days off from the hospital, I'd drive the girls to their activities—horseback riding, rowing, soccer, or gymnastics. On more than one occasion, when I'd been on call the previous night, I slept in the car instead of cheering them on. Names eluded me. I could remember teachers' names during the school year, and to my girls' chagrin, I couldn't recall their previous teachers. I also got their friends mixed up—and the babysitters. There was a Julie and a Julia, a Dani and a Danielle, a Katie and a Kristen, a Stephanie and a Stacie.

I dreaded the nights on call. I'd be away from the girls and Martin, which underscored my failure as a mother and wife. The little sleep I got would be in a dirty, unkempt, unguarded room, tucked far from the hospital wards. The patients arriving at night would often be dreadfully ill, and I worried constantly that I'd miss a diagnosis, forget some critical test, or order the wrong medicine.

Most hospital patients get better and go home, but those who do not keep you awake at night and stick in your mind years later. My first hospital patient was a twenty-eight-year-old woman dying of breast cancer. The cancer had spread to her brain, which made her speech delirious as she tossed her beautiful red hair back and forth on her hospital pillow. No one visited her, no family or friends, which added to the horror this young woman was experiencing. I'd linger with her a little longer than with other patients, listening to her babbling, but I had to see to my other patients and hurry home to my own red haired girls and pray they never had to experience this.

I cared for many other cancer patients, several of them unfairly young to have the disease. The patient experiences strengthened my interest in cancer prevention, but there was a personal connection for me, too. Cancer killed my grandmother and left her teenage daughters motherless and adrift. In turn, they damaged me.

In spite of the grueling residency schedule, I loved the patients. They allowed me fascinating glimpses into their lives, their loves, their passions. They were grateful for the care we gave them, even those of us in training who would have to check with the senior doctors to figure out what to do. Many faced serious health problems, but one way or another, the patients dealt with them. Their bravery inspired me and helped me find my calling; I wanted to continue caring for patients.

In the summer of 1992, when I had just completed my training, I began to look for clinical jobs. As I interviewed, I learned with dismay that the worst parts of medicine—the call nights and long hours in clinic—would be a part of the work as a new physician. Not wanting to neglect my family any longer, I had second thoughts about starting a medical practice. I widened my job search to include research positions. We didn't want to move the family again, so my choices were limited to the few academic and research institutions in Seattle. I made a lot of calls, left many messages, and received few responses. At the time, I had a couple of job offers in internal medicine practices and was ready to accept one simply because we needed the money.

One evening in August, the phone rang as I was cleaning up after dinner. The girls were doing homework at the kitchen table, and Martin was trying to raise their enthusiasm for their math problems. On the phone was the director of the Fred Hutchinson Cancer Research Center, Public Health Sciences division. I stretched the phone cord as far as possible away from the kitchen noise.

"There's a study you might be interested in. It's a clinical trial to test the effect of a low-fat diet on breast cancer risk," the director said. My family ignored me as I tried to signal them to quiet down so I could hear this important person.

"That sounds great," I said, meaning it.

"We've applied to the government to be the coordinating center for the whole study. We'll need someone to run the clinical side of the coordinating center if we're awarded the contract."

I thanked the ceiling. With my background in epidemiology and my brand new medical qualifications, this sounded like a perfect fit for me. I could run a clinical trial! I didn't stop to think that since I'd never directed a clinical trial, I might have a steep learning curve. Instead, I approached it like doctors in training approach everything—if your bosses tell you to do it, you do it, even if you don't know how.

"I'd like you to meet with Dr. Maureen Henderson," he said. "She's head of the program that you'll be working in here at the Hutch."

I thanked him profusely and agreed to contact Dr. Henderson the next day. Little did I know what I was getting into, but in hindsight it was the right decision for me and my family.

I was hired at the Fred Hutchinson Cancer Research Center as a staff scientist. Being female, I didn't negotiate money. So I started at a lower salary than I'd been offered for a job in a practice, but the hours were better for my personal life. I had some Cinderella moments when my staff arranged my office, phone, and computer, shocked at the fact that I had staff. Since I'd spent the previous seven years working out of a worn-out backpack, I was very excited to have a drawer where I could put my lunch. On my first morning, I stood behind my desk, deciding on the optimal placement of pencils and lined yellow pads for quick access, when Dr. Henderson marched in. She was my direct supervisor, one of the many bosses I'd have in the new study, which was called the Women's Health Initiative.

"Well, you're a bit above yourself, aren't you?" Her British accent made it sound like she'd caught me perpetrating a crime.

"What do you mean?" I asked, shaken.

"Your office is bigger than what we give staff scientists."

"This is what they assigned me," I replied. I was referring to the study administrators. I guess they thought more highly of me than my boss did. To them, my title of project director of the clinical unit of the Women's Health Initiative Clinical Coordinating Center held some sway. I was dismayed. I was off on the wrong foot on day one, and all I'd done was stow my lunch and think about pencils and paper.

I managed to keep on Dr. Henderson's good side on most days, although her management style of scolding me after the fact rather than teaching me ahead of time was eerily reminiscent of my childhood upbringing. What challenged me even more was that I had dozens of people who had the authority to tell me what to do—I was at the bottom of the pecking order in faculty status—and I didn't know to whom I should turn for advice. Still, I stayed with the study for almost a decade and learned how to design and conduct clinical trials.

The Women's Health Initiative study recruited over 160,000 women from across the United States to take part in one of the clinical trials or a separate follow-up study. In the diet modification trial, almost 20,000 women were placed in a program where they learned how to follow a low-fat diet. They were compared to almost 30,000 women who didn't change their diet, and both groups were followed for over a decade. In the end, the study found little protection against breast cancer from the low-fat diet, which was a great disappointment to scientists and women alike. The hormone replacement therapy trial changed medical practice around the world, as it found that taking menopausal hormones caused more harm than good. The Women's Health Initiative was a phenomenal study that required the work of thousands of doctors, scientists, and expert staff around the country.

For several years while working with the Women's Health Initiative, I saw patients one day per week, first at an inner-city hospital in Seattle, then at the University of Washington, and later at a private facility. Many of the patients had conditions that were caused by lifestyle—bad diets, too much food or alcohol, too little exercise. With my encouragement, several of these patients were able to change their eating and exercise patterns, and their measures of health always improved. Blood pressure decreased, cholesterol improved, and the patients felt better. But I found working with one patient at a time to be limiting, and there was insufficient time in a busy clinic schedule to adequately counsel patients. I decided to devote myself fully to research, find ways to change diet and exercise, and discover how these affect health.

After I'd worked with the Women's Health Initiative for several years, I decided that it was time for me to conduct my own, albeit smaller, trials. I wanted to explore whether exercise or weight loss could reduce risk for cancer and other diseases. With the help of hundreds of staff members and thousands of study participants, I've studied how weight loss and exercise affects our bodies in ways that can reduce risk of developing cancer. I've also studied how a healthful diet and exercise are associated with improved prognosis in people with cancer. I hope that my work will keep some children from losing a parent prematurely.

My mother and Margie came to visit in early fall of 1992, just after I'd begun my new job. I was sandwiched between two sets of sisters—my mother and aunt on one side, my daughters on the other—and marveled at the siblings' relationships. They understood each other in a way that I'll never experience as an only child. My mother and aunt talked about their mama; and I'm sure my daughters talked about me. But they squabbled over silly things; my mother and aunt fought as much as my daughters did, only they were meaner.

On one Saturday, the five of us drove to a local shopping mall. The girls needed school outfits, and my mother and aunt needed to look around. As we walked, I noticed that Margie's pace was very slow, as if she was moving through molasses. After about ten minutes, she sat down.

"What's wrong, Margie?" I asked.

"What do you mean?"

"You're walking awful slowly. Are you out of breath?"

"I'm fine," Margie replied, clearly not wanting me to worry.

The unfinished conversation sat around us for the rest of their visit. She enjoyed watching the girls as they played, read stories to the younger one, and picked at the food we served.

A couple of weeks after this visit, Margie called me to tell me that she had been diagnosed with lung cancer. My heart sank. I knew the statistics. She was sixty-seven years old—she would not live to be an old woman. Margie died two years later of her disease; my girls and I were by her side. With her death, my ties to my family of birth broke. Margie was my main connection, the reason I'd stop in Massachusetts when I was on a business trip back east. I stayed in touch with my mother while we settled Margie's estate, cleaned out her house, and sold her property. After that, my visits stopped.

Late one Sunday afternoon, my mother called. It was August of 1996, and our family was enjoying a rental video of *Pet Detective* and a pizza. My mother gave her usual litany of current irritations—illnesses, husband, stepdaughter—then asked me when our older daughter would be leaving for college.

"Tomorrow. Martin will fly out to Chicago with her. I hate that she's going," I said. I couldn't get the words out without a catch in my voice. I'd tried to prepare for this event for years, but how do you prepare to be separated from your baby by 2,000 miles?

"She must be looking forward to it," she said.

"She's a little nervous."

"Remember how nervous you'd get on Sunday afternoons when we had to take you back to Rosary Academy? You'd usually throw up. I'd have to drag you out of the house sometimes." My mother laughed, a real, thigh-slapping kind of laugh.

I froze. I didn't know how she could find humor in banishing her daughter from home, let alone the terror her little girl had experienced. And I was shocked that she would bring this up during another difficult time in my life—when my own daughter would be leaving home. She wasn't the type to use humor to get through difficult situations. I mumbled something about having to go, hung up, thought for a few seconds, and decided that I couldn't deal with my mother any longer. I wrote her a letter telling her of my decision, and why, and told her not to call. The link wasn't broken easily—she'd have doctors and irate neighbors call me from time to time—but I never spoke to her again.

I still conduct research studies at the Fred Hutchinson Cancer Research Center, hoping to find ways to prevent cancer and improve the prognosis for people with cancer. Food issues still dog me like the things you can see from the periphery of your vision. Chocolate is still my drug of choice, and in times of stress—work, family, life—I find myself reaching for its comfort. But I get a lot of exercise to counteract some of those extra calories and watch my calorie intake in general, so I am able to keep my weight in a healthy range.

Our daughters grew up, married, and had children. I love seeing the joy they now experience as mothers and I am so proud that they are better mothers than I was, and my mother before me. I nourished our daughters, and now they nourish their children. I never thought my life, and my heart, could be so full.

Epilogue

On Thanksgiving Day 2008, my husband and I traveled across the country to attend my mother's funeral. Our younger daughter flew up to Boston from New York City, and we drove together to Plymouth. In the birthplace of our nation's holiday devoted to food, we could find only one place to eat—a bar so old and close to the waterfront that you could feel the ancient mold on your tongue and in your nose—and the meal was no feast.

In Church the next morning, and later at the gravesite, my husband and daughter stood close on either side of me, the way an odd-shaped glass is positioned in the dishwasher so it won't fall over without extra support. I was an odd-shaped vessel at this funeral, which my mother had planned and paid for ahead of time—the prodigal daughter who had exited her mother's life some years before, the one who did not arrange the funeral, the relative who knew fewer than half of the people at the sparsely attended Mass.

After the graveside prayers were completed and her ashes lowered into a small hole under a bush behind a tree—her obscured grave satisfied me—people turned to talk to each other. The priest ignored me but spoke with my stepsister. It was as if the priest channeled my mother's spirit in that snub. I half expected him to stride over and slap my face in her memory. As if to counteract his slight, three of my second cousins surrounded me, completely blocking the November chill.

"Your mother was always so angry," the eldest said. That sentence could have been my mother's epitaph.

We left the cemetery and drove the slow Route 3A through Plymouth, up through Kingston where we stopped to visit Margie's grave. I cried while my daughter held my hand and my husband took notes from the gravestones for our genealogy database, helping me feel like I had family history as well as our own family present and future. Later that day we visited my husband's niece in Boston, who fed us Thanksgiving pumpkin pie. When we flew back to Seattle the next day, our older daughter and son-in-law surprised us with a belated Thanksgiving dinner, complete with engraved menus.

That Thanksgiving I was grateful for so many things. My husband and daughters took care of me through an event that evoked so many painful memories. I was thankful to have them, realizing they wouldn't abandon me or purposely hurt me. I appreciated those cousins who surrounded me with comfort—my memory of my mother was vindicated in that one profound statement about her anger. I was also grateful for the pumpkin pie and delayed Thanksgiving dinner, being nourished after being deprived.

Abandonment was passed through my family as powerfully as a dominant gene. My grandmother was isolated from her family in Ireland. As teenagers, my mother and Margie lost her forever. In turn, they deserted me physically and emotionally. My father's mother left him daily for alcohol, and he left me. But just as medicine can overcome genetic defects, I was able to choose and keep a steadfast husband. Now with our grandchildren, our unbreakable family bonds extend down through two generations. We will never abandon our children, and they will never abandon theirs.

As I think of the phone call from my mother's social worker portending her imminent death, I am reminded of other phone calls I've received over the years that delivered news of such shock and significance that I'd briefly wonder if my resulting heart palpitations were signs of a cardiac arrest. Nowadays, I have to include video calls, texting, messaging, and emails among the contacts that forever change a day, week, or life. Calls have informed me about the loss of loved ones and colleagues, sudden or expected. I've mourned all these losses in some way, several profoundly. Calls and emails have surprised me with news of an honor, or an award, or funding for a new study. But the most powerful, life-transforming missives were our daughters and sons-in-law informing us of new lives coming into our family: the long-distance call; the video chat that only worked one way—we saw the positive pregnancy stick, but our daughter couldn't see the joy on our faces; the emailed ultrasounds of little *in utero* people with arrows indicating important parts; the calls from sons-in-law telling us our daughters are fine and our new grandbabies are gorgeous and healthy.

The journey I made from an emotionally starved child led me to this point—my life, my loves, my family, and my work. Without the early famine, I would not have had the later feasts.